Essays

Historical and Historic

Kurt E. Marquart

TRUTH, SALVATORY AND CHURCHLY
Works of Kurt E. Marquart

Ken Schurb, Editor
Robert Paul, Assistant Editor

III
Essays
Historical and Historic

Luther Academy

The quotations from the Lutheran Confessions in this publication attributed to "Tappert" are from *The Book of Concord: The Confessions of the Evangelical Lutheran Church*, edited by Theodore G. Tappert, published in 1959 by Fortress Press.

The quotations from the Lutheran Confessions in this publication marked "K-W" are from *The Book of Concord: The Confessions of the Evangelical Lutheran Church*, edited by Robert Kolb and Timothy J. Wengert, published in 2000 by Fortress Press.

Quotations marked "AE" are from Luther's Works, American Edition volumes 1–55 (St. Louis: Concordia Publishing House and Philadelphia: Fortress Press, 1955–1986).

Scripture quotations marked NIV are from the Holy Bible, New International Version®, NIV®. Copyright ©1973, 1978, 1984, 2011 by Biblica, Inc.™ Used by permission of Zondervan. All rights reserved worldwide. www.zondervan.com The "NIV" and "New International Version" are trademarks registered in the United States Patent and Trademark Office by Biblica, Inc™.

Scripture quotations marked RSV are from the Revised Standard Version of the Bible, copyright 1952, © 1971 by the Division of Christian Education of the National Council of the Churches of Christ in the United States of America. Used by permission. All rights reserved.

ISBN: Hardcover: 978-1-935035-21-3, Paperback: 978-1-935035-22-0
Printed in the United States of America

"Truth for the Formula of Concord is salvatory and churchly. This means that it is neither a matter of individual, virtuoso brilliance nor one of social accommodation, academic nicety or bureaucratic formality. The truth is God's, and the church is God's, and he creates and cultivates his church by means of his truth. The church and the truth belong inseparably together."

~ Kurt E. Marquart
from his essay
"The Contemporary Significance of the Formula of Concord"

ABBREVIATIONS

AC	Augsburg Confession
AE	*Luther's Works* American Edition. 75 vols. Jaroslav Pelikan, Helmut T. Lehmann, and Christopher Boyd Brown, gen. editors. St. Louis: Concordia; Philadelphia: Fortress Press, 1955.
Ap	Apology of the Augsburg Confession
Br	*Briefwechsel* (Correspondence) volumes in WA
CTM	Concordia Theological Monthly
CTQ	*Concordia Theological Quarterly*
CTCR	Commission on Theology and Church Relations
CW	*Convention Workbook*
Ep	Epitome (of the Formula of Concord)
Examination I	Chemnitz, Martin. *Examination of the Council of Trent* Part I. Translated by Fred Kramer. St. Louis: Concordia Publishing House, 1971.
FC	Formula of Concord
KJV	King James Version
K-W	Kolb, Robert, and Timothy J. Wengert, editors. *The Book of Concord: The Confessions of the Evangelical Lutheran Church.* Minneapolis: Fortress Press, 2000.
LC	Large Catechism
NIV	New International Version
RSV	Revised Standard Version
SA	Smalcald Articles
SD	Solid Declaration (of the Formula of Concord)
St.L.	*Dr. Martin Luthers Saemmtliche Schriften.* 23 vols. Edited by Johann Georg Walch. St. Louis: Concordia, 1881–1910.
Tappert	Tappert, Theodore G., translator and editor in collaboration with Jaroslav Pelikan, Robert H. Fischer, and Arthur C. Piepkorn. *The Book of Concord: The Confessions of the Evangelical Lutheran Church.* Philadelphia: Fortress Press, 1959.
WA	*D. Martin Luthers Werke. Kritische Gesamtausgabe.* Weimar, 1883.

CONTENTS

FOREWORD

By Martin R. Noland

The essays in this volume give just a glimpse of the role that Dr. Kurt Erik Marquart played in the Lutheran Church during his ministry of forty-seven years.

In several ways, Marquart was a unique figure. I am not aware of any other native Eastern European who provided critical theological leadership in the twentieth century to both the Australian and North American Lutheran churches. His mastery of the orthodox Lutheran theological tradition was surpassed by only one man in the latter twentieth century—his former professor and later colleague, Dr. Robert Preus. Marquart was the first of many North American Lutherans to build "bridges" of ecclesiastical diplomacy to the East European Lutherans when the "iron curtain" dividing Europe collapsed. His perspective on modern apologetics was unique and could arguably be considered the most Lutheran approach to apologetics devised so far.

The reader who is interested in the personal history of Dr. Marquart should start with three essays in his *Festschrift*. The *Festschrift* was titled *Mysteria Dei: Essays in Honor of Kurt Marquart*, edited by Paul McCain and John Stephenson (Fort Wayne, IN: Concordia Theological Seminary Press, 1999). The three biographical essays are: "Kurt Marquart: A Brief Biography," by the editors; "Kurt Marquart: Faithful Steward of the Mysteries of God," by his Bronxville and St. Louis classmate, and dear friend, the Rev. Walter D. Otten; and "A Tribute to Kurt Marquart," by his colleague at the Fort Wayne Seminary, the Rev. Dr. Dean O. Wenthe.

The stories of Dr. Marquart's early life in Europe are fascinating. They remind me of the 1983 T.V. mini-series *Winds of War*, based on the novel by Herman Wouk. For example, sometime between September 1944 and April 1945, the ten-year old Kurt was walking the streets of Vienna near his parent's apartment, when he spotted a group of American bombers—B-

17s and B-24s of the U.S.A.A.F 15th Air Force—high in the cloudless sky, unmistakable with their light gray-blue undersides and white stars painted on blue circles. As the air raid sirens roared to life, and hot flak from the Austrian anti-aircraft guns started raining down in the city streets, his step-father, Baron George Meyendorff, grabbed Kurt and they ran pell-mell to the basement of their apartment. Soon thereafter Kurt, his siblings, and parents slipped away to the Western side of the front, eventually ending up in a refugee camp run by the British army in West Germany. While there, Kurt learned the "Queen's English" amidst his other studies.

Most of the seminary students at Concordia Theological Seminary, Fort Wayne had no idea about Dr. Marquart's personal history. We thought he was a native Australian, due to his authentic British dialect and his previous service as a pastor of a dual parish in Toowoomba, Queensland. Although he mentioned his Australian ministry when it pertained to a point of pastoral practice, he was too modest to entertain us with stories of his past. Besides, theology for him was serious business. For Dr. Marquart, the Word of God and the Marks of the Church contain the Light that enlightens every man (John 1:9). This is the real stuff of theological discourse, debate, and research, not the accidents of a person's own history.

After I had applied to the Fort Wayne seminary in 1979, I asked seven of its alumni, who came originally from my home congregation, which professors I should take for my courses. Every single one of them said, without hesitation, "Take Professor Marquart and take every course he offers! You can't do better than that." I followed their advice and was not disappointed, though I also grew to appreciate the many significant talents found in other members of the faculty.

My classmates will remember Marquart's daily quizzes at the beginning of the lecture period in his dogmatics courses. These quizzes forced us all to read Francis A. O. Pieper's four volume dogmatics textbooks on a semi-daily basis. There was no better way to get the future ministerium of The Lutheran Church-Missouri Synod "on the same page" theologically. It seemed to us that, of all of our professors, Marquart had the greatest appreciation for Pieper's dogmatics. Criticism of Pieper by students was welcome, but was always ably refuted by Marquart. It was only later that we realized that behind Marquart's and Pieper's theological position *stood the entire tradition of the greatest Lutheran systematicians:* Carl F. W. Walther, Johann W. Baier, Johann A. Quenstedt, Abraham Calov, Johann Gerhard, Leonhard Hutter, Martin Chemnitz, Philipp Melanchthon, etc., and Martin Luther himself.

Dr. Marquart had a significant network of relationships with Lutherans around the world. Most interesting was his relationship with Dr. Hermann Sasse who, during Marquart's tenure in Queensland, was professor of church history at Immanuel Seminary, North Adelaide, Australia. Sasse was at that time a member of the United Evangelical Lutheran Church of Australia (UELCA). Marquart's congregation was a member of the Evangelical Lutheran Church of Australia (hereafter ELCA). The two were brought together by church-merger negotiations from 1965 to 1972. Marquart's own recollection of Sasse, and their work together in those negotiations, is found in Marquart's essay "Hermann Sasse and the Mystery of Sacred Scripture," in *Hermann Sasse: A Man for Our Times?* (St. Louis: Concordia Publishing House, 1998). Another "essay" by Marquart about Sasse is found in the present volume.

Dr. Marquart's network of confessional Lutheran friends around the globe had an impact on the 1969 convention of The Lutheran Church-Missouri Synod in Denver. This was the convention at which J. A. O. Preus II was elected. It was a true crisis point in that synod's history. The impact was caused by a historic joint letter titled "An Earnest Fraternal Appeal," which is included in the present volume.

This appeal in letter form was received in May 1969 by LCMS President Oliver Harms from Professor William Oesch of the Oberursel seminary in Germany. The authors and signers had intended that it be published in the 1969 LCMS Convention Workbook. It was also published and widely distributed throughout the Missouri Synod by the conservative organization known as "Balance," and then was re-printed in the newspaper *Christian News*. If one reviews the names of those who signed "An Earnest Fraternal Appeal," Marquart's network is most obvious in the Australia signers. All were his friends in the Queensland district of the ELCA, including former Queensland district president F. W. Noack, Clarence Priebbenow, and Glen Zweck.

Less obvious was Marquart's connection to "Earnest Fraternal Appeal" signer William Oesch. Marquart and his St. Louis seminary friends, including David Scaer and Herman Otten, had significant correspondence in the late 1950s with Oesch. Oesch was known in the Missouri Synod as the chief publisher of the periodical *Lutherischer Rundblick* (1953–1976). Other signers from the Lutheran Free churches in Germany, France, Belgium, Finland, and Brazil added to the global scope of this "Earnest Fraternal Appeal."

Dr. Marquart's involvement in the theological struggles of the Missouri Synod went back to his seminary days in St. Louis (1954–1959). He was a recognized theological leader among the conservative seminary students, which was about half of the student body. When he took the call to Australia in April 1961, his seminary classmates and friends kept him informed about what was really happening inside the Missouri Synod. Articles he published in various newspapers and journals, including *Christian News*—edited and published by his former roommate Herman Otten, contributed immensely to the conservative cause in the LCMS in the 1960s and early 1970s.

In his Fort Wayne years (1975-2006), Dr. Marquart published numerous articles in his faculty's *Concordia Theological Quarterly*. He gave lectures for many Lutheran groups in the U.S., as well as around the world in places like Kenya, Latvia, Haiti, Kazakhstan, Germany, and Russia. His theological expertise was utilized extensively during his years on the Missouri Synod's Commission on Theology and Church Relations (CTCR) and in his last years as a board member of the Luther Academy.

Not least among Dr. Marquart's contributions were his lectures and articles devoted to the "public square." He wrote and lectured on abortion, becoming a leader in the right-to-life movement in the state of Indiana. Although many Lutherans may think it is improper for clergy to be involved in "politics" in any way whatsoever, the included Marquart essay on "Abortion and Luther's Two-Kingdom Theology" puts that concern to rest.

If I would have any advice to pastors, seminary students, and laymen interested in theology, I would paraphrase the advice given to me and say: "Read Professor Marquart and study every article he offers! You can't do better than that." When you are finished with Marquart's writings, then you will be ready for the grand tradition of orthodox Lutheran systematicians that he transmitted and epitomized.

EDITORIAL INTRODUCTION

One of Kurt Marquart's articles was entitled "Central Lutheran Thrusts for Today."* Those words could have served as a subtitle for most of his writings. While he strongly objected to trimming doctrinal content in any reductionist way, Marquart's evangelical theological compass kept him returning to the most *central* aspects of the biblical and *Lutheran* theological heritage. He called these *thrusts*, not mere limp claims. Marquart taught, defended, and proclaimed the salvatory and churchly truth in Christ which brings the Spirit and life to poor sinners *today*. He asserted this truth again and again, despite all sorts of opposition. Marquart spoke and wrote in a timely way, addressing real troubles in the church and the world.

Yet as Martin Noland points out in the foreword to this volume, behind Marquart stood the long tradition of the foremost Lutheran dogmaticians. For all his contemporaneity, Marquart turned out to be steeped in history—not any old history, to be sure, but the heritage through the years of proclaiming a Gospel that never gets old.

With Marquart's appreciation of history, especially the church's history, it comes as no surprise that his work sometimes had a distinct historical flavor. Even though he may not have been attempting to write history as such, his sense of context and his penetrating analysis still prove quite instructive. Those who set themselves the task of writing history in a more formal way would do well to consult Marquart. Several chapters in this volume amount to ripe historical fruit, waiting to be plucked. Occasionally Marquart also *made* history with what he wrote. You will find some of these historic essays in this volume too. In them you can get not only a feel for times past but also insight for confessing the faith today.

As with the previous volume in this series, some of the essays in the present volume have already been published, others not. Those which had not previously had the benefit of editorial attention have received it here. With the essays published before, the previous editing has been preserved as much as possible, resulting in slight differences of format from essay to essay.

Pastor Robert Paul's bibliography of Kurt Marquart's publications comes as an historical bonus. Although not exhaustive—it does not list,

---

* *Concordia Journal* 8 (May 1982):86–91.

for example, letters to the editors of newspapers—it will guide anyone interested into further reading.

In editing this entire series, I have gratefully utilized the libraries at Concordia Seminary, St. Louis; Concordia Theological Seminary, Fort Wayne; and the University of Missouri. I owe a particular debt to Concordia Historical Institute and the outstanding reference services provided there by Laura Marrs and Mark Bliese. Thank you!

Ken Schurb

Essays

Historical and Historic

Chapter One

HERMANN SASSE'S INFLUENCE ON THE LUTHERAN CHURCH OF AUSTRALIA

AN ORAL HISTORY

Editor's note: Unlike other pieces in the present three-volume set of Kurt Marquart works, this is the only one that was authored by Marquart without being written by him. It is an oral history interview with Marquart, reproduced here by the kind permission of the Concordia Theological Seminary Library. The interview was about Hermann Sasse, but it turns out to be informative also about Marquart himself. The Preface below is part of the oral history project.

ॐ

PREFACE

This transcript is the product of a tape-recorded interview conducted by Bill Hering for "The Church Since 1850" class, HIT 231. Dr. Heino Kadai was the class instructor.

Professor Kurt Marquart received his bachelor of divinity from Concordia Seminary, St. Louis, Missouri, in 1959. He then served as pastor at Trinity Lutheran Church in Weathersford, Texas, from 1959 to 1961. From there he accepted a call to Redeemer Lutheran Church in Toowoomba, Queensland, Australia. He served as a pastor in Toowoomba from 1961 to 1975. It is during this time period that Professor Marquart became acquainted with Dr. Hermann Sasse. Since 1975, Professor Marquart has been serving at Concordia Theological Seminary, now located in Fort Wayne, Indiana.

Readers of this oral history should keep in mind that the transcript reflects the spoken word, and that the narrator and interviewer have sought to preserve the informal, conversational style that is inherent in this type of historical resource. Due to the informal nature of the interview process, the reader ought to judge for himself/herself the factual accuracy of the document.

It is the hope of those involved in this effort that this resource will provide the reader with new insights into Hermann Sasse. It is from the perspective of a man who was an active parish pastor during much of Sasse's time in Australia. He had numerous opportunities to work and to correspond with Dr. Hermann Sasse. It also provides a reflection on the impact that Dr. Sasse made on the Lutheran Church, from a man well versed in Confessional Lutheran theology.

This transcript may be quoted or reproduced with the permission of the library at Concordia Theological Seminary in Fort Wayne, Indiana.

BH: An oral interview—or an oral history—with Professor Kurt Marquart, April 28, 1989, regarding Hermann Sasse and his influence on the Lutheran Church of Australia.

The purpose of this interview is to gain some perspective on Hermann Sasse and his influence in the Union of the Lutheran Churches in Australia and their development. I would like to begin by asking, when did you arrive in Australia?

KM: I arrived in Australia in the early part of '61, having been first a pastor in Texas for nearly two years.

BH: What was your role at this time?

KM: You mean in Australia?

BH: Uh-huh.

KM: I was called to the rather large parish in Toowoomba, which is quite a Lutheran center. When I first heard the name, I thought it was in Africa, but it turned out to be in Australia (laughing). And it was a large Lutheran parish with a Concordia Memorial College in it and all the faculty there also belonged to it. And it was the only ELCA [Evangelical Lutheran Church of Australia] church at that time in Toowoomba. The other Lutheran churches belong to the so-called UELCA, the United Evangelical Lutheran Church of Australia.

BH: OK, how would you assess the situation of the Lutheran Churches of Australia at this time?

KM: At that time?

BH: At the time you arrived there.

KM: Well at the time, and of course I didn't really realize or understand that until much later, but at the time they had been running parallel for about a hundred years out of fellowship with the exception of a brief decade, which fell apart later like our ALC–Missouri fellowship. So this time when the Union came, they were determined not merely to have altar and pulpit fellowship, but to have an actual merger so that they couldn't so easily fly apart again if things didn't work out straight away. But at the time they were in negotiations toward an agreement and the Australian Theses, the Theses of Agreement, had been worked out for some, oh, over a decade. [*Editor's note: The Theses of Agreement were adopted by a joint pastoral conference on August 27, 1956.*] And agreement had been reached on virtually everything that had been in dispute, except the matter of Church Fellowship.

BH: OK, what was your first encounter with Dr. Sasse?

KM: My first encounter was by mail, where I had sent to my parish a very good essay that Sasse had written about the Lutheran World Federation. And I was at the Helsinki assembly of the LWF in 1963, and when I came back, I distributed this paper to my parish. Too, because other people were claiming that the LWF was perfectly all right. You see, that was the position of the UELCA, and Sasse courageously testified within his own church. And this document had been given to me by, had been distributed to all our pastors by our official church office. So when I distributed it, I did not realize that Sasse thought it was confidential, and it embarrassed him to suddenly have this — receive such wide publicity. So we had a bit of correspondence to settle there. A little, what do you want to call it . . . (chuckle).

BH: OK, would you consider Dr. Sasse a key figure in the fellowship discussions which were part of the negotiations toward the Union?

KM: Oh, yes absolutely. I'm quite sure that without Sasse this whole union would not have happened. Because Sasse surely had an influence on one of our leading men, namely the late Henry P. Hamann. And then of course he wielded an enormous influence in the seminary in which he taught and the generation or so of clergy that have been educated there since, well, since about 1949–1950, when he got there.

BH: What influence if any, or what influence do you think he had on the merger of the two seminaries?

KM: Well there is no doubt that he was the ranking theologian; there was simply no one, he was simply head and shoulders above everyone else. There was no one there to equal him. And therefore he exerted a tremendous moral authority, also because of his own experiences both in the ecumenical movement and the Lutheran Church in Germany, which he left on conscientious grounds when they joined in the Union with the Reformed after the war. But because of that, Sasse had a clear perception of the doctrine of the Church, and of the function of the Augsburg Article 7. And he was able persuasively to impart this to both sides of the negotiations, and that is finally what brought them together in 1965.

BH: How was the Union being received by the pastors and the people in the parish?

KM: At that time, I remember we had a pastors' conference in, I think, it was 1964, and we had been told that there had been a dramatic break-through after years of negotiations. I'll backtrack a little bit. At our Melbourne convention, which I think was about 1963, our ELCA had decided, "Look it's enough talking; we are not getting anywhere. So we urge the inter-synodical committees to get together and maybe have a full week's meetings really to get to grips with these issues, and then if there is no break, if there is no agreement, then negotiations should be discontinued because we are simply wasting everybody's time. And the differences should simply be stated, and wait for a better time." And then, the two faculties came to a breakthrough, and I believe our Dr. Hamann was instrumental in that. For they were able to agree on the basic principle of fellowship which for all these years had stood in the way and they could never quite get to grips with it. And when that was agreed, the two faculties agreed and drafted the Document of Union. However, the first version of the Document of Union that came out had some very unfortunate wordings that immediately put up red flags of caution and protest, so that our conference in Queensland was quite opposed to it and fought it tooth and nail until the actual convention of our Church that adopted it in Toowoomba in March 1965.

BH: Did Sasse have any influence on the convention in Toowoomba?

KM: No, you see he belonged to the other Church, and this is our ELCA meeting, the General Convention of the ELCA.

BH: What did Sasse think of the new constitution?

KM: Well, he of course, having helped very much to bring about theological agreement, was disappointed, I understand. I don't have that from him directly but from sources close to him that he was disappointed at the way the constitution had a kind of unchurchly, as it seemed to him, principle of representation (so many people for so many in the parish, and the pastor if you like but not otherwise), and he felt it was an unchurchly constitution and therefore did not attend the opening convention — the constituting convention, or so I was told.

BH: Did that seem to make much of an impact?

KM: I don't think so. Sasse was not that sort of demonstrative person. He wasn't out waving flags. He just respected his conscience quietly, and as I say, I only heard about it indirectly; I didn't even realize that he wasn't there.

BH: To what extent did you have opportunities to work or to correspond with Dr. Sasse?

KM: Well, I've got quite a thick file of correspondence with him, actually. And most of it, I daresay, was in the aftermath of the Union, because I ended up being put on the theological commission of the new Church with the view to ironing out the difficulties that especially we in Queensland had seen, and we wanted desperately to avoid and forestall the kind of thing that was going on in the Missouri Synod that led to Seminex, and so on. So we tried to head off these matters of inerrancy and Genesis and so on. And since some seeds of division on that existed in both Churches — but these were never differences between the Churches — therefore it was thought fair that the new Church should take up these matters together. And it was in that context that Sasse and I often would meet and correspond to try to iron things out. And I must say that finally things were settled, under the blessing of God, despite some days when it looked absolutely hopeless and no way this could be resolved. So to me it is somewhat of a miracle that in 1972 the Commission was able to submit documents on Inerrancy and on Genesis, which, without compromising anything, were adopted unanimously by the convention, without dissenting vote. Yes, I think there were one or two pastors who voted against it, but they wanted something even stronger. They wanted the six days spelled out as natural days or something like that. Which of course the document did not do.

BH: To what extent did Sasse play a role within the final discourse that was accepted in '72?

KM: Well, he was there at all stages, even though he was retired and under modified service. But he always kept very, very active and he had a marvelous grasp of things going on everywhere in the Church. For example, there was a meeting of the Lutheran World Federation Commission on Church Cooperation in Adelaide in 1975, just before I came to Springfield, just before leaving Australia, and there was — you see, the UELCA had to leave the Lutheran World Federation for the sake of union with the ELCA. And so the World Federation has been wooing the Australian Church ever since. So they had this big meeting there, and we were invited to attend and to participate in the discussions, and one day Sasse came in, and it was the year he turned eighty. So when Sasse shuffled in, into that meeting, everybody got up and he got a long standing ovation from the audience and from people all over the world who of course knew of him. And in one session, I happened to be sitting next to him, and he always had a very sharp tongue, and so on this occasion as they were debating endlessly, not questions of truth and substance, but matters of structure and form — how many dollars sent here, how to do this, how to do that — Sasse leaned over and whispered into my ear, *"Sola structura"* (laughing), "only structure."

BH: That was the same year a book came out, *Theologia Crucis?*

KM: Yes, *Theologia Crucis,* that was a Festschrift to honor him on his eightieth birthday, edited by Henry Hamann of the faculty at Luther Seminary in Adelaide.

BH: How was that book received?

KM: Well, it was a scholarly work. I don't know if I can say anything more about it. It was of uneven quality. There were some very good things in it, and some more routine matters — like these fest ... that's how these things are.

BH: What do you think Sasse brought to the Australian Lutheran Church?

KM: I'm thinking here of what Henry Hamann wrote, in the introduction to that Festschrift, where he said that what he brought was sort of a global perspective, a broad point of view. Because Australia is so far removed from the rest of the world that it often becomes sort of a cultural backwater and no connection to the rest of the world. Sasse brought with him a direct connection to the rest of the ecclesiastical world and a sense of global perspective and responsibility, so he enlarged the vision of our churches in Australia.

BH: What were some of Sasse's unique accents?

KM: Well, I'm tempted, first of all, with a little pun, when you speak of accents. I'm told that when he first came to Australia, and of course I've never had him in class, so I wasn't in that vicinity at all, and I wasn't really a student of his in that sense. We were all students of his in another sense. But I am told that at first his English was so bad that the students could hardly understand him. He would, for example, speak of "the slaughter of the Aborigines," it was the "the Slufter of the Ab 'origines" (laughing). Quite! It had to be decoded, you see, but after a while. Uh, one of my prize possessions, incidentally, is a little pamphlet called *Australian Etiquette,* and I got it for about fifty cents from our library when it was getting rid of excess books. It had belonged to Sasse. It has Sasse's signature on it. And dated about 1949. So Sasse must have bought that book just when he got there, on Australian etiquette, exactly how to behave, and what to do for the right thing in this culture. And most of it was quite irrelevant because it had directions on how to act at a royal reception and how to respond to the Queen and the Governor General and this sort of thing. So it is an interesting testimony to the mores of that time, which unfortunately have been completely changed in the meantime. I suppose it could be of interest to mention that—that you know how providentially these things work. Humanly speaking, Sasse should have been called to St. Louis. But St. Louis in the 1940s was in the hands of ecumenical naifs in the sense of people who had been completely captivated by the charms of the State Church theologians whom they had discovered. People like [Theodore] Graebner and [F. E.] Mayer and so on. So when Sasse came, having just left the Bavarian State Church for conscientious reasons, and Sasse joined the little Free Church. When you think of the enormous standing which in Germany, a university professor had—that is really some major creature, a university professor—and a man of that caliber steps down, lays down his office and joins the small Free Church lacking all prestige! And then he came to America on a lecture tour and Dr. Behnken treated him very kindly. He was a lifelong friend. But the administration at the seminary treated him very badly. And he wrote letters complaining about how it hurt him. He tried to let everyone know the betrayal of the Lutheran Confessions that was going on in Europe in the State Church, and speak up for the Free Churches, but the seminary leaders were determined to get away from the little Free Churches that they despised and get on with the big established churches. They wanted to move in those circles. So this is why Sasse was virtually hounded out of St. Louis, treated shabbily there. He was never called there. He would have made a tremendous contribution there. But you see then he never would have got to Australia. So this way he got to Australia and accomplished the union of the two churches.

BH: Very good. Do you see any weaknesses in his outlook or thinking that we should keep in mind?

KM: Well, one has to speak with great care here. But experience teaches that all theologians have their blind spots. If you look in Pieper's *Dogmatics*, the best parts of the dogmatics always are those that he had to fight through in long years of theological disputation. Things on Conversion, Election, that kind of thing, on Justification, he is excellent. But no theologian can possibly know it all or be equally at home in absolutely everything. And so Sasse's great strength, his great strength because of his background, lay in the Doctrine of the Church, and the Ministry, and the Confession of the Church, and the Sacraments. These are the great strengths of his position, and these occupied him all during his life. And his writings on that are really treasure houses of carefully sifted information and balanced judgment. But things which he was not forced to address in such great detail — for example, some of the details on the doctrine of Scripture — probably because of his University of Erlangen background, he had inherited a certain bias, which is simply inbred in those circles, a certain bias against the seventeenth-century orthodox doctrine of inspiration, verbal inspiration. And he tended to caricature that the way our age simply has taught us to caricature these people. I noticed that Robert Preus, in his book *Inspiration of Scripture*, also to some extent corrects some of Sasse's impressions and calls on him to . . . not to take other people's word for it, but to examine these old fathers on their own terms and in the actual firsthand sources, original sources. So that was a kind of "lacuna" in Sasse's theology. And by the time the issue arose seriously, he was too old, I think, to start up this new thing. He made several attempts to cope with it. And he had some brilliant insights into some of it. For example, you see, he is generally disliked and suspected in some conservative circles because of his alleged liberalism on the doctrine of Scripture, but it wasn't really that. He was by no means a liberal on Scripture. But some of his language was not quite consistent. And one can notice a certain trend of development, a certain evolution, where he is actually getting better, whereas most people are actually getting worse (laughter) or things like that. Like Michael Reu you know, who started out criticizing inerrancy and ended up embracing it. Something like that I think happened in Sasse.

BH: You had mentioned some of the strengths; are there any particular strengths that you would like to emphasize, or that come to mind in regards to Dr. Sasse?

KM: Well, the particular sort of "theme song," if I may say so, is his great emphasis on Article 7 of the Augsburg Confession, which he called our Ecumenical Magna Carta of our Church. That sees quite clearly with clear evangelical perception that it is the pure Gospel and Sacraments alone that build the Church and keep it united and nothing else. And stressing that, and waking the whole Lutheran world, really waking it up to this reality and reminding of that again and there, by rendering a very, very signal service, because this whole matter of fellowship in the Church bothers all Lutheran Churches in the whole world. And Sasse drew attention to where the answers lie.

BH: In an earlier discussion you had made reference to a situation where he had shown some humility that you had thought was an admirable character; would you like to expound on that?

KM: Yes, Sasse was that rare bird, a theologian who could actually admit that he was wrong and learn something better. And even at his age, and even with his world reputation, I am thinking of again this inerrancy matter, and the inspiration of Scripture. When in the, I think it must have been in the early '50s or so or in the late '50s — anyhow, the student book shop in St. Louis was publishing and printing Sasse's earlier pronouncements on inspiration. And Sasse asked them to stop it, and couldn't get them to, and became very frustrated with them, very annoyed about it. And wrote a letter to *Lutheran News*, as it was then called, published there, that in the course of the Australian discussions toward union and agreement which resulted in the Theses of Agreement, he, Sasse, was unable to maintain all his positions and had to change some of them and therefore did not want this old paper to go forward as if nothing had happened. So in other words, the man was being honest and humble and not simply repeating and defending to the "*n*th degree" everything he had ever said. And it is very unfortunate, there is a book published after Sasse's death, *Corpus Christi*, the one by his friend and sort of testator who edited the two-volume *In Statu Confessionis*, pastor of our Free Church there, head of the mission — what was his name again? Well it escapes me. [*Editor's note:* Marquart may have been thinking of the Sasse collection *Sacra Scriptura: Studien zur Lehre von der Heiligen Schrift*, edited by Friedrich Wilhelm Hopf, who also edited *In Statu Confessionis*.] And there unfortunately, Sasse is presented in a way as though a change had never taken place. But if you compare his essays in the '50s, 1960, 1970, and later, you find that from an earlier view where he limited inerrancy just to theology, by 1970 he insists on inerrancy, factually in all matters. That was the sticking point, and that was thoroughly nailed down in a 1972 statement, and Sasse stuck to that. Well, the library has a letter that Sasse addressed to Jack Preus, who was then president and who had inquired about this very thing. And in that letter Sasse strongly exhorts him, he says you cannot give up inerrancy. You must stick to the inerrancy of Scripture. And you cannot give up that word. For it simply means that the Scripture is truthful and free from all error. Piepkorn has written some lengthy thing about it, and if Dr. Piepkorn had looked into the history of it, he would have seen that too and not given up that word.

BH: Do you see the writings and influence of Hermann Sasse having any influence on the Missouri Synod of this day?

KM: Well, yes, I think, I don't know of any thinking Missouri Synod theologian who has not been influenced by Hermann Sasse. I am reminded of C. S. Lewis, who said the best way to do mission work in our sort of culture is not to write another tract about Christianity but for a Christian physicist to write an excellent textbook in physics, or a Christian mathematician mathematics. So that when an unbeliever reads the textbooks, he is struck that the best textbooks are written by Christians. That will influence him. And something similar I think is going on with Sasse. If you see the three, these valuable three little paperbacks in the *We Confess* series, taken from *In Statu Confessionis* mainly, translated by Norman Nagel, himself an Australian. If you look at these books, there is material there, a depth of dimension, a depth of analysis, a depth of historical and theological perspective which you simply don't find anywhere else. So it's not simply the best book, but the only book that conveys that sort of information and that sort of perspective (in our circles). And in the philosophy of science, it is a well-known principle that the best proof of something is simply an explanation. If you can convince people of a certain explanation, that this is the way things are, you convince them that it is true. So Sasse is able to show things in their interconnections which continue the basic thrust of Lutheran confessional dogmatics. And anybody who reads that immediately sees and resonates to the consistent representation of the Lutheran confessional line. And there simply isn't anything else, yes there is Elert and people like that, but thinking people in the Missouri Synod who want to be responsible confessional theologians, who don't want to be ostriches with their heads in the sand, they have very few people besides Sasse to turn to.

BH: Do you see, kind of looking ahead, someone with that profound an influence as well as a necessity to keep the Lutheran Church–Missouri Synod or confessional Lutheran Church confessional?

KM: Well, we have of course experienced a great turnaround of the early '70s, and our present trouble is precisely in the doctrine of the Church and Ministry—where all the confusion remains, and this is where Sasse can help us most. And the first printing in English of Walther's great classic on *Church and Ministry*. So I am hoping that all these things will combine in the minds of the clergy of the Church, who are the public teachers of the Church, that this will ferment in our collective ministerial mind and will, by and by, create—what are they called?—antibodies, things that will fight the infections that are at the moment in our bloodstream.

BH: So you see the Church of the future, primarily looking back to documents written by theologians such as Sasse and Walther.

KM: Well, Sasse and Walther basically draw us back to our Confessions; we need to go back to our confessional heritage to see what that is; Sasse sometimes says how it would be comical, if it were not so tragic, that he would go to some meeting and the pastor there would complain, "Oh, we need some new confessions, because the old ones don't speak to this point," and then Sasse has to show them how the old Confessions do speak to many things that we don't think they speak to, because we don't know them well enough. So the best service that really writings like that can render is to make us reappropriate with fresh thought our own confessional heritage. It is not really anything new. And that is a process which is happening.

BH: Are there any concluding thoughts that you would like to share with me about your conception of Dr. Hermann Sasse?

KM: Well, it is difficult to find words adequate to the solemnity of this charge (laughter). I don't know how to sum all of this up. But I can only say that in my own experience, in my own little lifetime, that Sasse was a man of rare insight, of rare courage and integrity. Such men we cannot mass produce. They are simply given once in a while. I guess when we need them. I am profoundly thankful for everything I have learned from him, and also try to pass on as much as I can to the next generation.

BH: Thank you. Well, thank you very much, Professor Marquart, for sharing that with us. This concludes our interview with Professor Kurt Marquart, Department Chairman of Systematic Theology, Concordia Theological Seminary.

KM: Thank you very much.

Chapter Two

SOME IMPORTANT DOCTRINAL POINTS

Editor's note: This short piece is dated May 22, 1956. Kurt Marquart wrote it as a student at Concordia Seminary, St. Louis. The Dean of Students had asked him to draw up a list of controverted doctrinal points on the campus over which he and others were concerned. These points give today's reader a glimpse into theological trouble signs at the St. Louis seminary nearly two decades before the Walkout of February 1974. Already midway through his studies at the seminary, Marquart was demonstrating his theological abilities and writing something historic.

THE HOLY SCRIPTURES

1. Whether the Holy Scriptures are, in all their parts and words, the very Word of God, communicated to the sacred writers by the Holy Ghost.
2. Whether these Holy Scriptures are entirely true and without error in all matters of which they treat, including geographical, historical, and other secular matters.
3. Whether all the events described in the first few chapters of the Book of Genesis, including the Creation, Adam and Eve, the Fall into Sin, etc., are historically and literally factual and correct, as described.
4. Whether there is any objection to the *Brief Statement*'s formulation of Verbal Inspiration (Paragraphs 1–3).

MINISTRY AND ORDINATION

1. Whether the spiritual priests of a Christian congregation are the original and immediate possessors of all Church power (i.e., administration of all the means of grace), or whether this power, or any part thereof, is originally and immediately vested in the ministerium.
2. Whether the office of the ministry is validly conferred by the call of a Christian Congregation, even without the imposition of hands by an ordained clergyman in Holy Ordination.
3. Whether God confers the ministerial office through the congregation's delegation of its priestly powers, or through the imposition of hands by a clergyman.*

4. Whether, other things being equal, the Ordination imparted by a clergyman who is himself unordained or improperly ordained is valid.

5. Whether the Holy Sacraments are always valid, and efficacious whenever administered under the auspices of the orthodox Confession, irrespective of the administrant's ordination or lack of it.

THE HOLY TRINITY

1. Whether the term "Person" in the confessional formula "Three Persons in one Godhead" is to be taken as meaning a distinct "I" (Ego) or self-consciousness.

2. Whether the corresponding antithesis is to be regarded as a denial of the doctrine.

THE REAL PRESENCE

1. Whether the heavenly elements of the true body and true blood of our Lord Jesus Christ are actually and substantially present, by virtue of sacramental union, with the earthly Eucharistic elements of the bread and wine respectively.

2. Whether this presence of the heavenly elements of our Lord's body and blood is unique to the Sacrament of the Altar, i.e., not merely of the nature of Christ's presence with the Word, or in the hearts of His believers, or in the universe in general.

3. Whether the true body and blood of Christ are received in the Sacrament with the mouth of the body, so that this oral reception is essentially distinct from the reception of Christ by faith in the heart.

4. Whether the true body and blood of Christ are orally received in the Sacrament by all communicants, also by the impenitent and the unworthy, namely to their judgment.

---

* *Editor's note:* Marquart once told me that in retrospect, he wondered whether these theses made it seem that spiritual powers were being delegated individually. That, of course, was not his mature position. (See *The Church,* 118: "By her call, the church does not gather individual functions into one cumulative bouquet. Rather, she conveys the public administration of her common possessions, that public administration being itself a divinely instituted office, and as such also part and parcel of the church's treasures.") Yet it might be noted, despite any second thoughts Marquart may have had, that the immediately preceding point 2 said the Office of the Ministry is being conferred when a congregation calls.

Chapter Three

AN EARNEST FRATERNAL APPEAL FROM OVERSEAS

To Our Fellow-Believers in The Lutheran Church—Missouri Synod on the Eve of the Denver Convention

Editor's note: Some of the background for what follows is provided by Martin Noland in his Fore-word to this volume. It might be added that in addition to the election of J. A. O. Preus as presi-dent, the other headline-grabbing decision that the Missouri Synod made at its 1969 (Denver) convention was to enter into altar and pulpit fellowship with the American Lutheran Church.

Editorially, this historic piece has hardly been touched, to preserve its distinctive look as it came from Marquart's typewriter. All the notes for the piece have been provided by me. These provide fuller bibliographic information. Marquart used abbreviations which are no longer current:

A.L.C. = American Lutheran Church   *L.W.F. = Lutheran World Federation*
L.C.A. = Lutheran Church in America   *W.C.C. = World Council of Churches*
L.C.U.S.A. = Lutheran Council in the United States of America

ॐ

In the Name of Jesus. Amen.

CRISIS AND TEMPTATION

From time to time individuals, nations, and churches are convulsed by elemental crises which shape their whole subsequent courses.

Our dear Lord went through such a crisis after His Baptism, when, fasting in the wilderness, He prepared Himself for His public Ministry. The Gospel for Invocavit (St. Matthew 4:1–11) tells how the Devil came and tempted Christ with all sorts of grandiose plans for a successful career. The Lord now faced the most basic decisions about His whole life's work. The issues could be confused (even with Bible texts!), and made to appear harmless, but at bottom they were as simple as they were crucial: faith or unbelief, obedience or disobedience, Cross or no Cross!

Christ's Church continues to be assailed by Satan. His temptations thicken with especial seductiveness at certain focal, pivotal points in her history. For as the tensions in the earth's crust are said to build up till they trigger an earthquake, so the pressures of nothing more than, e.g., years of theological hesitation and indecision accumulate until they produce a crisis which can no longer be postponed or evaded.

Nicaea, in A.D. 325, was such a crisis. Yet there were well-meaning "moderates" who thought that a compromise was possible. Even years after the Council, they portrayed the dispute as a needless quarrel over one single letter of the alphabet—Yes, but that one letter spelt the difference between confessing Christ as God and reducing Him to an idol "like" God!

Again, in Reformation times, Luther was under terrific pressure to agree to a hushing up of the issues for the sake of peace, love, unity, etc. No doubt Satan whispered, "Think of all the good you could do for the Church later—perhaps as a Cardinal!" Luther, like his Master, chose the foolishness of the Cross—and triumphed over the wisdom of men!

And after Luther's death, a dangerous conspiracy of secret Calvinists, intent on robbing the Lutheran Church of the Sacrament, very nearly succeeded in gaining the upper hand right at Wittenberg University. (See Bente's *Historical Introductions to the Book of Concord*, pp. 172–192.)[1]

Your Synod's great hour of crisis is coming at the Denver Convention in July. How will you face your fateful moment of truth?

We, the undersigned, some of your fellow-believers overseas, acting not officially on behalf of our churches, but simply as concerned individuals, herewith implore you by our common Faith to see what is really at stake, and to insist that everything be examined honestly and openly in the light of the Lord's own victorious "It is written"! Specifically, we beg and entreat you in Christ:

I.

Resist the Ecumenical Lure of "All the Kingdoms of the World, and the Glory of Them" (St. Matthew 4:8)!

In the Temptation, Satan did not ask Christ to change His formal doctrinal position. "Keep Your principles," he urged in effect, "only bend Your practice a little bit!"

The same soothing assurance is given in respect of the proposed declaration of fellowship with the A.L.C.—as if orthodoxy were a cheap paper currency, and practice didn't matter! But to deal with the A.L.C. while turning a blind eye to its various Ecumenical connections (L.C.A., L.W.F., W.C.C.) is like trying to deal with Poland as if there were no Warsaw Pact!

---

1. F. Bente, *Historical Introductions to the Book of Concord* (St. Louis: Concordia Publishing House, reprint, 1965).

L.W.F. and the Sacrament

In Article VII, Par. 33, of the Formula of Concord (Solid Declaration), the Lutheran Church makes its own the confession of Martin Luther:

> I reckon them all as belonging together (that is, as Sacramentarians and enthusiasts), for that is what they are who will not believe that the Lord's bread in the Supper is his true, natural body, which the godless or Judas receive orally as well as St. Peter and all the saints. Whoever, I say, will not believe this, will please let me alone and expect no fellowship from me. This is final.[2]

This is the official position of the Lutheran Church. But the exact opposite is the official position of the nominally "Lutheran" territorial churches of Europe, all of which are members, in excellent standing, of the "Lutheran" World Federation!

In the homeland of the Reformation all the formerly Lutheran territorial churches joined, in 1948, with the Reformed (Calvinist-Zwinglian) and the United churches (those giving equal rights to the Real Presence and its denial) into one single administrative unit, The Evangelical Church in Germany (EKiD). Some quibble that this is only a federation. That is beside the point. The point is that this joint body officially practises indiscriminate altar and pulpit fellowship. No wonder Dr. H. Sasse wrote: "In Eisenach, at the foot of the Wartburg, the Lutheran Church of Germany was buried in 1948. Loehe's dream-vision of the burial of the Lutheran Church by its own pastors had become a reality" (*In Statu Confessionis*, p. 63).[3]

The same is true of the national "Lutheran" churches of Scandinavia. (See Attachment 1, A, for a summary of the European situation by Dr. H. Sasse, himself a former professor at Erlangen University from 1933 to 1948.)

L.W.F. and Christ

On these grounds alone (surrender of the Real Presence, as officially confessed by the Lutheran Church) it is impossible to recognise the European territorial and national churches, and their agent, the L.W.F., as Lutheran. But of course much more is at stake now than the Real Presence.

---

2. Tappert, 575.
3. Hermann Sasse, "Der Siebente Artikel der Augustana in der gegenwärtigne Krisis des Luthertums," *In Statu Confessionis: Gesammelte Aufsätze von Hermann Sasse*, hrsg. Friedrich Wilhelm Hopf (Berlin, Hamburg: Lutherisches Verlagshaus, 1966); English translation in Hermann Sasse, *Letters to Lutheran Pastors: Volume III: 1957–1969*, ed. and trans. Matthew C. Harrison (St. Louis: Concordia Publishing House, 2015), 268.

What meaning can the Sacrament possibly have if the Divinity of Christ, the Redemption, or even the very existence of a personal God are in doubt?

The following sobering words were written from a deep personal knowledge of the situation by the late Dr. Hans Asmussen, President of the Chancery of the Evangelical Church in Germany between 1946 and 1948:

> But this is in fact the picture of wide sectors of our Lutheran Church to-day: clergymen read aloud the Christmas story, which they consider a fairytale. They read aloud the Easter story, to which they find access only after several reinterpretations. At the grave, they witness to the resurrection of the dead, which they consider a myth. (*Lutheran World,* Vol. XIII, No. 2, p. 186)[4]

Thank God, reform movements have of late been taking shape (e.g., the "No Other Gospel" movement in Germany). But you cannot help them by making common cause with the global church-political machine, which has sold its soul to the established, liberal university "theology"! You would be helping the enemy to tighten his grip on the poor Church he oppresses!

Is L.W.F. a Church?

Of course it will be said: But the L.W.F. is not a church; therefore it is not wrong to belong to it, even if its member churches are full of apostasy!

Some appear to believe that the 1963 Assembly of the L.W.F. at Helsinki made it clear, even by way of constitutional amendment, that the L.W.F. is not a church. This confuses two things:

1. a "super-church" in the Roman or Anglican sense of an administrative structure with power to compel; and
2. a church in the theological sense of a body, however loosely organised, doing joint church work, i.e., worship, teaching, administration of the Means of Grace.

At Helsinki the L.W.F. made it quite clear that on the one hand it does not at this stage wish to be a "super-church" in the administrative sense, but that on the other hand it is and must be a church in the theological sense. Thus the new Article III, Par. 1, of the constitution as amended at Helsinki, says that the L.W.F. "shall not exercise churchly functions on its own authority." This means that the L.W.F. is not to act as a "super-church." But that the L.W.F. has and must have "churchly functions," and

---

4. Hans Asmussen, "The Dogma of the Holy Scriptures," *Lutheran World* 13 (1966):186.

is therefore, theologically, a church, was taken for granted as self-evident at Helsinki! (See Attachment I, B.)

After Helsinki, Prof. Hans Liermann of Erlangen University, the noted expert in ecclesiastical law, writing in the L.W.F.'s own official organ, concluded, after a painstaking analysis, that "the Lutheran World Federation is a church in every sense of the word. It possesses a confession and fulfils churchly tasks. It is entrusted with direct proclamation of the word"[5]

Next year's L.W.F. Assembly in Porto Alegre, Brazil, has even been urged by Prof. E. Clifford Nelson, writing editorially in the L.W.F.'s official organ, to declare itself "to be the Lutheran *church* on an international level"![6]

The Ecumenical Spell

This was only the barest outline of the case against the L.W.F. And the latter's doctrinal tragedies are multiplied many times in the World Council of Churches, of which, after all, the L.W.F., run from the same headquarters in Geneva, is but an aspect.

So long as the A.L.C. continues in the L.W.F. and the W.C.C., it is therefore utterly fatuous to talk about any "consensus in the Gospel." Membership in these organisations is in and of itself a serious violation of the Gospel!

Satan evades specific objections by purring his ancient enticements:

"Don't quibble about details! Look at the needs of millions!" And so Christ becomes a Bread-King, and His Gospel is twisted into a revolutionary social action programme, as at Uppsala! No! "It is written: Man shall not live by bread alone, but by *every* word that proceedeth out of the mouth of God!"

"Never mind the prophets of doom! Jump in with faith and courage, and trust in the Holy Spirit!" No! "It is written again, Thou shalt not tempt the Lord thy God!"

"All those nations are yours to influence, evangelise, yes, save! Only join the big Ecumenical Movement— otherwise you will be too weak and small!" No! "Get thee hence, Satan: for it is written, Thou shalt worship the Lord thy God, and Him only shalt thou serve."

To break the hypnotic spell of the great Ecumenical Imitation Church with a clear "It is written," it is necessary to have a good grasp of the true

---

5. Hans Liermann, "The Legal Nature and Constitution of the Lutheran World Federation," *Lutheran World* 11 (April 1964):198.
6. E. Clifford Nelson, "Looking to Porto Alegre 1970" (editorial), *Lutheran World* 15 (1968):323.

Biblical doctrine of what the Church really is, as this is so beautifully set forth in Articles 7 and 8 of the Augsburg Confession and its Apology, in the Smalcald Articles and the Tractate, and in the Large Catechism.

From the Bible it is quite clear that as a pile of stones is not yet a church, so a pile of churches is not the Church! Only that is the Church which is "built on the foundation of the apostles and prophets, Jesus Christ Himself being the chief corner stone" (Eph. 2:20). Anything else is human or demonic imitation—even though many good men and true are tragically caught in the false systems as in a Babylonian Captivity!

The real Church, the Mystical Body of Christ, is and remains hidden from human view, under the cross and many weaknesses, sins, and offences. We may *see* the Devil's mirage of "all the kingdoms of the world," but we must *believe* the Church—she is an article of Faith! We find her not by sight, amid the trappings of a self-important ecclesiasticism, but only by faith in her pure Marks, the pure Gospel and Sacraments of Christ!

As the creature of the Word, the Church always remains under that Word. The pure doctrine of Christ's Gospel comes first, and determines what is Church and what is not—not as in the Ecumenical Movement, where the institutional "church" comes first, and then advertises the concoctions of its own theological alchemy as the "Gospel"!

Judged not by numbers, power, prestige, names, and other false standards, but by the true Marks of the Church, the pure Word and Sacraments, the Ecumenical Movement's claims collapse like a house of cards.

These are compelling grounds for repudiating L.C.U.S.A., L.W.F, and W.C.C., and refusing to consider the A.L.C.'s offer of fellowship until it has severed its Ecumenical connections.

II.

Do Not Allow Satan to Disarm You, by Robbing You of Your Only Weapon, Christ's "It Is Written"!

Even Satan did not dare to attack Holy Scripture directly by questioning Christ's firm "It is written." But the liberal, rationalising theology of the last two centuries insists without any shame that the Bible is not as such God's Word, much less inerrant! This "theology," particularly in the form of "Neo-Orthodoxy," and more recently as the "New Hermeneutics," has eaten deeply into both the Lutheran Church in America and the American Lutheran Church—and, alas, your own St. Louis seminary!

---

7. *Who Can This Be? Studies in Christology* (New York: Division of Theological Studies, Lutheran Council in the U.S.A., 1968).

The L.C.U.S.A. report "Who Can This Be?" wishes to "reflect the conviction that biblical criticism is here to stay" (p. 10).[7] This means of course not merely textual criticism, but freedom to attack the very substance of the Bible.

The L.C.A.'s prominent theologian, Dr. Joseph Sittler, had already in 1948 rejected inspiration and inerrancy in his book, *The Doctrine of the Word*, published by the Board of Publications of the then United Lutheran Church in America! Sittler said, for example: "If we equate the Word of God with the Scripture, we are confusing things heavenly with things historical" (p. 11).[8]

These and much more radical views abound in the L.C.A., with which the A.L.C. has become spiritually one, through declared fellowship. And of course the A.L.C. itself is adrift on the same seas of anti-Biblical modernism. (See Attachment II.)

Dr. Otto Heick, writing in the joint L.C.A.-A.L.C. publication *Lutheran Quarterly* (February, 1968), confesses himself a Liberal and observes:

To the Liberals of the old and new school, the Bible is essentially a classical document of man's religion, whereas in the eyes of the Orthodox, Evangelicals, and Fundamentalists, the Scriptures are a communication from God to man, vervally [*sic*] inspired, and therefore inerrant in every detail. This divergent view of Scripture is the most incisive element dividing American Protestantism, including the Lutheran churches in America. The men around *Christianity Today* as well as *Lutheran News*, search the Bible for infallible doctrines. They regard every statement in the Bible as accurate.[9]

Somewhat embarrassing to the liberals is the A.L.C.'s constitution, which speaks of the Bible as "the divinely inspired, revealed, and inerrant Word of God." The A.L.C.'s President, Dr. F. Schiotz, has officially explained this away in his essay "The Church's Confessional Stand Relative to the Scriptures." He writes: "The A.L.C. holds that the inerrancy referred to here does not apply to the text but to the truths revealed for our faith, doctrine, and life."

This must ultimately mean that what is inerrant is not the Bible itself and as such, but only its "truths," that is to say, the arbitrary, subjective constructs of those infallible modern popes, the theologians!

---

8. Joseph Sittler, *The Doctrine of the Word in the Structure of Lutheran Theology* (Philadelphia: Muhlenberg Press, 1948).

9. Otto Heick, "Biblical Inerrancy and the Hebrew Mode of Speech," *Lutheran Quarterly* (old series) 20 (February 1968):7.

A Vast Difference

But if the Missouri Synod is infected with such views too, what is the real difference between the two synods? Why not declare fellowship, and then "deal" with the matter together?

The difference is vast. In the A.L.C. the liberal view of Scripture officially rules and predominates. In Missouri, it is still a minority voice challenging the official position. Certainly, no Missouri Synod President has ever said, as Dr. Schiotz has, that inerrancy "does not apply to the text," that is, not to Scripture as such! Missouri's detailed position on Biblical inspiration and inerrancy is sound and clear—only it must be put into effect in terms of discipline.

A recent survey of more than ten thousand clergymen, published in the July/August 1967 number of *Transaction* (Washington University), showed that only 23 percent of the clergy of the A.L.C. accept the inerrancy of Scripture, while 78 percent of the Missouri Synod's clergy do so.

This means that your Synod could still reassert inerrancy, and "make it stick," whereas the A.L.C. cannot. But put the two together, mix them thoroughly with the L.C.A., declare fellowship, and the inevitable result will be L.C.U.S.A.'s bet: "Biblical criticism is here to stay"!

Let not Satan rob you of the Reformation's great Scripture-principle, *sola scriptura* (Scripture alone): "The Word of God shall establish articles of faith, and no one else, not even an angel!" (Smalcald Articles II ii 15).

If not even an angel can establish articles of faith, then certainly human reason, science, and speculation cannot do it. But the moment the inerrancy of Scripture is in any way denied, and "Biblical criticism" admitted, human reason is enthroned as final judge of what in Scripture is true and what not. That is the end of *sola scriptura*, for human reason is now in command. But then the whole foundation is gone, and instead of the rock of God's Word, we have the shifting sands of human opinion! Firm doctrine is no longer possible on this basis, and the only alternative left is the eternal Ecumenical guessing-game, which the Apostle describes as being "tossed to and fro, and carried about with every wind of doctrine, by the sleight of men, and cunning craftiness" (Eph. 4:14).

Declaring fellowship would be tantamount to embracing the A.L.C.–L.C.A.'s denial of Biblical inerrancy and authority! But you cannot resist the Ecumenical or any other temptation, once you have surrendered your only weapon: "It is written"!

Nor can you safely ignore your Synod's internal threats to the Scripture-principle. Many warning voices have been raised for years. In your own midst there are learned and faithful men like Dr. Robert Preus (essays on Scripture and A.L.C. fellowship), and Dr. John Warwick Montgomery (*Crisis in Lutheran Theology*, 2 volumes).[10] Then there are the sainted Dr. J. W. Behnken's unanswered *Questions* directed to your St. Louis seminary, and the cautiously understated admission of your Theological Commission itself, in its Report on Revelation, Inspiration, and Inerrancy, that doctrinal differences (Position A., Position B.) exist among you in this vital area. From overseas, there are the letters of Dr. H. Sasse, the *Memorandum Inter Nos* by Dr. W. M. Oesch, statements and pleas from the faithful Churches in Finland, Belgium, and France, the fraternal letter of admonition directed by the former Evangelical Lutheran Church of Australia's Melbourne Synod (1962) to your 1962 Cleveland Convention, and other Australian documents.

May the Lord grant you strength for effective remedial action!

III.

"Launch Out into the Deep, and Let Down Your Nets for a Draught" (St. Luke 5:4)

There are scattered throughout the world congregations and churches faithful to Scripture and Confession. For a hundred years your great Missouri Synod was the acknowledged leader and champion of those churches. But as your Synod became troubled by the problems of liberalism, its administrative apparatus at any rate turned its attention more and more toward the worldly-wise Ecumenical Movement, and neglected the Synod's former brothers-in-arms in other countries. As a result, the formerly solid Confessional front is in danger of fragmentation. Certainly, if you join in fellowship with A.L.C.-L.C.A., you will break up our world-wide Confessional fellowship. Make no mistake about that. But surely you will not abandon those with whom you are one, in order to join those with whom you are not one in doctrine?

Many of you, dear brothers, have a great love and zeal for God's Word. You see the great needs of the world and of the Church, and you are anxious to bring the Gospel of Christ to bear on them. You want to share your heritage, not to hoard it. You want passionately to bring a changeless Christ to a changing world!

---

10. Robert D. Preus, *Doctrine Is Life*, 2 vols., ed. Klemet I. Preus (St. Louis: Concordia Publishing House, 2006); John Warwick Montgomery, ed., *Crisis in Lutheran Theology: The Validity and Relevance of Historic Lutheranism vs. its Contemporary Rivals*, 2 vols. (Grand Rapids: Baker Book House, 1967).

All this is deeply Christian, Biblical, Lutheran. But Satan, who poses as an angel of light, tries to exploit even our noblest desires. He holds before you the shining illusion of a great doctrinal unity among Lutherans in America, and beyond that in the world, and urges you to widen the straight gate and broaden the narrow way, and to exchange the modesty of the Bride of Christ for the pomp and worldly power of the Scarlet Woman (Rev. 17), who rules in collusion with the Beast.

Surely the tremendous energies and resources of your Synod must not be dissipated in this way. Let them, instead, be devoted to the genuinely ecumenical task of strengthening everywhere the forces of real, Biblical, Confessional Lutheranism, so that the voice of Christ's pure Gospel can again sound forth in a great worldwide consensus, and undo to some extent the damage done by those who claim to speak for the Church, but do not and cannot.

This would be truly ecumenical because whatever promotes the truth of the Gospel, which alone builds the Church, thereby also advances real Christian unity; and whatever distorts or compromises the doctrine of the Gospel, destroys unity and the Church itself—even if it builds up large numbers! Keep and defend the real, God-given oneness of His people (Eph. 4:1 ff.)!

Such a genuinely ecumenical programme may not seem spectacular. But it will have Christ's blessing. He Who so signally blessed Peter's obedient, but apparently hopeless efforts (St. Luke 5:4 ff.), will also richly prosper, in many unexpected ways, your launching out into the deep, not in carnal ambition, as men-pleasers, but in obedient trust in His Word!

We and our churches owe much to your Synod. You have in the past strengthened us. Now we pray for you, that you may be guided safely away from the brink of the bottomless Ecumenical abyss, and that, having won the victory with a firm "It is written," you may in turn strengthen us. Let the Saviour's own prayer be fulfilled anew:

"SIMON, BEHOLD, SATAN HATH DESIRED TO HAVE YOU, THAT HE MAY SIFT YOU AS WHEAT: BUT I HAVE PRAYED FOR THEE, THAT THY FAITH FAIL NOT: AND WHEN THOU ART CONVERTED, STRENGTHEN THY BRETHREN" (St. Luke 22:31–32)! AMEN!

Note: The list of signatures which follow is selective, not exhaustive. No attempt has been made to reach the many who would have signed this appeal. Such a difficult task is not necessary to dramatise the gravity of this fraternal appeal. [Editor's note: The signatures are not being included here.]

ATTACHMENT I

A.

Dr. H. Sasse on European Lutheranism

"The Lutheran territorial churches of Germany have been dissolved into the 'Evangelical Church in Germany,' whose Council has just decided that in every member church, all members of the EKiD, without regard to their Confession, must be admitted to the Lord's Supper. The Churches of Sweden and Finland are in intercommunion with the Church of England. An Anglican bishop participates in every episcopal consecration. Bishop Stephen Neill, who 'equalises' German students and missionaries at the supposedly Lutheran Faculty of Hamburg, keeps book about how many German bishops already possess apostolic succession. On top of this, Sweden has now solemnly introduced intercommunion with the Church of Scotland, which is practised also by Denmark and Norway. How all this works out in the formerly Lutheran mission fields, above all in Africa and India, is well known. The Church in the Palatinate has solemnly accepted intercommunion with the Congregational Union of England and Wales and the related American sects, but demands that all German Lutherans moving into the Palatinate communicate at the Reformed Communion Table of the Church of the Palatinate. In Holland, altar fellowship between the Lutheran and the Reformed territorial churches has been solemnly confirmed. France will follow. And no one takes offence at this. The German professors go from Tuebingen to Zurich, from Zurich to Goettingen, from Bonn to Erlangen, from Erlangen to Mainz. For 'the Confessional Age is over,' as they assure us. That their students must someday swear an Ordination Vow does not interest them" (*Lutherische Blaetter*, December 1966, p. 84).[11]

B.

Helsinki and the L.W.F. as Church

+ Helsinki did not reject Prof. Peter Brunner's argument that the L.W.F. was constantly having to make decisions involving teaching, but that teaching is "the one absolutely central commission of the Church of Christ. When it teaches, it is undoubtedly acting as a church" (*Lutheran World*, December 1960).[12]

---

11. English translation in Sasse, *Letters to Lutheran Pastors* III, 422–423.
12. Peter Brunner, "The Lutheran World Federation as Ecclesiological Problem," *Lutheran World* 7 (December 1960):245.

◆ Helsinki, while declining the unworkable suggestion of an official commentary on the constitution, did not reject the theology of the official report of its Commission on Theology on "The Nature of the Lutheran World Federation," which took for granted the L.W.F.'s "churchly tasks," and even concluded: "Therefore, these churches are spiritually obligated, above and beyond their having come together in the L.W.F., to enter into mutual church fellowship" (Helsinki Assembly, 1963, Document No. 4).

◆ Helsinki reacted with tumultuous applause to Prof. E. Clifford Nelson's lecture, in which he also underscored that theologically the L.W.F. was a church. He said:

> No doubt the leaders of the Lutheran World Convention and the Lutheran World Federation felt they were acting wisely in making disclaimers of intentions to being or becoming 'a church' in a constitutional sense. But, that organised world Lutheranism was an expression of the *ekklesia*, had already been recognised (Jørgensen: 'It is a Church'). Nevertheless, a prudential concern dictated then that haste be made slowly, in order to dissipate anxieties and to avoid shattering by precipitous action, what had already been achieved.

C.

Dr. H. Sasse on L.W.F. and Missouri

"If the Missouri Synod were to join the World Federation . . . nothing would change in the World Federation, but everything would change in Missouri. This great Church would cease to be a Confessional Church. Who would be served thereby? The great global church politicians perhaps, but no one else, neither the congregations, nor the pastors. Whether a Church might perhaps break up, many thousands of consciences be injured, hearts be broken, and souls lost, about that the Oecumene does not ask" (Letter No. 52, *Lutherische Blaetter*, Advent 1960, p. 137).[13]

---

13. English translation in Sasse, Letters to Lutheran Pastors III, 244–245.
    English translation in Sasse, Letters to Lutheran Pastors III, 244–245.

ATTACHMENT II

The Meaning of L.C.U.S.A.'s Dictum,
"Biblical Criticism Is Here to Stay"

+ *Theology in the Life of the Church* (Fortress Press, 1963), edited by Prof. Robert Bertram and sponsored by "the Conference of Lutheran Professors of Theology" (A.L.C., L.C.A., and L.C.-M.S.), contains a chapter on the Bible (pp. 22–39), by Prof. Warren A. Quanbeck, professor of systematic theology at the A.L.C.'s. largest seminary, Luther, at St. Paul, Minnesota. Quanbeck says that in the past, Lutheran "theologians read the Bible as a collection of revealed propositions unfolding the truth about God, the world, and man." He rejects this position, arguing that there "can be no absolute expression of the truth, even in the language of theology" (p. 25).

+ *The Bible: Book of Faith* (Augsburg Publishing House, 1964), was issued by the A.L.C.'s Board of Parish Education, and was defended by the A.L.C. as such in Convention assembled. That book advocates biblical criticism and a cautious modernism. For example: "The infallibility of the Scriptures is the infallibility of Jesus Christ, and not the infallibility of the written text" (p. 148).

+ *Theological Perspectives*, published by Luther College (A.L.C.) says:

> Luke is definitely wrong in saying that Paul agreed to these requirements [i.e., those of the Apostolic Council, Acts 15:28–29].
>
> The opening of the heavens, the descent of the Spirit, and the voice from heaven are not objective events accessible to the eyes and ears of the observer. They are the theological interpretation of the meaning of Jesus' baptism by John.
>
> Some remarkable sayings are attributed to Jesus in the gospel of John: "I am the bread of life ... I am the resurrection and the life; he who believes in me, though he die, yet shall he live, and whoever lives and believes in me shall never die" (John 11:25–26). These are the words of the risen Lord speaking through the confessions of the church and not the words of the Jesus of history.[14]

---

14. Wilfred F. Bunge, "The Historical-Critical Method and the New Testament," *Theological Perspectives: A Discussion of Contemporary Issues in Lutheran Theology* (Decorah, Iowa: Luther College Press, n.d.) 42, 43–44, 46.

(In other words, Jesus never said that! The Church invented it later, and put these words into His mouth!)

+ *Luther*, the quarterly organ of that same Luther College, Decorah, Iowa (A.L.C.), in its Spring 1967 issue, contained Prof. Paul Jersild's article, "What Are Those Theologians Saying?" Prof. Jersild said:

> Our American Lutheran Church is rather obviously divided to-day on certain theological issues. . . . We who teach at Luther College cannot subscribe to scriptural inerrancy because our knowledge of Scripture prevents us from making such a claim.[15]

+ "Miracle Stories—Testimony to Faith or Credibility Gap?" (*Journal of the Lutheran School of Theology at Chicago*, Spring/Summer 1968) argues that the miracles never happened, but were merely literary devices to express the "theological meanings" of events. Also this:

> I just don't think we have need of the miraculous today. Perhaps there was a time when people needed it, maybe for psychological or sociological reasons. But I don't think we need it today. . . . I think the miracles emphasize that which is contrary to the Gospel of Christ.
>
> But to believe today that God would do such a God-awful thing as separate the waters of the sea so that the Hebrews can escape and the Egyptians get it— I think this is very ungodly of him!"[16]

---

15. *Luther* 4 (Spring 1967):9.
16. Morris Niedenthal, ed. "Text in Context: Miracle Stories — Testimony to Faith or Credibility Gap?" Context 1 (Spring/Summer 1968):36–37, 38, quoting Carl Uehling.

Chapter Four

THE SWING OF THE PENDULUM

An Attempt to Understand the St. Louis "Affirmations and Discussions"

Editor's note: As The Lutheran Church—Missouri Synod's crucial 1973 convention approached, many preparations were being made. For this convention would receive the synodical president's "Blue Book" report of September 1, 1972. This report was informed by the work of the Fact Finding Committee that had been appointed by President J. A. O. Preus to investigate doctrinal problems at Concordia Seminary, St. Louis. It carried a theological document, "A Statement of Scriptural and Confessional Principles," released by President Preus to the Synod earlier in 1972. (This material is readily available to the contemporary reader in Paul A. Zimmerman, A Seminary in Crisis: The Inside Story of the Preus Fact Finding Committee [St. Louis: Concordia Publishing House, 2007].)

In early January of 1973, Concordia Seminary disseminated to the pastors and congregations of the Synod its own two-volume document. The essay below concerns the first volume, which was called Faithful to Our Calling, Faithful to Our Lord: An Affirmation in Two Parts *by the Faculty of Concordia Seminary, St. Louis, Missouri. Part I — A Witness to Our Faith: A Joint Statement and Discussion of Issues (N.p., n.d.). Within this volume were both "Affirmations" and "Discussions."*

Acting on a request from District Presidents, in March 1973 the Synod's Commission on Theology and Church Relations evaluated this first volume. The Commission's evaluation was included in the 1973 Missouri Synod Convention Workbook *(on pages 39–40).*

At about the same time in Australia, Kurt Marquart was diligently writing his own analysis, which turned out to be much more detailed. This is the essay that follows, which originally appeared in Occasional Papers *(published by Affirm), Spring 1973. It remains the most incisive single evaluation of the seminary document, and perhaps of the then-faculty majority's theological position.*

Editorial changes have been deliberately minimized in the present publication, so today's reader can see what others first saw in 1973. Bibliographic information has been filled out for a number of the sources cited, and words that Marquart had emphasized by placing them in all capital letters in the original have been italicized here.

Throughout this essay Marquart makes reference to a couple of documents that may not be as well known today as they were to him or his readers in 1973. One is the "Statement of the Forty-Four," sometimes called the "1945 Statement" or the "Chicago Statement." It may be found in Concordia Historical Institute Quarterly *XLIII (November 1970):150–152.*

The other document to which Marquart sometimes refers here is "The Theses of Agreement and Inerrancy," on which he had worked as a member of the Lutheran Church of Australia's theological commission. These theses were eventually published in the United States in The Springfielder *38 (September 1973):84 ff. A subsection of this* Springfielder *piece is titled "Genesis 1–3: A Doctrinal Statement."*

෧෨

PRELIMINARY ORIENTATION

Since the Seminary document did not fall from Heaven into Luther Tower, a historical-critical study of its intended meaning and function is indicated.

Standing back for a bit of perspective, it seems best to start with the thinking of Theodore Graebner, one of the finest intellects the Missouri Synod has produced. Like Melanchthon before him, T. G. was prodigiously learned and analytical. The breadth of his outlook is reflected in his classic *God and the Cosmos*, which no doubt whetted and shaped the philosophical and theological appetites of many of us. And also like Melanchthon, Graebner gave impetus to developments the outcome of which he could neither foresee nor approve.

As I see it, the 1945 *Statement* was concerned, in a somewhat stifling atmosphere, to assert two great Reformation truths and their consequences for inter-Lutheran relations: (1) the absolute centrality of Christ and His Atonement for all doctrine and theology; and (2) the exclusive normativeness of Scripture itself, as distinct from mere exegetical opinions and traditions. In other words, we have here a concern for the material and the formal principles, and for their proper correlation.

Behind the *Statement* is Graebner's theologically much more adequate *The Historic Lutheran Position in Non-Fundamentals*, issued by C.P.H. (Concordia Publishing House) in 1939. It deserves a lot more attention than it seems to have acquired. And I must add in all candor that this judgment would probably not have occurred to me without and before the salutary discipline of our intensive Inerrancy-Genesis discussions in Australia, particularly within our Commission on Theology and Inter-Church Relations, which led to the fruitful Biblical-Confessional agreement documented in the relevant statements of our 1972 General Synod at Horsham, Victoria. Although I shall be quoting these documents, I do not want to suggest that the unavoidable judgments expressed in the present paper represent any sort of official or unofficial Australian consensus. I speak for myself alone.

Graebner's book on non-fundamentals arose out of the abortive fellowship discussions with the old American Lutheran Church. What bothered Graebner was a tendency to elevate all sorts of exegetical details and inferences to the level of church-divisive doctrine — for example, the thousand years of Revelation 20, the conversion of the Jews, etc. As a way out of this dilemma he drew attention to the time-honored Lutheran scheme of the threefold foundation of the Faith, the substantial, the dogmatic, and the organic or instrumental. The substantial foundation is of course the Triune God Himself and His saving work in Christ. The dogmatic foundation is the Gospel in a nutshell, the *articulus stantis et cadentis ecclesiae,* justification *propter Christum, sola gratia, sola fide.* This Gospel, however, is not an isolated abstraction, but necessarily presupposes certain articles (e.g., Trinity, Creation, Original Sin, Incarnation) and entails others (Church, Means of Grace), so that to attack any of these is to subvert the Gospel itself. The organic foundation, finally, is the Scriptural Word of God in its twofold role of source and norm for both *fides qua* (the individual's act of believing, personal, saving faith) and *fides quae* (the objective content of faith, doctrine, theology).

It is clear that the dogmatic foundation is the same as the material principle, and that the organic foundation is the formal principle, which includes the plenary inspiration, authority, inerrancy, clarity, sufficiency, etc., of Scripture. These then are not two (or three) different things, but distinct yet inseparable aspects of the one saving work of God in Christ: the divine-human reality which constitutes and sustains it (substantial foundation), the teaching which describes this reality (dogmatic foundation), and the divine source, authority and power guaranteeing the truth of the teaching and through it communicating the reality itself (organic foundation).

The point of the scheme for church-fellowship is that only what subverts the threefold foundation of the Faith may be regarded as divisive. Walther himself wrote: "The Church has never reached a higher degree of unity than a fundamental one, and only a fanatical chiliast could hope that the Church would ever reach a higher degree."[1]

This eminently Biblical, evangelical approach (1 Cor. 3:11, 12; Eph. 2:20) fully safeguards the dogmatic substance of the Christian Faith, without fossilizing all exegetical and theological discussion into a rigid immobility. It leaves generous room for responsible differences under the discipline of God's Word. For example, one may be convinced that a certain

---

1.   Quoted in Theodore Graebner, *The Historic Lutheran Position in Non-Fundamentals* (St. Louis: Concordia Publishing House, 1939), 22.

exegetical opinion (e.g., non-normal Creation days) is dead wrong or a doctrinal formulation clumsy (e.g., the means of grace as the "visible side" of the church), and then one must by all means say so. But this would not threaten the fraternal bonds of church-fellowship, *provided* that there is no violation of anything that belongs to the integrity of the dogmatic foundation (the doctrine of the Gospel "in all its articles," *FC SD X, 31*) or of the organic foundation (full Biblical authority). On the other hand, of course, the humblest non-fundamental ceases to be that and becomes church-divisive the moment it is asserted in conscious opposition to the Biblical text, for then the organic foundation is denied.

But this "de-militarized" theological discussion zone is no longer spacious enough for Dr. Graebner's successors. With one-sided zeal for the dogmatic foundation, the Seminary document has jettisoned the organic foundation. As a result, the Gospel itself is in principle de-natured.

Having roughly defined some historical and dogmatic reference points, we must note a few general hermeneutical points about the document under discussion. Since that document explicitly intends "to address the issues under discussion in the Synod," which in turn are most comprehensively summarized in President Preus' [*Statement of*] *Biblical and Confessional Principles* and in his Fact Finding Committee's Report, and since the Seminary also explicitly rejects the theology of these documents, it is clear that the *Affirmations* and *Discussions* are meant as answers, even alternatives to President Preus' documents, and must be so understood.

Further, the *Affirmations* are meant "as assurance to the church that we teach in accord with Article II of Synod's Constitution" in the face of the contrary claim by the Fact Finding Committee. Failure to achieve this stated purpose could have drastic personal and institutional consequences. One must assume therefore that the formulations put their very best foot forward. Their tendency will be maximal, i.e., to say the most that can be said, and to say it as reassuringly as possible, in terms of traditional Missouri Synod thinking. This means that disturbing elements contrary to this intention will tend to be understated, and must therefore be given especial weight whenever they appear. On the other hand, "good" statements appearing only in the *Discussions* but not in the *Affirmations*, must be discounted to some extent, since the *Discussions* do not necessarily represent the "precise wording" which the faculty majority would unanimously accept "as the only or the best way to formulate the answers. We are agreed that other wordings or expressions are not excluded" (Preamble).

The document's split-level structure is no doubt meant to suggest that the controversial "questions at issue in the Synod" concern only a secondary,

Discussions-level, and do not threaten doctrinal agreement where it counts. But no literary partitions can protect the *Affirmations* from the *Discussions*, since the latter really define what is meant, or allowed, by the former.

Finally, charity towards the faculty demands that we accept their good faith with the simplicity of the dove, while charity towards the church compels us also to be wise as serpents in taking account of possibilities like the one reported by the managing editor of the *Concordia Theological Monthly*: "Some weeks ago a trusted friend advised us to stick to broad theological issues in the pages of this journal and to avoid all the pressing present problems in the Lutheran Church–Missouri Synod. 'Fill the church full of Gospel,' he said, 'so that there will be no room left for non-Gospel problems'" (Herbert T. Mayer, "Which Birds" *CTM* XLIII [September 1972]:438).

HISTORICAL-CRITICAL METHODOLOGY

The validity of the historical-critical approach to Scripture is the basic point at issue in the whole document. Although the matter is not explicitly dealt with until *Discussion Nine*, it permeates and shapes the entire presentation, as we shall see. In fact the document itself illustrates the falsity of the crucial assumption that "in and of itself the so-called 'historical critical' methodology is neutral."

Let us consider *Discussion Nine*'s claim that "basically all the techniques associated with 'historical-critical' methodology, such as source analysis, form history, and redaction history, are legitimated by the fact that God chose to use as His written Word human documents written by human beings in human language."

At least four related issues arise here: (1) the distinction between the servant-use and the master-use of reason; (2) the scholarly validity of representative critical techniques; (3) the theological validity of the critical approach; (4) the question of controls or limits.

Servant-Reason or Master-Reason?

The talk about neutral "techniques" suggests that the objection to the historical-critical approach arises from an obscurantist inability or unwillingness to exercise responsible scholarship. But no responsible Lutheran doubts that the exegete must make competent use of all relevant scientific equipment in the service of the Biblical text. The principle is not new, and is certainly not the distinctive contribution of historical criticism, nor the point at which it becomes objectionable. Thus our Australian Genesis statement says:

This does not mean that we reject either reason or scholarship. Quite on the contrary. We hold that it is the function of Biblical interpretation to understand and apply the Bible as a whole and in all its parts. But everyone who takes the Reformation's *sola scriptura* seriously must insist that the proper function of reason, and thus of scholarship, is in every respect *under* and not *over* Scripture — as handmaid, and not as mistress. As emphatically as we reject any use of reason as master or judge over Scripture, so we affirm the fullest use of reason, with all its scholarly tools, as a servant, to understand and make clear what the sacred text says and means.

But the *Discussions* in effect reverse this. When it comes to the proper, servant-use of reason, we are discouraged from drawing substantive inferences from Genesis, since the Biblical materials "speak primarily to our faith rather than our intellect" (*Discussion One*). This false opposition reflects the typically neo-orthodox-existentialist aversion to "Aristotelian" inconveniences like logic, definition, precision, propositions (doctrine!), and clear thinking generally. The irony is that we have here a form of the Thomistic illusion that the Biblical contrast is between grace and *nature* (e.g., reason, the body, matter, and other scapegoats) when actually it is between grace and *sin* (e.g., the rebellious autonomy of reason)!

Yet when it really is a question of reason acting as master and judge over Scripture, in the historical-critical approach as well-nigh universally understood and practiced today the Seminary document yields almost unconditionally, and is firm only in its defense of this yielding! And that is the real issue.

How Scholarly?

While nobody objects to genuine scholarship, yielding palpable facts and information, much of what passes for neutral "tools" and "methods" is really nothing of the sort. The *Discussions* nowhere hint at this state of affairs. In fact the "techniques" they list ("source analysis, form history, and redaction history") are particularly good examples of procedures often governed by a minimum of factual evidence and a maximum of imaginative speculation, flavored with a good bit of philosophical bias to boot.

Take that senior sacred cow, the J-E-D-P source hypothesis, which Cyrus Gordon of Brandeis University has, while rejecting it on scientific grounds, aptly styled the "badge of inter-confessional academic respectability."[2] Pro-

---

2. Quoted in Raymond Surburg, "Implications of the Historico-Critical Method in Interpreting the Old Testament," *Crisis in Lutheran Theology*, ed. J. W. Montgomery (Grand Rapids: *Baker*, 1967), 2:56.

fessor U. Cassuto, of the Hebrew University in Jerusalem, demonstrated in painstaking textual detail the complete untenability of the accepted documentary scheme and of the techniques with which it is deduced.[3]

Prof. J. W. Montgomery, whose meticulously documented studies are, incredibly, nowhere referred to in the *Discussions'* suggestions "For Further Study," comments:

> The use of parallel critical methods in other academic fields has proven so unfruitful that these techniques have been largely discredited outside of biblical scholarship.... As to the continued presence of "such niggling word-baiting" in biblical criticism, Yamauchi of Rutgers has stated at the close of a recent lecture which has been expanded into an exceedingly important monograph: "If we applied the criterion of 'Divine Names' to Ugaritic, Egyptian, or Arabic texts, we would see that the principle was not valid. I could multiply examples for all the other criteria of the documentary hypothesis."[4]

And the Liverpool University Orientalist, K. A. Kitchen, is very critical of "the literary-critical theories of the composition of the Pentateuch in particular" which were based ultimately "on the dilettante speculations of the eighteenth century" and "are still dominant in Old Testament studies today." Kitchen, who brings to bear a fascinating wealth of actual archaeological evidence, complains that the reigning Old Testament scholarship continues to spin its speculations in almost total independence of the known facts:

> For, worst of all, the documentary theory in its many variations has throughout been elaborated *in a vacuum,* without any proper reference to other Ancient Oriental literatures to find out whether they had been created in this singular manner. In the eighteenth and earlier part of the nineteenth centuries, of course, no comparative data were available from the Ancient Near East; but from the late nineteenth century onward, Egyptian, Mesopotamian and even West-Semitic material became increasingly available, and the failure of Wellhausen and almost all of his earlier and later contemporaries to heed this material is inexcusable. It is a most serious omission, because — in the forms actually preserved to us in the extant

---

3. U. Cassuto, *The Documentary Hypothesis* (Jerusalem: Magnes Press, Hebrew University, 1961). U. Cassuto, *Commentary on Genesis,* 2 vols. (Jerusalem: Magnes Press, 1961 & 1964).

4. J. W. Montgomery, "Theological Issues and Problems of Biblical Interpretation Now Facing The Lutheran Church — Missouri Synod," *Crisis in Lutheran Theology,* ed. J. W. Montgomery (Grand Rapids: Baker, 1967), 1:85–86.

Old Testament—Hebrew literature shows very close external stylistic similarities to the other Ancient Oriental literatures among which (and as part of which) it grew up. Now, nowhere in the Ancient Orient is there anything which is definitely known to parallel the elaborate history of fragmentary composition and conflation of Hebrew literature (or marked by just such criteria) as the documentary hypotheses would postulate. And conversely, any attempt to apply the criteria of the documentary theorists to Ancient Oriental compositions that have known histories but exhibit the same literary phenomena results in manifest absurdities.[5]

And then there is that form-critical invention, "*Gemeindetheologie.*" The basic idea is that certain things reported in the New Testament never actually happened, but were invented by the preaching, confession, or theology of the early church in response to its own needs. For example: "We know darn well something was happening, maybe not to a group of people standing in a boat watching Jesus, but something was happening somewhere in the life of the early community that made it seem desirable to put in something like this, which is undoubtedly rooted in experience but which also has been embellished."[6]

W. F. Bunge, of Luther College, Decorah, Iowa, virtually identifies this approach with "the historical-critical method" which is "indispensable" if we are to "read the literary deposit of early Christianity with comprehension."[7] The essence of this "comprehension" is that the New Testament is not a report of what actually happened, but a "confessional interpretation." This means, for instance, that Jesus never uttered the great "I am" sayings of St. John's Gospel: "These are the words of the risen Lord speaking through the confession of the church and not the words of the Jesus of history." Here "the post-resurrection theological insights of a particular group within the early church are read back into the history of Jesus of Nazareth."

Now, what genuine scholarly validity attaches to this whole notion of "*Gemeindetheologie*"? Prof. W. Kuenneth of the University of Erlangen refers to Prof. Schadewald of Tuebingen, whom he describes as an "outstanding Graecist" who knows "the entire literature of antiquity":

---

5. K. A. Kitchen, *Ancient Orient and Old Testament* (London: Tyndale, 1966), 112, 114–115, italics original.

6. M. Niedenthal, ed., "Text in Context: Miracle Stories — Testimony to Faith or Credibility Gap?" *Context* 1 (Spring/Summer 1968):36 ff. [Quote from Philip Hefner, p. 40.]

7. Luther College Religion Department, eds., *Theological Perspectives* (Decorah: Luther College Press, 1968), 49.

He pointed out that precisely in the New Testament we have before us the best conceivable historical sources. He stated further that there can be no question at all of a production of a *"Gemeindetheologie."* I personally want to designate this popular talk of a *"Gemeindetheologie"* as a modern myth. Schadewald made it plain that precisely in the New Testament recollection plays a decisive role. Recollection has an interest in holding on to and preserving verbatim all that Jesus said and did. Therefore there can be no suggestion of a legend at all. If all that is legend, that's about how Schadewald puts it, then no scholarly study of ancient history exists at all.[8]

And H.-J. Kraus, in the most thorough history known to me of the historical-critical study of the Old Testament, repeatedly draws attention to the decisive influence of philosophical premises, e.g., rationalism, romanticism, idealism, evolutionism, historicism, etc.[9] To these must be added the existentialism of the New Hermeneutic, which tries to "warm up" the coldly destructive vagaries of "scientific" criticism with yet another massive dose of subjectivism! Montgomery shows that contrary to the fashionable belief, the "vicious circle" hermeneutics of today corresponds not to Luther's exegesis, but precisely to the medieval, tradition-dominated method which he rejected; and that it is the *"sola scriptura"* hermeneutics of orthodoxy which really corresponds to Luther's exegesis![10]

Criticism's Hidden Doctrines and Theology

The preceding points to the heart, soul, and essence of historical criticism: the subjection of Scripture and its content to the magisterial judgment of human reason. It is this *Sachkritik*, the criticism of substance or content according to human, philosophical assumptions, rather than any scholarly refinement, which constitutes the distinguishing feature of the historical-critical approach and methodology. Already in 1805 Johann Philipp Gabler, one of the most influential historical-critical thinkers, put it quite plainly: It is

impossible nowadays to be satisfied with the mere fact that an ancient author reported an event and considered it to be true. It is right to ask and investigate: But is it true? And if it *cannot* have happened like this, then

---

8. W. Kuenneth, *Die Grundlagenkrisis der Theologie heute.* Essay presented to the Council of the European Evangelical Alliance, London, September 1968, 11.

9. H.-J. Kraus, *Geschichte der historisch-kritischen Erforschung das Alten Testaments,* 2nd ed. (Neukirchener Verlag, 1969), passim.

10. J. W. Montgomery, "Lutheran Hermeneutics and Hermeneutics Today," *Crisis* 1:64.

one investigates further: How did the author get the idea? Is something true perhaps at the bottom of it? If so, what? And what prompted him to make the additions? Or is the whole thing only fiction? Deliberate — the invention of a deceiver or a fanatic? Or merely well-intentioned fiction? Philosophical or poetic myth?

And:

> A more exact study of nature and especially of man, and a worthier view of God and of his attributes, have spread truer concepts in the whole realm of religion; and these no longer permitted belief in the letter of the Bible.[11]

This quintessence of the critical orientation, which it would be fatuous to restrict to the "age of rationalism," is completely bagatellized in *Discussion Nine*: "Criticism does not mean sitting in judgment over others but involves making a studied decision on the basis of all available evidence." What a prim Victorian stork-story! If it refers simply to intelligent efforts to determine what the text says and means, then it is quite beside the point, for that is not at issue. If, however, it means to describe the typical operations of historical-critical methodology, then it is plainly false. For the "studied decision on the basis of all available evidence" involves treating Biblical and non-Biblical "evidence" as equals, so that the latter is in principle "sitting in judgment" over the former!

I doubt that one could find a more authoritative definition of criticism than that of Abraham Kuenen's 1880 essay on "Critical Methods." The leading historian of the historical-critical methodology as applied to the Old Testament takes this essay to represent "the 'methodology' of historical-critical scholarship at the apex of its unfolding."[12] Says Kuenen: "'Criticism' means the art of judging. Very well then, let us envisage the man who bears his name from this his activity, a judge!"[13] And then he goes on to describe in detail how it is necessary to view all evidence and examine and cross-examine all witnesses impartially (without granting any special status or privilege to Biblical materials!), in order to determine what actually did take place. It is clear that man's reason is judge here, and Scripture, far from being "the only judge, rule, and norm" (FC), is one among other witnesses at best, and a suspect or defendant at worst. "The biblical witnesses are first and foremost witnesses of a historical process

---

11. C. Hartlich and W. Sachs, *Der Ursprung des Mythosbegriffes in der modernen Bibelwissenschaft* (Tuebingen: Siebeck, 1952), 87–89.
12. Kraus, 249.
13. Kraus, 253.

which the 'judge' must reconstruct, because he is dealing — and that is the secret presupposition of all research with Kuenen —with the 'case' of a 'false historiography' in the Old Testament." So Kraus comments, adding that Kuenen's essay represents "the real vital nerve of historical-critical research at the stage of its mighty unfolding," and a "masterpiece" illustrating "the innermost impulse of scientific questing and questioning."[14]

And this is precisely the typical approach today. The following recent theses formed the basis for a discussion between the assistants of the Roman Catholic and Protestant theological faculties, respectively, at the University of Munich:

> 4. If exegesis is to be practised historico-critically, it must use the methods of secular historical science, i.e., criticism which allows only probable judgments, and the principles of analogy and correlation (cf. Troeltsch). Thereby it subjects itself in principle to secular-historical judgment.
>
> 6. Historical-critical exegesis presupposes the equal historical value of all sources, i.e., it prescinds from the self-witness or the special status of a writing. . . . The biblical books count as ancient near-eastern sources, and the concepts contained in them are ancient near-eastern. . . .
>
> 8. From the historical integration into general history there follows the religio-historical integration. Yahweh is a Semitic divinity (about whose introduction into Israel the historian may offer conjectures); this applies in principle also to the *Theos* of the N.T. Phenomena and concepts (e.g., charismatics, kingship, prophecy, discipleship, apostolate; commandments, ethos, prayer, virgin birth, resurrection, ascension) are subject to the principles of correlation and analogy. Jesus is a late-Jewish figure. The forms of religion in the biblical texts count, since they developed historically, as syncretistic.
>
> 10. Through the abolition of the boundary of the canon for historical research, the concept "unity" or "centre of Scripture" becomes questionable.
>
> 13. If historical-critical exegesis subjects its findings to secular-historical judgment [as by definition it must, cf. thesis 4. K. M.] then the demand to bind it to an ecclesiastical teaching office or to confessional writings, contradicts its very starting point [*Ansatz*].[15]

Against this monolithic critical reality *Discussion Nine* half-heartedly pits the illusion that it is simply a question of getting at "the intended

---

14. Kraus, 254.

15. *Korrespondenzblatt* (Pfarrerverein in Bavaria), 1969, 128 ff.

meaning of the written Word of God as we have it." I say "half-heartedly," because the inerrancy of Scripture was surrendered already in *Discussion Eight*, and the critical leaven is at work throughout the document, from *Discussion One's* relativizing of Genesis through *Discussion Three's* dispensation from "an absolute acceptance of each detail of the miracle, precisely as it is reported," to the final denouement in *Discussion Nine*. The surrender of inerrancy can mean only that the interpreter is free to disagree with direct assertions of the Biblical text, and to that extent with "the intended meaning of the written Word of God as we have it." And as Dr. Franzmann points out, even a "conservative" critic like K. Froer feels free to "interpret against the intention of the evangelist." Comments Franzmann:

> A principle, or a method, is not to be applied "conservatively" or "radically" — it should simply be applied *consistently*. Therefore the more "radical" practitioners of the method can always reproach the more "conservative" ones with inconsistency. It is therefore not unfair to cite examples of a more "radical" use of the method in order to illustrate its tendency and its consequences.[16]

It is not surprising therefore that the critical scholar Kraus himself repeatedly stresses the incompatibility of the orthodox doctrine of inspiration with the historical-critical approach, and rejects "the optimistic illusion that the historical-critical study of Scripture is merely an implementation of the Reformation's Scripture-principle."[17]

Meaningful Controls

No doubt Prof. H. Hummel is right in arguing that it is simplistic to speak of "*the* historical-critical method," as if there were only one uniform version of it.[18] At the same time, historical-critical *methodology*, as distinct from this or that particular method, covers, as we have seen, a multitude of sins, the identifiable common denominator of which is the rejection of Biblical authority. This is the *proprium* which distinguishes critical methodology from *bona fide* interpretation. It is therefore doubly wrong of *Discussion Nine* simply to whitewash "so-called historical-critical methodology" as such, without any further ado.

---

16. Martin H. Franzmann, "The Hermeneutical Dilemma: Dualism in the Interpretation of Holy Scripture," *CTM* XXXVI (September 1965):507–508.
17. Kraus, 390.
18. H. D. Hummel, "The Outside Limits of Lutheran Confessionalism in Contemporary Biblical Interpretation: Part III (1) History and Revelation" *The Springfielder* XXXVI (June 1972):44, italics original.

Dr. Hummel hits the critical nail on the head when he writes:

> It is the presence or absence of the overall *hermeneutical* framework (Scripture interpreting itself) alongside our intensified historical investigations which determines whether or not the latter are simply extensions of the Reformation accent on the "grammatical sense" or something *toto caelo* different.[19]

Exactly. Of obedient exploration of the text we can never have enough. But of the critical elevation of scholarship as master and judge over Scripture, even a little bit is too much. Since, as that master critic, Troeltsch, insisted, the historical-critical methodology "once applied to biblical science and church history, is a leaven which transforms everything, and finally bursts the entire previous form of theological methods,"[20] the point is not to keep that leaven down to a small amount, or to muddle through with a moderate use of it, but to exclude it completely and in principle.

And Dr. Hummel's essay indicates the sort of tough-minded specifics which are necessary for a meaningful dissertation of Biblical and confessional authority here. Amazingly enough, his highly competent and relevant contributions do not even rate a mention in the Seminary document's bibliographical notes, while much less significant articles do. Dr. Franzmann likewise has published uniquely perceptive papers on the subject, which, like his essay on "The Hermeneutical Dilemma,"[21] are not mentioned (although two anti-traditional pieces in the same issue of the *Concordia Theological Monthly* as the "Dilemma" article are listed). To be fair, it must be said that Dr. Franzmann's exquisite "Seven Theses on Reformation Hermeneutics" is listed "For Further Study,"[22] as is Dr. R. Preus' splendidly comprehensive systematic analysis, "Notes on the Inerrancy of Scripture."[23] But their content is ignored by the *Discussions*, which proceed as if these and other trenchant contributions by responsible theologians simply didn't exist. Our Australian Church's 1972 "Doctrinal Statement" on Genesis indicates, I believe, the kind of specifics which are necessary:

> We therefore find ourselves opposed to many assumptions of "higher" criticism, assumptions which have increasingly shaped the methods and

---

19. Hummel, 41, italics original.
20. Kraus, 392.
21. Franzmann, 502–533.
22. Martin H. Franzmann, "Seven Theses on Reformation Hermeneutics," *CTM* XL (April 1969):233–246.
23. *CTM* XXXVIII (June 1967):363–375.

conclusions of Biblical scholarship in the last two hundred years. Some of these assumptions are:

a. That the Biblical documents must be treated in principle like all other historical documents, without regard for their claim to inspiration and authority;

b. That science, history, and other disciplines are valid and legitimate norms and standards by which the truthfulness and reliability of Biblical statements can and must be judged;

c. That the miraculous aspects of the witness of the Biblical writers may be discounted as an element of primitive culture;

d. That the Apostles' and even our Blessed Lord's Own understanding and interpretation of particular texts of Scripture may in principle be regarded as defective or questionable, and as subject to progressive correction by subsequent Biblical scholarship.

Such assumptions as these constitute an attack not only on the apostolicity of the Church (Eph. 2:20), but on the very Lordship of Christ. For this reason we reject them unconditionally.

Discussion Nine, by contrast, speaks blandly about Christian or Lutheran or "reverent" presuppositions, but says nothing more specific about them than that they "include: (1) the centrality of the Gospel in the Scriptures; (2) the distinction between the Law which always accuses and the Promise which always assures; (3) the Spirit's gift of faith as the prerequisite to receive the Promise and obey the commandments of God." In terms of the actual issues these formulations are the very soul of vagueness. They restrain historical criticism about as much as a net restrains water. What is worse, the most radical Bultmannite could embrace them, if not from *critical* necessity, then at least with *hermeneutical* relish!

Incredibly, the "presuppositions" do not even mention the authority of Scripture! The sentence, "The Scriptures are in a unique sense the written Word of God and deserve due reverence," occurs, but nothing concrete follows from it (indeed, the next sentence begins with "But ...."!). The divine authority of Scripture seems to have nothing whatever to say to the historical-critical enterprise. On the contrary, "all the techniques" of the latter are simply declared "legitimated by the fact that God chose to use as His written Word human documents written by human beings in human language." But this is like deriving a court's powers and jurisdiction from the human rights of the judge as a private person! What distinguishes Scripture from other books surely is not its humanity, but its divinity, which establishes a qualitative "distinction between the holy Scripture of the Old and New Testaments and all other writings" (FC Ep Rule and Norm, 7). *Discussion Nine's* oddly adoptionist language — as if God found ready-made human documents and then decided to "use" them as His Word! — falls far short of this.

If Biblical authority in the exegetical enterprise is to be more than a phrase, it must involve inerrancy "in the normal sense of freedom from all error and contradiction, 'factual' as well as 'theological,'" as our 1972 Australian statement, "The Theses of Agreement and Inerrancy," puts it. The quotation marks around "factual" and "theological" mean to suggest that this popular opposition is rejected. The document also refuses to separate divine from human elements in Scripture, confessing instead the inseparable "rich complexity of the Holy Scriptures as Word of God in all its parts and aspects and also word of man in all its parts and aspects." As Dr. Hummel puts it, so succinctly: "the most elementary faithfulness to the Lutheran Reformation requires that *any and every* dichotomization of Scripture be uncompromisingly rejected."[24]

The relevant thrust of inerrancy is that while it is wrong to treat the Bible "as though its divine authority rendered historical investigation unimportant or irrelevant," it is also wrong "to hold that what according to clear biblical statements 'actually is or actually happened,' may be regarded as" something which "actually is *not* or actually did *not* happen" (Australian Inerrancy statement, rejections 7 and 2 respectively).

But the *Discussions*, having yielded on inerrancy, avoid specifics and maintain a laissez faire stance towards historical criticism. St. Louis Prof. E. Krentz, for instance, is convinced that *sola scriptura* "is not in any sense a hermeneutical principle that determines *methods* in interpreting this single authority. . . . It is not contrary to any theory of sources."[25] There are indications in the article that Dr. Krentz doesn't really mean quite what he actually says here, but as it stands the formulation is wrong. It is precisely the characteristic *methods* of historical criticism which, as we have seen, *required* the abandonment of Biblical authority, in obedience to alternative dogmas, i.e., those of the Enlightenment. If *sola scriptura* is to express more than a meaningless ceremonial reigning, with the "ministers of the crown" doing exactly as they please in the crown's name, then the

---

24. Horace D. Hummel, "The Outside Limits of Lutheran Confessionalism in Contemporary Biblical Interpretation: Part II Gospel Versus Bible," The Springfielder XXXV (March 1972):266, italics original.
25. Edgar Krentz, "Hermeneutics and the Teacher of Theology," *CTM* XLII (May 1971):280.

customs ministry, as it were, must strictly enforce the royal regulations for all "methodological" imports. If the mere label "methods" automatically guarantees diplomatic immunity from inspection, it will soon be used to smuggle in subversive doctrine! Dr. R. Preus' restriction is surely both methodological and necessary:

> Specifically, any literary genre that would in itself be immoral or involve deceit or error is not compatible with Biblical inerrancy and is not to be found in Scripture, for example, myth, etiological tale, midrash, legend or saga according to the usual designation of these forms.[26]

The trouble is that the antiseptic scholarly jargon tends to hide, sometimes intentionally, the real theological issue of faith vs. unbelief. Nowhere is this truer than in Dr. Krentz's example of source theories. J, E, D, and P, and their datings seem such demure methodological technicalities. But when the great critic Friedrich Delitzsch as a student heard his famous Old Testament professor lecture on Deuteronomy and date it seven centuries after Moses, he saw the disturbing implications. Visiting his professor that very same day, he blurted out, "So then the fifth Book of Moses is what is called a forgery? The reply was: 'For God's sake! That's no doubt true, but one can't say a thing like that!' This word, especially his 'for God's sake!' keeps ringing in my ears till the present day. . . . For I have never understood why one should not, in such serious matters, also express that which is true."[27]

Since authority without "teeth" is no authority, *bona fide* confession of Biblical authority must have concrete hermeneutical and methodological "teeth," even for source theories, along the lines, for instance, of the Australian Genesis statement:

> It is contrary to the form of sound doctrine . . . b) to reduce the stature of Moses, in opposition to the New Testament (John 1:17; the Transfiguration), by holding that the Pentateuch is not essentially Mosaic, or by questioning the historical value of what the Pentateuch attributes to him, or by denying that he wrote of Christ (John 5:45, 46); c) to throw doubt in general on the historicity of the persons and facts mentioned in the Pentateuch.

Quite startling is *Discussion Nine's* assertion that "the fundamental principles of interpretation" including "'Scripture interprets Scripture'

---

26. *CTM* XXXVIII (June 1967):370.
27. Kraus, 312.

... are not laid down in the Scriptures. Furthermore, these rules are not unique to the study of the Scriptures, but apply to the interpretation of any ancient document." This is completely un-Lutheran and untheological. Lutheran theology[28] has always insisted on Scripture's self-interpretation because of its unique status as a sole authority. In this strict sense the rule does not apply simply to documents in general (note FC SD VII 41!). But in the Bible's case there simply is no alternative if "no human being's writings dare be put on a par with it, but ... everything must be subjected to it" (FC SD Rule and Norm, 9). As the divine light and lamp (Ps. 119:105) Scripture must give and not receive illumination. It is a matter of God's Word versus man's (Matt. 15:9) "private interpretation" (2 Pet. 1:20).

THE ORGANIC FOUNDATION
Solus Christus — Sola Scriptura

Inspiration and Inerrancy

Under pressure from its prior commitment to historical criticism, *Discussion Eight* gives up the inerrancy of Scripture. The issue is defined quite unmistakably: "Does the inspired character of the Scriptures guarantee ... the complete inerrancy of all materials in the Scriptures?" Although the answer is not equally straight-forward, since it quibbles about "twentieth century standards of factuality" and "this kind of 'inerrancy'" (as if a disguised efficacy were another kind!), it is quite clearly negative.

Come to think of it, our age of mass-mediated lies and propaganda on an unprecedented scale is hardly in a position to give itself superior airs about its "standards of factuality." On the other hand, St. Luke already had rather solid standards (1:1–4), as also did St. John (1 Jn. 1:1–3), not to mention St. Paul's total realism about the difference between fact and wishful thinking in 1 Corinthians 15. Even Bultmann grudgingly admits that here at least Paul "wants to secure the miracles of the resurrection as a historical event by enumerating the eye-witnesses."[29] Nor is there anything vague or foggy about standards of factuality in a popular sixteenth

---

28. Cf. quotations in C. F. W. Walther, *Die evangelisch-lutherische Kirche, die wahre sichtbare Kirche Gottes auf Erden* (St. Louis: Concordia Publishing House, 1891), esp. Theses XIII ff. [*Editor's note:* C. F. W. Walther, *The True Visible Church*, trans. John Theodore Mueller (St. Louis: Concordia Publishing House, 2005), 50 ff.] Also: R. D. Preus, *The Theology of Post-Reformation Lutheranism* (St. Louis: Concordia Publishing House, 1970), 329 ff.

29. Quoted in G. Gloege, *Mythologie und Luthertum* (Goettingen: Vandenhoeck & Ruprecht, 1963), 79.

century piece like Luther's explanation of the Eighth Commandment in his Large Catechism.

The conflict is not between antiquity and modernity at all, but between faith and unbelief. No doubt those medieval Popes of whom the Apology says that "many openly ridicule all religions, or if they accept anything, accept only what agrees with human reason and regard the rest as mythology, like the tragedies of the poets" (VII/VIII 27), also appealed to superior standards of factuality. So it is not from any lack of sophistication in this regard that Luther and with him the Lutheran Church give the only possible definition of inerrancy: *"I and my neighbor can err and deceive, but God's Word can neither err nor deceive"* (LC Baptism, 57 [italics added]).

Although there is even among some conservatives a certain dissatisfaction with the term "inerrancy," no one has as yet suggested a better one. That that concept "inerrant" is not made explicit in the compressed axiom of John 10:35, as some have urged, is merely a technicality, since the concept "incontrovertible" or "uncontradictable" (which must include "inerrant") certainly is the major thrust of that text, as Luther,[30] Gerhard,[31] and all other honest exegetes insist.

But of course the real argument is not about the term, but about the substance. And the challenge often takes not the form of a direct frontal attack but that of a bored indifference, which focuses only on the empirical-inductive aspects of Biblical difficulties, and regards it as unimportant whether these should be called "errors" or "problems." I have never seen a more trenchant reply to this thinking than Prof. Hummel's:

> No doubt, the difficulties and the possible solutions in and of themselves often remain the same, regardless of what one calls them, but *hermeneutically* it does ultimately make a *world* of difference whether they are construed as God's inability to reveal adequately or as man's inability to understand completely![32]

This, in a nutshell, is the real theological burden — and necessity — of inerrancy.

Inerrancy then is an instant litmus-test which shows whether the term "inspiration" is being used seriously and meaningfully, or merely emotively and rhetorically. For to distinguish within Scripture between what

---

30. St.L. 4, 1307.
31. Chemnitz, Leyser, Gerhard, *Harmoniae Quatuor Evangelistarum* (Frankfurt and Hamburg, 1652), 1:1255–56.
32. Hummel, *Springfielder* XXXV (March 1972):270, italics original.

is and what is not correct is obviously to distinguish between what is and what is not God's Word. Conversely, to say that something is God's Word is to say that it is beyond human correction, i.e., inerrant. But to say that something is both God's inspired, authoritative Word, and at the same time in error and subject to human correction, is to use language without meaning. The effect of the following sample is distinctly lunatic, even in the original German: "Since [St. Luke's] interpretation of the parable [8:4–15] is not factually correct [*sachgemaess*], it dare not determine the sermon. But since it is, after all, written there, it must also be heard and taken seriously as God's Word"![33]

Since inerrancy is rejected, *Discussion Eight* can manage only a half-hearted non-definition of inspiration: "Accordingly the inspiration of the written Word pertains to the effective power of the Scriptures to bring men and women to salvation through the Gospel. We affirm, therefore, that the Scriptures are the inspired Word of God." Why not "therefore" affirm, in exactly the same sense, that the Catechisms are the inspired Word of God? We have here a confusion of a thing itself with its ultimate purpose. And inerrancy is redefined in exactly the same way. But that is as disastrous as defining marriage, for instance, as "pertaining" to the happiness of two people — although the latter is undoubtedly a correct statement of the basic purpose of marriage. The open invitation to chaos is obvious, and no less so in the case of inspiration and inerrancy.

There are other confusions on inspiration in *Discussion Eight*. It is rightly admitted that 2 Timothy 3:16 "actually applies the term 'inspired' to the Sacred Scriptures as such." In other words, the primary object of inspiration is the Biblical text itself, not the persons of the writers. But in the very next paragraph we are told not to "focus on the how of inspiration" since "throughout the Scriptures little is said about precisely how the prophets or apostles were inspired." The intent, transparently, is to sanction a vague, ill-defined use of the term "inspiration," while sweeping all inconvenient doctrinal precision under the carpet of the "how." The fact of course is that full, verbal, plenary inspiration belongs not to any speculative "how," but to the exegetical and dogmatic "what" ("*all* Scripture")!

Equally ill-starred is the attempt to construe an implied "therefore" between verses 15 and 16: "All of this is true because, first of all, the Scriptures are able through the Spirit, 'to instruct you for salvation through faith in Christ Jesus' (2 Tim. 3:15)." If this is an example of historical-critical exegesis (new hermeneutics, more likely), it again illustrates the

---

33. Quoted in *Lutherischer Rundblick* 18 (1970):325.

cavalier straight-jacketing of the text into existentialist preconceptions. No respectable grammatical and syntactical analysis would tolerate such a procedure. If anything, verse 16 gives the reason for verse 15, rather than the other way 'round.

Gospel vs. Scripture

With the abandonment of meaningful notions of inspiration and inerrancy, the whole Scripture principle of Lutheran theology evaporates, as Dr. C. F. W. Walther clearly saw:

> It is absolutely necessary that we maintain the doctrine of inspiration as taught by our orthodox dogmaticians. If the possibility that Scripture contained the least error were admitted, it would become the business of *man* to sift the truth from the error. That places man *over Scripture,* and Scripture is *no longer* the source and norm of doctrine. Human reason is made the *norma* of truth, and Scripture is degraded to the position of a *norma normata.* The least deviation from the old inspiration doctrine introduces a rationalistic germ into theology and infects the whole body of doctrine.[34]

To St. Louis Professor C. S. Meyer it seems that Walther's doctrine of the Word "was not wholly Christocentric but tended toward biblicism."[35] To Walther's successors at the Seminary, the Scripture principle is simply no longer comprehensible. By an odd oversight, the term *sola scriptura* does not even occur in the document, although *sola gratia* and *sola fide* do, and although it is on the doctrine of Scripture that reassurance is especially needed.

But even if that old shibboleth had been mentioned, it would have been but a perfunctory shadow of its former self, as "reinterpreted" as inspiration and inerrancy. For the *Discussions* take the honor of the *sola* from Scripture and bestow it on something else. They distinguish between "Gospel" and "Scripture," and are designed as "a demonstration of how we employ the Gospel as the governing principle in our theology." The *Preamble* — it isn't clear whether this is "affirmed" or merely "discussed" — pointedly asks:

> "Is the Gospel alone sufficient as the ground of faith and the governing principle for Lutheran theology? Or is something else required as a neces-

---

34. Quoted in Theodore Engelder, "Walther a Christian Theologian," *Walther and the Church,* ed. Theodore Engelder (St. Louis: Concordia Publishing House, 1938), 14, italics original.
35. C. S. Meyer, "Walther's Theology of the Word," *CTM* XLIII (April 1972):262.

sary condition?" The "something else" here is obviously the same as *Discussion Four's* "even if that something else be the Bible itself." Having set up the choice between "the Gospel alone" and "something else" (Scripture as such), the *Preamble* decides: "any effort, however subtle, to supplement the Gospel, so that it is no longer the sole ground of our faith or the governing principle for our theology is to be rejected as un-Lutheran, contrary to our confession. . . ."

The formal principle then is not Scripture as such but "the Gospel" abstracted from it. While Scripture is once or twice called "the *norm* for faith and life," it is clearly demoted to a subsidiary *norma normata*, subject to another and higher "governing principle": "The Gospel gives the Scriptures their normative character, not vice versa" (*Discussion Four*); "the Gospel is the norm . . . of the Scriptures. . . ." (*Discussion Six*). Any genuinely objective scholarship would admit that what the document here condemns as un-Lutheran and "contrary to our confession," is of the very bone and marrow not just of this or that great Lutheran theologian, but of the Lutheran Confessions themselves:

> *In this way the distinction between the Holy Scripture of the Old and New Testaments and all other writings* [including quintessence-of-Gospel documents like Creeds and Catechisms! K. M.] *is maintained, and Holy Scripture remains the only judge, rule, and norm according to which as the only touchstone all doctrines should and must be understood and judged as good or evil, right or wrong.* (FC Ep Rule and Norm 7 [italics added])

It is very clear then just how far left the pendulum has swung since the days of Theodore Graebner. He strongly maintained the organic foundation, the Scripture principle, citing N. Hunnius' conviction that one might deny certain non-fundamentals without loss of saving faith "so long only as he cannot perceive their foundation in Scripture."[36] And the second thesis of the Chicago *Statement* insists: "We *affirm our faith in the great Lutheran principle of the inerrancy, certainty, and all-sufficiency of Holy Writ.* We therefore deplore a tendency in our synod to substitute human judgments, synodical resolutions, or other sources of authority for the supreme authority of Scripture." What seemed bold then, seems positively reactionary now, side by side with the 1972 *Discussions*, which have joined the critical revolution against inerrancy!

---

36. Graebner, 10.

It is a pity that the *Statement's* original thrust of "back to the text!" came to be twisted into a doctrinal dismantling programme. Yet the one man in Missouri whose contributions have probably faced the challenge most constructively, never wavered in his allegiance to strict Biblical authority. Although the depth and awareness of Stoeckhardt's generation should not be underestimated, the *Concordia Theological Monthly's* editorial tribute to Dr. Franzmann is no doubt quite valid for recent times:

> He was among the first to introduce genuine historical awareness to our church's study of Holy Scripture and thus enabled us to break out of an interpretive methodology that read the sacred record as if it were merely a collection of dogmatic propositions. But at the same time he constantly opposed his intuitive feeling for the rich poetic quality of Biblical language to the equally arid pedantry of mere historicising exegesis.[37]

Nor is it merely "intuitive feeling," as a certain anti-dogmatic bias would have it. The fact is that while Dr. Franzmann has effectively counteracted a certain dry, doctrinaire schematism, he has always consistently continued to oppose the fashionable devaluation of Biblical authority: "The interpreter is not critic. . . . There is no place where the interpreter can stand (if he is acting in *mimesis* of the apostle) and exert critical leverage."[38] Taken seriously, this cuts the ground from under the whole conception of the *Discussions!*

Formal and Material Principles

The writers of the *Discussions* no doubt believe that they have, with Luther and the New Testament, liberated the Gospel itself, the material principle, from a false, scholastic-intellectualistic dependence on the formal principle (*sola scriptura*), so that the Gospel may now stand on its own feet.

But the real opposition comes not from the material principle at all but from the demands of historical criticism. It is reason exercising "critical leverage" against a misunderstood formal principle, under cover of a misunderstood material principle:

> Any tendency to make the doctrine of the inspiration or the inerrancy of the Scriptures a prior truth which guarantees the truth of the Gospel or

---

37. Richard Jungkuntz, "Preface" (editorial), *CTM*, XLII (September 1972):483.
38. "The Posture of the Interpreter," p. 10, *Proceedings*, Conference of Theologians, Oakland, Calif., 1959.

gives support to our faith is sectarian. The Gospel gives the Scriptures their normative character, not vice versa. We are saved by grace through faith in Christ alone, not through faith in Christ and something else, even if that something else be the Bible itself. (*Discussion Four*)

The main fallacies here are, first, that it is misleading to make it seem that inerrancy is being rejected only as a "prior truth" when in fact the argument is about whether it is a valid truth at all. Second, the term "prior truth" is equivocal: it could mean "prior" in several senses, some right, some wrong. As part of God's objective act in Christ, Biblical inerrancy certainly is *ante et extra nos* (before and outside us), and thus "gives support to our faith." But if it suggests something constructed somehow independently of faith, by rational proof, then it is an irrelevant strawman, representing not even the old orthodox dogmaticians, but only the Wolffian-rationalist precursors of historical-critical methodology! Third, the phrase "normative character" by-passes and confuses the vital difference between the objective, "prior" *fact* of the Bible's authority (normative authority), and its *power* to convince people of this fact as part of Christian faith (causative authority). Fourth, the "not vice versa" is clearly false (Acts 17:11; 1 Cor. 15:3, 4). Fifth, without a historical-critical abortion of its meaning, the statement that "the Gospel gives the Scriptures their normative character" must imply inerrancy. Sixth, Christ nowhere allows a contrast, in principle, between faith in Him, and faith in His direct (Matt. 24:35) or mediated (John 15:20) Word. Seventh, the bare minimum of what is necessary for salvation is not a source or norm for doctrine. The thief on the cross was saved without Baptism, but this does not mean that the doctrine of Baptism is a superfluous luxury in theology.

The confusion is spelled out in great detail by St. Louis Prof. E. H. Schroeder.[39] He alleges that in the 1954 book *The Religious Bodies of America*, the late Prof. F. E. Mayer "completely reversed" his 1937 stand that as Schroeder puts it, "the material principle *follows from* and is *dependent upon* the formal principle *in principle!*" But apart from an improved balance, there is not the slightest difference in principle between Mayer's 1937 and 1954 positions.

What Schroeder takes as evidence of a false "dependence" is simply Mayer's point that in contrast to Rome and Calvin, Luther did not impose a material principle on Scripture, but got his *sola gratia from* Scripture

---

39. Edward H. Schroeder, "Law-Gospel Reductionism in the History of The Lutheran Church — Missouri Synod," *CTM* XLIII (April 1972):245.

itself! And this is vital. Law-Gospel or justification is not some kind of *a priori* Lutheran bias read *into* Scripture (that would be sectarian!), but the central Biblical demand, read *out of* the normative text. It is therefore misleading to describe this inner-Biblical stress as a "critical judgment,"[40] as if it came from without. The popular habit of relying on the Confessions as a *hermeneutical* antidote of the *historical-critical* destruction of Biblical authority is totally misconceived, and reverses the roles of Scriptures and Confessions. To believe and accept something just because it is "Lutheran," i.e., taught by Luther or the Confessions, is fundamentally un-Lutheran and anti-Lutheran (FC SD Rule and Norm, 5)!

The real gulf of "complete reversal" must be placed not between Mayer, 1937 and Mayer, 1954, but between Mayer, 1954, who accepts, in Schroeder's own citation, "the absolute authority of the Scriptures" and "the Bible as Christ's inerrant and final word," and the *Discussions*, 1972, which accept nothing of the sort. Despite the earlier one-sidedness at Bad Boll, at least as quoted by Schroeder, Mayer in his 1954 book holds strictly to the formal principle, and insists that "when speaking of the material principle of theology, Lutherans do not have in mind a basic principle according to which a body of doctrines may be developed. The material principle of Lutheran theology is in reality only a synopsis and summary of the Christian truth."[41] The *Discussions* follow precisely the approach which Mayer rejects: the formal principle is given up, and the material, "the Gospel alone," becomes instead "the governing principle for Lutheran theology!" Mayer insists on the Lutheran axiom: "*The Word of God shall establish articles of faith and no one else, not even an angel*" (SA II ii 15 [italics added]). The *Discussions* in effect reverse this into: "The articles of faith shall establish the Word of God, and nothing else, not even the Bible!"

To top it all off, Schroeder even projects the confusion into Francis Pieper's mind, who is said to be "of two minds about the question," since he insists on the necessity of both inerrancy and the Law-Gospel distinction. This is supposed to create the problem of "how both inerrancy and the distinction are *the* one *articulus stantis et cadentis Christianae.*"[42] But the conflict is just as spurious as that between "Christ alone" and "faith alone" or between "faith alone" and the means of grace. Not everything that is necessary to theology thereby becomes "*the* one *articulus.*" If "the

---

40. *CTM* XLII, 5, p. 278.
41. F. E. Mayer, *The Religious Bodies of America*, 2nd ed. (St. Louis: Concordia Publishing House, 1956), 144.
42. Schroeder, op. cit., 242.

acceptance of doctrine about an inerrant Bible has no necessary connection to salvation," neither does such mere "acceptance of doctrine" about the Blessed Trinity. Not even "the one *articulus*" saves if it is merely intellectually accepted as doctrine. And of Bultmann, who denies every substantive doctrine, Gloege says that his "*basic theme is rooted in Luther's distinction between Law and Gospel.*"[43] Is he therefore the theological apex of Lutheranism?

In Ephesians 2:20 ("the foundation of the apostles and prophets, Jesus Christ Himself being the chief Cornerstone" [KJV]) the substantial, dogmatic, and organic foundations, or the formal and material principles, subsist in perfect, harmonious "interpenetration." There is no conflict or rivalry here, but "Christ teaches (about) Christ most purely" (Luther). No Word but Christ's — and no Christ but the Word's! Full apostolic-prophetic authority is not some optional "extra" (e.g., an irrelevant "accuracy of ancient historians," *Discussion Five!*) but part and parcel of God's one and indivisible saving act in Christ. And neither the "offensive" humility of the Incarnation (Matt. 11:2–6; John 6:42) nor the corresponding human-historical concreteness of the Biblical text may be surrendered to the profanations of secular-critical thought. Note therefore how the Lutheran Confessions insist not only on the centrality of the Gospel, but also on the total authority of the whole Scripture, commending Abraham because "he gave God the honor of truthfulness" and refused to evade the plain meaning of God's Word through "a tolerable and loose interpretation," despite the fact that "these words were patently contrary not only to reason and to divine and natural law but also to the eminent article of faith concerning the promised seed, Christ" (FC SD VII 46)!

Finally, it is pure dilettantism to prattle about Law and Gospel while wrecking Biblical authority. It is precisely the application of Law and Gospel which necessitates the kind of doctrinal certainty which only clear divine authority— the formal principle! — can provide. "It is inherent in man to despise God and to doubt his Word with its threats and promises" (Ap IV 35). And faith is not an easy optimism which readily believes itself forgiven or is satisfied with hearsay or theological catchphrases. Only total Gospel-certitude can reassure anyone in the wake of seriously applied Law. Therefore "good consciences cry for the truth and proper instruction from God's Word, and to them death is not as bitter as it is to doubt in one point" (Ap XII 129; German). Faith must have "a very definite Word of God" (Ap IV 262), of which it can be sure that it is not

---

43. Gloege, 41, italics original.

illusion or "commandments of men" (Matt. 15:9). Only the divinely-given apostolic-prophetic Scripture, "written that you may believe" (John 20:31), can ultimately support such assurance. But note that this is *not* a demand for "rational proof"! Faith takes God at His Word — that is its nature. But it must have and be sure of that Word. It is this totally Christ-centered, Biblical, confessional, and pastoral concern for spiritual-doctrinal certainty, explained in the fourth lecture of Walther's much-touted but little-heeded book on *Law and Gospel*, which demands what C. S. Meyer misunderstands as Walther's "biblicism."

Much of this discussion has moved in the area of *prolegomena*, i.e., the very nature and first principles of theology. As Luther comments on Galatians 5:9: "In philosophy, if a small error is made in the beginning, a very great error comes of it in the end. So in theology a small error overturns the whole doctrine."[44] How much more a tissue of big errors in first principles! And today it is the most basic axioms and foundations that are under attack. The whole crisis could be called the "Prolegomenistic Controversy." It is therefore theologically incredible, however understandable it might be church-politically, that a Seminary President can dismiss prolegomena as of secondary importance![45] On the contrary, this is where the meaning and value of everything that follows is decided. (The *Formula of Concord* already prefaces its numbered articles with an introductory section, which treats of Scripture, Confession, and their correlation.) Prof. Kuenneth rightly says that today the Devil uses not so much "great might" as "deep guile" in seducing theologians and church-leaders away from the very foundations:

> The same familiar biblical words, names, and concepts which are used by existentialist theology, do not mean the same thing, but have another content. . . . Bultmann was once asked if he considered it warranted to formulate a new Creed in place of the Apostles' Creed. He said: NO, that isn't necessary at all, since the new formulations can't be believed either. . . . The boundless confusion which arises out of such a theological posture is incalculable. People speak of the Creed, but don't believe one sentence of it.[46]

All the talk about "the saving event" then becomes, as G. Bornkamm has put it, a mere "tissue of significances, it dissolves into a mere *Signifi-*

---

44. St.L. IX, 644. [*Editor's note:* See AE 27, 37.]
45. J. H. Tietjen, *Fact Finding Or Fault Finding?: An Analysis of President J. A. O. Preus' Investigation of Concordia Seminary* (N.p., n.d.), 6.
46. Kuenneth, 15.

cat and has lost the force of the *Est*."[47] This dissolution is the necessary and predictable end-result of the denial of the organic foundation, or the formal principle.

THE DOGMATIC FOUNDATION
Solus Christus — Sola Gratia, Sola Fide

The Gospel, agreement in which is necessary for the true unity of the Church (AC VII), is not an isolated abstraction or slogan, but involves Christian doctrine "in all its articles" (FC SD X 31). Three of the four Gospels formally trace the evangel back to the beginnings of Genesis: Matthew to Abraham, Luke to Adam, and John to cosmic creation. We shall follow the Trinitarian arrangement of the *Affirmations*.

The First Article

The question of the existence of angels touches the Christ-center of the Faith at three points: the formal principle, which will not allow angels to be dismissed as literary devices or aspects of "the theological machinery of the Jews";[48] the implications for the Fall; and the reality of angelic and demonic activity in the redemptive life, teaching, and ministry of our Lord Himself. Since this doctrinal concern was explicitly raised by the Fact Finding Committee, it should have been clarified in the Seminary document.[49] The *Affirmations* do not mention angels, and the *Discussions* use the term once in passing. The term "demonic forces" or "powers" occurs three times, but usually refers to things like racism. (At the same time there is a curious emphasis not on the "one blood" of Acts 17:26, but on a concreated "identity" of "races" [*Discussion Seven*].)

Genesis 1 is placed, in principle, on the same level as "the minds of scientists, the imagination of poets, and the faith of worshippers for centuries" straining "with human words to describe God creating through His Word"; except that the "biblical men of faith," though "operating with the same limitations of human language in a given culture, were moved by the Spirit to portray the creative work of God in diverse ways" (*Discussion One*).

---

47. Quoted in Gloege, 183.
48. Gabler, quoted in Hartlich-Sachs, 66.
49. *Report of the Synodical President to The Lutheran Church — Missouri Synod in compliance with Resolution 2-28 of the 49th Regular Convention of the Synod, held at Milwaukee, Wisconsin, July 9–16, 1971* (St. Louis: The Lutheran Church — Missouri Synod, 1972), 83. [*Editor's note:* See Paul A. Zimmerman, *A Seminary in Crisis: The Inside Story of the Preus Fact Finding Committee* (St. Louis: Concordia Publishing House, 2007), 322.]

In other words, there is no real doctrine of creation at all in the old sense, but only a series of "diverse" Biblical "pictures," though these are sometimes given the public relations title of "descriptions." And of course Scripture is "not a textbook on science." But to say that "any discussion of the relationship of biblical pictures of creation to scientific theories is secondary" is going too far. In our cultural context it amounts to kowtowing to the "scientific theories" on behalf of the "biblical pictures."

We have here a facile evasion of three stubborn facts: (1) As Hartlich and Sachs show in their significant monograph, the "surrender of the historical-factual" aspect of Genesis 1–3 was due not to any textual considerations, but to the incompatibility of Genesis with the alleged "newly won scientific and historical discoveries concerning the initial state of the world and of mankind."[50] (2) The reigning "scientific theories" of origins are to a surprising degree extra-scientific and even anti-scientific.[51] The mainspring of evolutionism is not empirical observation but anti-theistic bias;[52] it is in short a philosophical rationalization of sinful man's instinctive flight from God (Rom. 1:18–23). (3) The ever-valid Word of God in Genesis is not interpreted but evaded if it is allowed to demythologize only safely dead divinities like Marduk and Tiamat, and not also those prospering twin gods of modern evolutionary mythology: Time and Chance! Human guess-work must not be granted even the appearance of equality with, let alone precedence over, divine truth: "In this confused age the Church must reflect serene confidence in Genesis as the Creator's own account of what happened in the beginning" (Lutheran Church of Australia, *Doctrinal Statement on Genesis*).

Discussion One's approach is in fact hard to distinguish from that of Gabler, one of the eighteenth century rationalist founders of the historical-critical methodology: ". . . The first document [of Genesis] was an old poetic picture and the second an old philosophical myth. — Nothing in it is divine truth except the sentence: God is the Originator of the whole world. — It would be quite contrary to the intention of the Bible to determine scientific data from it."[53]

---

50. Hartlich-Sachs, 35.

51. A. E. Wilder Smith, *The Creation of Life: A Cybernetic Approach to Evolution* (Wheaton: Harold Shaw, 1970). G. A. Kerkut, *Implications of Evolution* (Oxford; Pergamon, 1960). A. Ch. v. Guttenberg, *Biologie als Weltanschauung.* (Ratingen: A. Henn, 1967).

52. R. J. Rushdoony, *The Mythology of Science* (Nutley: Craig Press), 1967. R. T. Clark and J. D. Bales, *Why Scientists Accept Evolution* (Grand Rapids: Baker, 1966).

53. Hartlich-Sachs, 46.

Discussion Two extends this approach to Adam and Eve, whom "many within our Synod" take to be "two specific individuals known as Adam and Eve," but "others" don't. Of course it is not stated as bluntly as Prof. W. Bartling's famous outburst: "One thing they caught most of us on is 'Were Adam and Eve historical persons?' I don't know. I don't think so. It is not important."[54]

The claim that all this is purely a matter of "differences of opinion about the kind of literature involved," and not about the "doctrinal content of the passage" is demonstrably false. In his massively Biblical-evangelical essay on inspiration and proto-history Prof. W. M. Oesch writes of Genesis:

> This is to be heard, instead of preventing the hearing by riddling about how this divine revelation might have been invented by men. The statements, especially about creation, the original state, and the fall, are indissolubly connected with the saving New Testament message, yes, it is just here that the Old and New Testaments stand together as one front in such a way that they can be rejected only together.[55]

Romans 5 and 1 Corinthians 15 alone establish an indissoluble nexus between Genesis and the very heart of the Gospel:

> Clearly therefore the factual-historical framework of the Genesis narrative is the indispensable foundation not only for the history of the People of God which follows, but for the very Incarnation and Redemption. Within this framework figurative elements are no doubt to be found. But we must reject all interpretations which in any way undermine the facticity of the framework itself, e.g., the suggestion that the creation and fall of Adam and Eve may be taken to represent not actual persons and events, but timeless myths or parables of what happens to every man. (*Australian Genesis Statement*)

Having, with others, devoted "blood, sweat, and tears" to this whole matter for years, I was surprised and delighted subsequently to find Dr. Hummel's succinct and independent formulation, which parallels rather closely one of the major concerns and conclusions of our Australian discussions: "There seems no way around the argument that the Adam-Christ typology (not mere analogy!), as well as, in a way, the entire *ordo*

---

54. *Alternatives Information-Action-Line*, 15 June 1972, quoted in *Christian News*, 31 July 1972.
55. W. M. Oesch, "Die Lehre von der Inspiration und ihre Anwendung auf die Urgeschichte," *Fuldaer Heft*, No. 13, 1960, 51.

salutis, makes a historical element (in the ordinary sense of the term) a *sine qua non* for both Adam and the Fall."[56] Amazingly, this superbly reasoned essay is not listed "for further study" in the *Discussions,* although two far less significant articles in the same issue of the *Concordia Theological Monthly* are cited.

The whole scheme of sacrificing the history while retaining the idea, i.e., "the truth about Everyman . . . and every woman," is deeply anti-Biblical. It is the worst feature of that very "Greek" approach, about which existentialists of all descriptions are forever huffing and puffing. There seems to be no recognition of the doctrinal problems involved: "This sinfulness is present in every individual from the beginning of his existence as a human being and persists throughout his life." Was there then never a state of sinlessness, from which man fell? If there was, then this is obviously not a "truth about Everyman" today. But if there was not, what becomes of the Fall? Or why does everyone become sinful now? If Adam is "Everyman," do we all start out sinless? True, there is a reference to the fact that in "Romans 5 . . . Paul states that sin and death enter the world through one man. . . ." But how can this be brought into harmony with the sacrifice of Adam's historicity?

The Second Article

The second set of *Affirmations* seems to me to be the most explicit of the three. Christ is affirmed to be "our Lord and our God." Normally one would not query this further. Since *Discussion Five* however suggests W. Bouman's essay on "History and Dogma in Christology"[57] for further study, it is necessary to point out that this essay tends towards a dangerous functionalism which would make the term "God" meaningless. Bouman's criticism of Article VII of the Formula of Concord [sic] is far more substantive than he admits. If taken literally and seriously, Bouman's key contention—that a critically "stringent" historical investigation of what Jesus actually said and did "defines what the church is saying when it confesses that Jesus, the man, is God"—is heretical. Clearly when St. John calls Christ "God" in the first verse of his Gospel, he is not saying that the definition of the term "God" depends on the history which follows—quite apart from the fact that a "stringent" historical study of the critical type would disallow most of it anyway! And Bouman

---

56. H. Hummel, "Critical Methodology and the Lutheran Symbols' Treatment of the Genesis Creation Accounts," *CTM* XLIII (September 1972):545, italics original.

57. *CTM* XLII (April 1971):203–221. [Marquart quotes from p. 220.]

suggests that it is the divinity, not just the humanity of Christ, which is to be "defined" in this way.

Now, take just such a "stringent" investigation of St. Mark's Gospel. Prof. J. S. Setzer argues that an examination of Mark's "Petrine stratum" shows that "Jesus' own christology was adoptionistic" — in the sense that "there is nothing to be heard about a second person of a divine trinity, nothing of a virgin birth" or "about the descent of a heavenly being to become Messiah. We hear, rather, about a marvelous but human child of God."[58] Now, is this an example of how stringent historical investigation defines what we mean by saying that Jesus is God? Since "all the techniques associated with 'historical-critical' methodology" are "legitimated" (*Discussion Nine*), what is wrong with Setzer's technique? Would Bouman exclude it? If so, how and why? And how would the *Affirmations* and *Discussions* protect their confession that Jesus is God from this sort of "definition" by stringent historical investigation? To this sort of probing, in terms of relevant current issues, the document is as unresponsive as the Sphinx.

In the vital matter of messianic prophecy, the historical-critical commitments of the *Discussions* again show themselves to be something less and other than objective, neutral tools. *Discussion Six* rightly stresses the importance of typology and it avoids the untenable extreme of insisting on a rather specific understanding of the content of the divine Promise on the part of the average believer under the Old Covenant. After all, even the Apostles, after three years of seminary plus the Resurrection, were still rather wide of the mark (Acts 1:6). It was only when the Spirit-fulness of Pentecost broke in upon them that they were released from the politicizing misconceptions to which the World Council of Churches has now returned with such a vengeance!

But the other, much more dangerous extreme of denying direct, predictive messianic prophecy altogether, seems to worry the *Discussions* not at all. To say that "in the light of their fulfilment a new dimension is added to the meaning of Old Testament promises of God" fails to do justice to the New Testament's understanding of the Old. It suggests not so much exegesis as eisegesis, reading things into the text that are not really there. This is clearly not the sort of thing that Christ meant when He said that Abraham rejoiced to see His day, that he saw it and was glad (John 8:56), or what St. John meant by saying that Isaiah saw His glory and spoke of Him (12:41). St. Paul's refrain, "according to the Scrip-

---

58. J. S. Setzer, "A Fresh Look at Jesus' Eschatology and Christology in Mark's Petrine Stratum," *Lutheran Quarterly* 24 (August 1972):252–253.

tures" (1 Cor. 15:3–4), echoed in the Nicene Creed, clearly refers not to any kind of subtle afterthought, but to actual prediction and fulfilment, in the sense of Peter's Pentecost sermons: David, "being a prophet" (Acts 2:30 KJV), spoke not of himself, but foresaw and predicted the Resurrection (v. 31) and Ascension (v. 34) of Christ. The *Discussions* nowhere assert this sort of thing. It is the critical methodology which obstructs faithful imitation of the Apostles here:

> If modern Old Testament exegesis has rarefied the nexus between the Testaments to the point where it bears only a shadowy resemblance to that massive and living connection posited by the apostles; if it has made dubious and problematical what is for the apostles certain and axiomatic, the methodological question inevitably arises: If modern methodology in Old Testament exegesis has brought men to the point where they can no longer "imitate" the apostles, may it not be that we are in the last stages of a grandiose aberration, comparable to the age-long domination of the four-fold sense in patristic and medieval exegesis?[59]

The decisive text, to my mind, is 1 Peter 1:10–12:

> It was this salvation that the prophets were looking and searching so hard for; their prophecies were about the grace which was to come to you. The Spirit of Christ which was in them foretold the sufferings of Christ and the glories that would come after them, and they tried to find out at what time and in what circumstances all this was to be expected. It was revealed to them that the news they brought . . . was for you and not for themselves. (*Jerusalem Bible*)

If the Gospel were really "the governing principle" of the *Discussions'* theology, and not merely a stalking-horse for critical methodology, should not *Discussion Six* imitate and embrace with delight St. Peter's positively aggressive insistence on direct prophecies of Christ? After all, what could be more gloriously Christ-centered and Gospel-oriented? Instead, we find the whole issue skirted with cautious ambiguities! We are even warned "not to leap prematurely into the New Testament to find the meaning of Old Testament passages." This is because the "Old Testament deserves to be thoroughly studied on its own terms and in its own historical context first of all." But again the concern is not really for the Old Testament "on its own terms," but for certain historical-critical reconstructions of it. Thus,

---

59. "Posture of the Interpreter," pp. 10–11.

no attempt at all is made to defend the historicity of Genesis, in *Discussions One* and *Two*, against current critical fashions. On the contrary!

The real "governing principle" is the dead hand of historical criticism. And although the critical acids have eaten more deeply into the *Discussions'* treatment of the Old Testament, the New is by no means exempt. Nor is this surprising. Since the Old and New Testaments form "one front," they cannot be separated into water-tight—or corrosion-proof—compartments. Hartlich and Sachs show in their authoritative monograph that the notion of "myth," once introduced into the first chapters of Genesis, could not be contained there, but soon demanded, and got, entry-rights into the rest of the Old Testament, and into the New as well.[60] And whether the term "myth" is explicitly used or not, the idea behind it is an inner necessity for historical criticism, since that approach cannot remain true to itself while allowing special status or privilege to Biblical accounts. Hence Kuenneth is right when he says that "in Bultmann we find the completion [*Zuendefuehrung*] and perfection of historical criticism."[61]

In the field of New Testament history the *Discussions* try to hunt with the critical hounds while running with a somewhat emaciated gospel-hare. On the whole they clearly mean to assert the factual-historical "infrastructure" of the Incarnation and Redemption. So for instance the Resurrection is described as one of the "hard core events of human history." (The Empty Grave is affirmed, but in the more non-committal *Discussions* rather than in the *Affirmations*. Perhaps this is an oversight.) But on the other hand there is a persistent tendency to denigrate factual elements in the Biblical narrative. False and dangerous oppositions are set up, for instance: "central meaning of the miracle accounts" vs. "dwelling on the authenticity of isolated miraculous details"; "the need for historical factuality" vs. "the primary need for Christ"; "faith alone" vs. "verification of historical details," "promise of a faithful God" vs. "the accuracy of ancient historians" (i.e., the Biblical writers)! And critical slaps are directed at "an absolute acceptance of each detail of the miracle, precisely as it is reported," and "public acceptance of the historicity of every detail of the life of Jesus as recorded by the evangelists" and "the historical accuracy of one element of the Gospel narratives."

Questioning mere "details" sounds very harmless. But what is a "detail"? Anything, it seems, which one wants to get rid of. So for instance

---

60. Hartlich-Sachs, passim, and esp. 6 ff.
61. Kuenneth, 9.

Discussion Two, having placed the historicity of Adam and Eve on the free list, urges a de-historicized doctrinal lesson "regardless of how we interpret the details of Genesis 3." In other words, the very historical existence of Adam and Eve is dismissed here as "details"! Nor can the problem be waved away with the magic wand of "Law and Promise." The category "Promise," as used in the *Discussions*, turns out to have no necessary connection with fact and history. *Discussion Six* says: "The Promise in the Old Testament assumes many forms," and then cites Adam, Cain, and Noah. Unfortunately, as we have seen, Adam's existence was sacrificed already in *Discussion Two*. This no doubt settles Cain's fate as well, and Noah's critical status is not encouraging. Now, how can "Promise" (or "Gospel") safeguard a single historical fact about Christ when it can obviously make do equally well with completely unhistorical, non-existent people, and mere literary devices?

Noteworthy in all this is the fact that actual argumentation in the *Discussions* regularly leads to "permissive" conclusions about historical factuality, while "conservative" statements just appear, like Melchisedek, out of nowhere. They are simply asserted, without any grounding in argument. But if the *Discussions* are really meant to illustrate "how the Gospel [rather than *sola scriptura*] governs our handling of theological topics," then we have a right to expect a clear procedure to be spelt out for determining which facts are essential to the Gospel, and which not, and why. Otherwise we are forced to conclude once more that the Gospel doesn't govern at all, but is merely used as window-dressing for the historical-critical disposition of "theological topics." How for instance does the Gospel require the Resurrection to be a "hard core" event of history, when equally competent and sincere practitioners of the critical method think otherwise, yet insist that they too care only about "Law and Gospel"? Or why not this notion of "hard core event": "Take the Exodus for example. Something happened, to be sure. But I tend to believe that much of the miraculous that is associated with the event was an embellishment of it"?[62] More "details"?

If the important thing is the "central meaning of the miracle accounts" rather than "dwelling on the authenticity of isolated miraculous details," then why not say with the above article from *Context* that the miracles never happened at all, but that "these stories were the authors' way of emphasizing the importance of God's activity and the importance of Jesus as the Christ"? Isn't that even "Christo-centric"? And surely the Luther-

---

62. Niedenthal, ed., 38 [quoting Carl Uehling].

an School of Theology at Chicago, whose official organ *Context* is, also knows all about Law and Gospel! Does the St. Louis Seminary object to church-fellowship with the Chicago school, or are these regarded as tolerable differences of opinion? Or why, apart from the Scripture-principle, is it wrong to say further with the same *Context* piece: "we know darn well something was happening, maybe not to a group of people standing in a boat watching Jesus, but something was happening somewhere in the life of the early community that made it seem desirable to put in something like this, which is undoubtedly rooted in experience but which also has been embellished"?

In short, if the Gospel allows us to take liberties with the "details," how does one know what belongs to the Gospel and what not? How can such a historically permissive Gospel show that the New Testament is more valid than, say, Israeli Supreme Court Justice Haim Cohn's fascinating thesis that the Jewish leaders, far from seeking Jesus' Crucifixion, did their best to prevent it? Cohn uses "Christian" interpreters to argue: "In short, the Gospel traditions are 'messages of faith and not historiography'; any historical material in their hands the authors used 'to add detail and graphic quality,' but, on the whole, they freely exercised their fantasy 'in presenting, and in meaning to present, not history but theology.'"[63] Is it a sufficient answer merely to substitute "Risen Lord" for "fantasy"?

It is clear that the *Discussions'* persistent ambivalence towards "mere" facts reflects neo-orthodox bias and orientation. From liberalism neo-orthodoxy has inherited the habit of regarding Scripture as one of the "products of man's religious life," none of which "is in itself infallible or a direct, unmediated result of divine activity."[64] The same authoritative source says: "Neo-orthodoxy agrees with liberalism that the whole area of spatio-temporal fact and event is the valid object of scientific inquiry, with the result that the hypotheses of science in the area of natural and historical fact are regarded as authoritative." Hence, "to the contemporary thinker theological doctrines are statements containing symbolic rather than literal truth, propositions pointing to the religious dimensions of events rather than propositions containing factual information about events." This explains, to quote a book by Dean Hazelton, highly

---

63. H. Cohn, *The Trial and Death of Jesus* (London: Weidenfeld and Nicolson, 1972), xv.

64. M. Halverson and A. Cohen, *A Handbook of Christian Theology* (London: Collins, 1958), 261.

recommended by Jaroslav Pelikan, "the simple fact that what most biblical theologians mean by history is just what historians themselves are wont to call myth, saga, or legend — almost the very opposite of history as they understand it."[65]

How odd that the very people who talk most about the "mighty acts" of the "God who acts," then reduce acts and facts to meanings, and history to ideals! The *Discussions*' double-mindedness gravitates along this neo-orthodox incline, which leads inevitably to the full-blown schizophrenia described by L. Gilkey:

> Suddenly a vast panoply of divine deeds and events recorded in Scripture are no longer regarded as having actually happened . . . all these "acts" vanish from the plane of historical reality and enter the never-never land of "religious interpretation" by the Hebrew people. . . . The difference between this view of the Bible as a parable illustrative of Hebrew religious faith and the view of the Bible as a direct narrative of God's actual deeds and words is so vast that it scarcely needs comment. . . . What has happened is that, as modern men perusing the Scriptures, we have rejected as invalid all the innumerable cases of God's acting and speaking; but as neo-orthodox men looking for a word from the Bible, we have induced from all these cases the theological generalization that God is he who acts and speaks. This general truth about God we then assert while denying all the particular cases on the basis of which the generalization was first made. Consequently, biblical theology is left with a set of theological abstractions, more abstract than the dogmas of scholasticism, for these are concepts with no known concreteness.[66]

President Preus' *Principles* show that these contours of the contemporary theological landscape have been thoroughly grasped. The *Discussions* sleepwalk by comparison. What does it mean, for instance, that a "promise depends on a relationship of trust, not a series of rational proof" (*Discussion Five*), and that the "promise is ours by faith alone, not by the verification of historical details" (*Discussion Four*)? Aren't these shoes all on the wrong feet? These formulations suggest that the orthodox, formal principle approach demands "rational proofs" and the "verification of historical details," while the *Discussions* represent "faith alone"

---

65. R. Hazelton, *New Accents in Contemporary Theology* (New York: Harper, 1960), 66.
66. L. B. Gilkey, "Cosmology, Ontology, and the Travail of Biblical Language," *CTM* XXXIII (March 1962):145–152.

and a "relationship of trust." But in fact the reverse is true: orthodox faith accepts the "historical details" of the text without any "rational proofs" or "verification," simply because of its "relationship of trust" to Christ and His Word, the Bible. The *Discussions* meanwhile defend historical criticism, which accepts nothing on authority, but insists on "rational proofs" and "verification" of all "historical details"! And *Discussion Five*'s attempted contrast between "merely a passing agreement to keep an appointment or do an assignment" and "a word of commitment from the depths of someone's being" misfires too. For it is just the formal principle approach which accepts in trust God's full "commitment" in the Bible, and *therefore* trusts the details. God is not an absent-minded professor, who might with the best of intentions overlook a minor appointment. It is not only irrational but sacrilegious to pretend to trust His Word in "large matters," while suspecting the reliability of His Word in "small matters" (cf. Luke 16:10)!

This again illustrates the consistent pattern of the *Discussions*: "faith," that is, the material principle, which has no quarrel whatever with its own historical details, is being used as a battering ram to make way for the historical-critical approach, which, as soon as it is admitted, starts gnawing away at the "details" of the very Gospel in the name of which it gained entry! The *Discussions* ought not to pretend that the dispute is about whether faith is *more* than the acceptance of historical facts, when the real thrust of the critical approach is that it is *less*!

The "ultimate purpose" of Scripture and the "central meaning" of particular texts may not be played off against intermediate purposes and "details." The broader truth must illuminate, not eliminate, the narrower. To the extent that the "details" are sacrificed, the general truths become vacuous abstractions, quite contrary to the incarnational-sacramental mystery of the Biblical narrative. Without historical and geographical details there simply was no Incarnation. To say, for instance, that the Lake Gennesaret must be understood not as a geographical, but as a "theological place,"[67] is to embrace the very spirit of antichrist, who denies that Jesus is come "in the *flesh*" (1 Jn. 4:2–3, italics added)! The Good News, after all, is not about shadows but about en-flesh-ment, reality, body (John 1:14–17; Col. 2:9–17), and glories precisely in these!

John's symbolism, therefore, does not compromise history but presupposes it; for him there is no tension between the symbolic and the factual:

---

67. Cited in Kuenneth, 6.

his symbols are the real events of history, and his symbolism is inherent in these events; his symbolism not only explains the inner meaning of these historic events, but to John, the privileged witness of the incarnate Word, all this symbolism would be useless if these events had not taken place (*Jerusalem Bible*, Introduction to St. John).

That our holy Faith is the religion of the Word doesn't mean that it is a religion of words. To the life-giving Gospel's "output" of Word *and* Sacrament there corresponds the "input" of the Savior's teaching *and* action. To paraphrase Luther on Baptism: The Biblical facts are not simple history only, but they are the history comprehended in God's command and connected with God's Word. This sacred "sacramental union" between words and acts, doctrine and fact, is irrevocably fixed in the once-and-for-all-ness of God's saving act in Christ. And the eternal inviolability of this sanctuary extends to its concrete particulars, to what human reason might dismiss as "peripheral details" (Mark 14:9)! Here faith must take its stand, and with the flaming Sword of the Spirit defiantly bar the way to every abomination of desolation or desecration, under whatever methodological guise!

The Third Article

The definition of the church as "communities" in the third set of *Affirmations* foreshadows the relevant *Discussions*' failure to confess explicitly (1) the distinction between the Church properly speaking and the Church in the wider sense of the word, i.e., the "fellowship of outward ties and rites"; (2) the *pure* marks of the Church; (3) the difference between orthodox and heterodox churches; and (4) the distinction between the Two Kingdoms. These confusions appear to be in the service of a "social action" oriented ecumenicism.

The *Affirmations* do refer once to the Lord's "body and blood in the Sacrament of the Altar." But nothing is said to ward off denials and compromises of the Real Presence, like *Marburg Revisited* and the *Leuenberg Concord*. Indeed, I understand that St. Louis faculty members are publicly on record as favoring Lutheran-Reformed intercommunion on such a basis. All the more alarming, therefore, to read in *Discussion Seven*: "In all of this we must trust the Spirit to lead Christians of all churches into all truth and not try to impose our particular way of wording the Gospel upon them. We affirm the Lutheran Confessions as a true exposition of God's Word; our Confessions, however, are not intended to be barriers between denominations, but bold affirmations of Christ, His Gospel and the unity of His Church."

But the Confessions themselves repudiate such a misleadingly optimistic one-sidedness:

> We mean specifically to condemn only false and seductive doctrines and their stiff-necked proponents and blasphemers. These we do not by any means intend to tolerate in our lands, churches, and schools inasmuch as such teachings are contrary to the expressed Word of God and cannot co-exist with it. . . . But we have no doubt at all that one can find many pious, innocent people even in those churches which have up to now admittedly not come to agreement with us. . . . It is furthermore to be hoped that when they are rightly instructed in this doctrine, they will, through the guidance of the Holy Spirit, turn to the infallible truth of the divine Word and unite with us and our churches and schools. (*Preface, Book of Concord*)
>
> We consider this Confession [the Augsburg Confession] a genuinely Christian symbol which all true Christians ought to accept next to the Word of God (FC SD General . . . Restatement, 4).
>
> This symbol distinguishes our reformed churches from the papacy and from other condemned sects and heresies. (FC SD Rule and Norm, 5)
>
> We reject and condemn all the sects and heresies that are rejected in the aforementioned documents. (FC SD Rule and Norm, 18)

Note also FC SD VII 33!

But perhaps none of this is binding in the view of the *Discussions:* "Our commitment to the Lutheran Confessions means that we adopt their governing theological principles and engage in the theological enterprise in the same way the confessors did" (*Discussion Four*). This switch from the "what" to the "how" of the Confessions, makes confessional subscription practically meaningless. And the *Concordia Theological Monthly,* edited by the St. Louis faculty, permits itself to say *editorially:* "It is no part of the doctrinal contents of the Lutheran Confessions (which alone is binding) *that they are to be used today as a rule and norm for Christian faith and life*" (italics in original)![68] Compare this with, say, FC SD Rule and Norm 10:

> Our intention was only to have a single, universally accepted, certain, and common form of doctrine which all our Evangelical churches subscribe and from which and according to which, because it is drawn from the Word of God, all other writings are to be approved and accepted, judged and regulated.

---

68. C. E. Huber, "The Gospel Needs Protection," *CTM* XLII (May 1971):259.

Highly relevant to the *Discussions'* stance is the part played by the Historical-Critical Method in bringing about the facile Lutheran-Reformed "agreement" in the Arnoldshain Theses, the precursor of the Leuenberg Concord:

> For about two hundred years German theologians had been leaders in developing the so-called "historical-critical" study of the Bible. Prior to this time the Bible had been looked upon as a divinely inspired book which contained eternal truths and no uncertainties or errors. . . . German scholars began to examine the Bible in much the same way that they would examine any ancient document. . . . The Lord's Supper became one of the things examined in the light of the historical-critical method. . . . We should also realize that this new approach to the Bible ultimately determined the course of the discussions and the formulation of the Theses.[69]

The Leuenberg Concord too documents not a real agreement between *churches* adhering to the Lutheran and the Reformed Confessions respectively, but a kind of esoteric professional understanding that has in essence existed among the practitioners of historical criticism all along anyway. Highly applicable to the St. Louis Discussions is the critique of Leuenberg from within the Bavarian Lutheran Territorial Church:

> The body of doctrine of both churches is distorted because contrary to the confessional claim (*Epitome,* Rule and Norm, 1) the function of rule and norm . . . is attributed not to Scripture as a whole, but only to the message of justification. Thereby the message of justification is transformed from the chief article (*Smalcald Articles*) into a principle of selection. The expression "chief article," by contrast, implies the independent right of other articles besides it. Through this overemphasis the body of doctrine is dangerously distorted. When no longer the fullness of revelation, but an abstract doctrine is the measure of proclamation, then the church enters upon the path of the sects, which also overstress a doctrine which is correct in itself.[70]

---

69. E. M. Skibbe, *Protestant Agreement on the Lord's Supper* (Minneapolis: Augsburg, 1968), 77–79; cited in T. N. Teigen, "A Proper Basis for a Discussion of the Lord's Supper," *Lutheran Synod Quarterly* 9 (Summer 1969):41–43.

70. *"Steilungnahme des Theologischen Ausschusses der Gesellschaft fuer Innere und Aeussere Mission im Sinne der lutherischen Kirche zur Leuenberger, Konkordie"* 1972, p. 6.

SUMMARY AND CONCLUSION

Since the St. Louis faculty themselves have publicly opposed their position to that of President Preus, and have described his theology as un-Lutheran and un-Biblical, they must agree that, as the *Formula of Concord* puts it, the controversy is not a mere matter of misunderstandings (these may of course be involved too) but one of basic doctrinal conflict, so "that the opinions of the erring party cannot be tolerated in the church of God, much less be excused and defended" (FC SD General . . . Restatement, 9).

Moreover, the *Affirmations* and *Discussions* do not really attempt to refute the particulars of President Preus' *Principles* and of his Fact Finding Committee's *Report*, but try to present the whole situation in a different light or perspective. This perspective is shaped ostensibly by the Gospel, the material principle, but actually by historical-critical methodology. This methodology is defended as a strictly neutral tool of interpretation, and some controls are indicated, but in the most general terms, which fall far short of an adequate and relevant defense against the known perils.

Actually the *Discussions* themselves illustrate the fact that the critical methodology they champion is far from doctrinally neutral. It succeeds not only in abrogating the formal principle *sola scriptura* completely, but even in exacting heavy tribute from the material principle, the Gospel itself, in terms of disastrous concessions in all three articles of the Creed. In this the *Discussions* represent a "swing of the pendulum" way beyond what was originally intended by the protest of Theodore Graebner and others against a certain ingrown traditionalism and rigidity. For despite some ecclesiological short circuits, which were exploited later, Graebner never wavered in principle from total commitment to both the organic and the dogmatic foundations of the Faith, which define the pure marks of the Church and thus the legitimate limits of church-fellowship.

In reaching these conclusions I have tried scrupulously to be fair, in terms of clearly and openly stated Biblical and confessional commitments. I have not maliciously twisted anyone's words. If I have misjudged this or that particular, I humbly apologize and submit to better instruction.

The *Discussions* urge the "freedom of the Gospel." But as C. S. Lewis observed somewhere, my freedom to play chess depends on the absolute rigidity of the squares and of the moves. In the case of the Gospel this precondition of freedom is destroyed when one makes common cause with historical criticism, which rebels against the Lord and His Anointed, saying: "Let us burst their bonds asunder, and cast their cords from us" (Ps. 2 [RSV]). This unilateral declaration of independence not from synodical statements, but from Biblical authority itself, spells not the freedom of the Gospel, but freedom from the Gospel. And the Gospel itself is tied hand and foot to the Procrustes' bed of criticism! The *Discussions* are here turning off the lights as Chesterton put it, fondly imagining that they are turning them on. But the fact that the secular tyrannies are accepted in good faith, without any apparent intention or sense of treason, does not alter the objective consequences.

"Method," observed that brilliant conservative controversialist, Bill Buckley, "is the fleshpot of those who live in metaphysical deserts." And criticism is the method of our sceptical wilderness. In a very useful book not immediately accessible to me, Harry Blamires distinguishes between a shallow and a deeper scepticism. He illustrates the difference with the typical crime novel: Scotland Yard detectives, representing routine, bureaucratic scepticism, question and suspect everyone, but fail to solve the mystery. Then along comes the hero, the brilliant amateur, and by questioning the conventional surface scepticism of the professionals, solves the murder. Similarly, says Blamires, the typical critical, liberal attitude to religion is a smug, superficial scepticism which is blind to its own prejudices. The dogmatic approach of faith, on the other hand, questions the easy, optimistic illusions of current fashion. Orthodox faith is not more but less gullible than self-congratulatory criticism, for it is much more realistic and therefore humble about the nature and scope of human knowledge and wisdom. [*Editor's note:* Harry Blamires, *A Defence of Dogmatism* (London, SPCK, 1965), 60 ff.] It comes down to Law and Gospel again: real faith, having had its self-assured critical stuffings knocked out of it by the Law as an awesome reality, not a paper-tiger phrase, is in no mood to tangle or tamper with the Word of the Almighty. And having received all from the Gospel, faith knows perfectly well Who is trustworthy in case of conflict: "Let God be true, and every man a liar!" (Rom. 3:4). Therefore faith looks for freedom not to a revolutionary "*Offenbarungsueberdruss*" (being sick and tired of revelation) and its "rational liberation front," historical criticism, but to that *magna charta* of Christian liberty, the divine Scriptures. And He Who healed the paralytics, and Who here in His Word offers full release even from the final paralysis of death, certainly also releases the minds of His People from all degrading and paralyzing subservience to the "elements of this world," including the historical-critical *rigor mortis!*

And here lies the deepest tragedy of the *Discussions*. It is not any technical proficiency that is lacking in them, but a sense of theology. That profound Christian thinker, Etienne Gilson, a great mind and generous spirit, has in his memoirs described much that is acutely relevant also to the decay of doctrinal substance in Lutheran churches. Here is a striking excerpt:

We had no doubt that, if he was a Catholic, a philosopher was thereby a theologian. That is why so many people dabbled in theology in an amateurish way without being aware of incurring any risk. A case in point was a most devout Christian, capable of holding both a chair of philosophy and a chair of mathematics, who did not hesitate to expound the most intricate theological problems. He even undertook to explain to the Church the nature of religious dogmas, as though she had not been promulgating them for centuries. His ignorance of theology was as complete as ours. Doctrinal condemnations were to be expected, but when they came, they took that small world by surprise. Those condemned simply considered themselves persecuted by backward theologians.[71]

Quite apart from President Preus' *Principles*, the theological faculty of St. Louis ought long ago to have recognized and faithfully warned against American Lutheranism's Gadarene descent into chaos and unbelief, as documented in purely empirical studies like L. Kersten's *The Lutheran Ethic*. Instead, the faculty, and especially its current President, Dr. Tietjen, have done their level best to promote a deceptive outward union even with those "Lutheran" bodies in which the disease has obviously reached the terminal stages. President Preus and the church he represents have every right to expect their chief Seminary to take a clear, decisive stand on the great theological issues of today. The *Discussions* partly evade these issues, and partly seek to justify their compromise with the historical-critical root-evil. And doxological phrases ("common chorus of adoration") are no substitute for unambiguous theological substance.

But the Missouri Synod has and must have the freedom to confess the Gospel according to Scripture and Confessions, and to define what this means in the face of internal and external aberrations. Article II of Synod's constitution is an instrument of confession, not a waxen nose, which allows anything that pays lip-service to Scripture and Confessions. If God's Word, "as becometh it," is not to be bound, but to "have free course and be preached to the joy and edifying of Christ's holy people," then the pseudo-freedom of the *Discussions* must be rejected.

If misunderstandings do exist, then let them be faced. There is no reason why, if the faculty have genuine Biblical, confessional objections to this or that particular point of the *Principles*, these could not be clearly pointed out and satisfactorily adjusted. But the issue cannot be left unresolved. When

---

71. E. Gilson, *The Philosopher and Theology* (New York: Random House, 1962), 64.

Pelagius' companion, Coelestius, gave evasive answers before a North African Council, the latter demanded that he explicitly reject particular points of false doctrine which had been attributed to him. When he refused, the Council excommunicated him for heresy. This ecclesiastical decisiveness is not a matter of "casuistry," as Dr. Tietjen seems to suggest,[72] but belongs to the integrity of the church and of her very reason for being. What to do about someone who is personally confused or wrong about some point of Christian doctrine, can be a very complex pastoral problem. But what must be done about a public teacher who spreads such confusion and errors, perhaps even among the future clergy, is a very clean *doctrinal* question!

Certainly that great theologian of the Cross, Martin Luther, knew the meaning of Law and Gospel, and of Christian freedom. And like St. Paul (Gal. 1:8–9) he did not confuse the Gospel with a soft permissiveness, but insisted on the difference between a confessing church and a discussion club. When Prof. George Major was shocked at Luther's sign, above his study-door: "Our professors must be examined regarding the Lord's Supper," the great Reformer explained:

> You make yourself suspect with your silence and covering up. But if you believe as you speak before me, then speak thus also in the church, in the public lectures, in sermons and private conversations, and strengthen your brethren and help the erring back to the right path, and contradict the wilful spirits; otherwise your confession is only a masquerade and of no use. He who regards his doctrine, faith, and confession as true, right, and certain, cannot stand in one stall with others who hold false doctrine or are given to it, nor constantly pay compliments to the devil and his works. A teacher who keeps silent about the errors, and nevertheless wants to be a true teacher, is worse than a public fanatic, and with his hypocrisy does more damage than a heretic, and he is not to be trusted. He is a wolf and a fox, a hireling and a belly-server, and dares to despise and surrender doctrine, Word, faith, Sacrament, churches and schools. He either lies secretly under one blanket with the enemies, or he is a doubter and weathervane, and wants to see how things will turn out, whether Christ or the devil will win out; or he is totally uncertain in himself, and not worthy to be called a student, much less a teacher, and doesn't want to offend anyone, neither speak His Word for Christ, nor hurt the devil and the world.[73]

---

72. Tietjen, *op. cit.*, 6.
73. Cited in C. F. W. Walther, *Der Concordienformel Kern und Stern* (St. Louis: Concordia Publishing House, 1906), 40–41.

Chapter Five

C. F. W. WALTHER IN FACT AND FICTION

Editor's note: The previous essay had been written before the 1973 Missouri Synod convention at New Orleans. The one below was written afterwards, seemingly early in 1974, before the Walkout of faculty and students at Concordia Seminary, St. Louis on February 19. It responds to the December 3 and December 24, 1973 issues of Missouri in Perspective. *This article by Marquart appeared in Affirm 4 (April 18, 1974).*

What is noteworthy about this quickly composed response is its depth of research. Marquart was making far more than a passing attempt to set the record straight regarding a theologian he deeply respected, C. F. W. Walther. Unlike others who quoted the Missouri Synod's first president superficially or, still worse, merely mentioned his name, Marquart seriously appropriated Walther. No doubt, this appreciation had started with an intense reading that positioned Marquart to put his finger on relevant Walther statements for ready deployment, as here, in historically informed ecclesiastical polemics. One can only admire his command of the material.

Early on, the article enumerated six "fictions" about Walther. Then followed six sections, each of which was marked with a Roman numeral. These Roman numerals correspond to the numbering of the "fictions" listed toward the beginning of the article. Within each section marked by a Roman numeral various "facts" are also numbered. Readers should be aware that the numbering of these "facts" does not match up with the numbering of the "fictions." Also, at points below, guidance from the editor to the reader is given in brackets.

ༀ

In the December 3, 1973, issue of *Missouri in Perspective* Erwin L. Lueker purports to present Dr. Walther's answer to the question: "What is a Lutheran?" What we actually get, however, is something like Tietjen's answer, clumsily disguised as Walther's.

Dr. Tietjen and his allies, as is well known, have been claiming for some time that they are defending the real Christ-centered Gospel against the "sub-Biblical" and "un-Lutheran" legalistic Biblicism and traditionalism of Dr. Preus.

Now, since Dr. Walther was an eminently Biblical, Lutheran theologian, his writings abound with the polished gems of Christ-centered, truly evangelical confession and exposition. By breaking a few such jewels out of their total setting, and forcing them through the "moderate" sieve, it is easy to present a censored, filtered, diluted "Walther" who looks in fact like Tietjen's identical twin!

The main illusion then is that Walther legitimizes Tietjen's claim that "the Gospel" (that is, the latter's own ambiguous slogans about it) is "enough," and that President Preus and the synod are wrong in making "other" and "additional" demands on the Seminary.

This illusion-by-selection is reinforced by placing the Walther-snippets into new and misleading contexts. Superficial verbal resemblances and false distinctions suggest to the reader an application to the present controversy which would have horrified the original author. Let us examine this technique in detail.

The reader is clearly meant to infer:

Fiction 1: That President Preus' stress on the Gospel as "a narrative, an historical account" is really "Reformed," while the Tietjen faculty's historical-critical evasions, ambiguities, and surrenders are in harmony with Walther's emphasis on "the Gospel"!

Fiction 2: That the insistence on precise, concrete "points of doctrine" is "Reformed," while the "moderates'" pietistic slogans and generalities represent Walther's stress on Christ and faith.

Fiction 3: That the Seminary is the innocent victim of that pseudo-orthodoxy which Walther condemned, viz., "attacking every apparent heretic and everything which had the appearance of being ecclesiastical laxity with utmost ferocity." Again the anti-Walther villains are, naturally, Preus and New Orleans!

Fiction 4: That the new St. Louis Seminary theology stands with Walther against the "Biblicism" of Schmucker—and Preus!

Fiction 5: That the "moderates" are, with Walther, "person-centered," while Dr. Preus and the synod are — contrary to Walther— "book-centered."

Fiction 6: That since all American Lutheran bodies now subscribe to the Augsburg Confession, Walther would have favored union on this basis. The "ecumenically" oriented "moderates" naturally agree with Walther, while Preus and his intransigents stand in the way of true unity by insisting on narrower and more exclusive "theses" and "statements."

These, clearly, are the intended insinuations — otherwise the whole article would be pointless and irrelevant. Indeed, If Dr. Walther's words had been intended in their true and original sense —well, then Dr. Lueker would have written them up for *Affirm*, rather than for a publication dedicated to the reversal of New Orleans and to the defense of the "moderate" theological novelties.

We owe it to the blessed memory of that great man of God, and to his unsullied reputation as an orthodox Lutheran theologian, to examine the above imputations carefully in the light of the real facts both about the real Dr. Walther and about the real nature of the conflict in Missouri today. The facts that follow are grouped in six sections, corresponding to the six misinterpretations.

I.

Fact 1: Walther insists on the principle expressed thus by Aegidius Hunnius:

> To be sure he is a heretic who denies an article of faith; yet not only such a one, but also he who denies a historical narration of the Holy Spirit. (*True Visible Church,* under Thesis XVIII C; also: "The False Props of the Modern Theory of Open Questions," *Lehre und Wehre,* 1868, p. 103)

Fact 2: Walther scathingly rejects all compromise with the historical-critical approach, for instance in his 1871 *Lehre und Wehre* series, "What do the newer, would-be orthodox theologians teach concerning inspiration?":[1]

> Therefore Mr. [Friedrich A.] Tholuck looks down, with a pitying smile, on the older exegetes, for whom, by virtue of their acceptance of an *inspiratio litteralis* (i.e., verbal inspiration) the absolute inerrancy of the New Testament writers stood firm as indubitable presupposition. For those fools the interpretation of the Old Testament given in the New Testament was normative!! While scientific exegetes like Tholuck have long ago given up this childish opinion. [sic] These redoubtable men explain the Old Testament without recourse to the New; they excuse the dear Apostles for not having interpreted quite scientifically, on account of their kinship with the rabbinical schools . . . For that Ex. 3:6 really refers to the resurrection of the dead, Mr. Tholuck by no means believes, although the living God Himself asserts it in Matt. 22:32. Rather, this man, who calls himself a

---

1. *Editor's note:* The following block quotes consist of a few snippets from Walther, as translated by Marquart. In this article, Marquart relied a great deal on quotations from Walther like these, adding little or no comment to most of them. Note that in several of these quotes, Walther was being sarcastic.

doctor of divinity, dares to judge thus of the authentic explanation of his God: "One Old Testament interpretation has given the impression of rabbinical subtlety, not quite without reason. It is Matthew 22:32." (p. 42)

Of the five books of Moses, which the Lord and the Apostles attribute to Moses in more than twenty places, Delitzsch teaches that they are a *mixtum compositum* from all sorts of different workshops. (p. 101)

A man who makes a novel out of the first chapter of Genesis must necessarily find the inerrancy of the Bible inconvenient. (p. 106)

But an unknown forger had the impertinence to invent visions and to spread them among the people under the fraudulent name of Daniel ... Certainly Mr. [Karl F. A.] Kahnis has proved with this his disquisition that he believes in the Lord Himself as little as in the writings of Daniel. He — the Lord, after all — said to His Christians (Matt. 24:15): "When now you see the abomination of desolation of which it was spoken through the prophet Daniel" ... Here Christ not only attests the genuineness and truthfulness of the prophecies of Daniel, but also draws from this an important conclusion ... I do not know whom Mr. Kahnis takes the Lord to be. But he who regards Him as the Son of God must regard Mr. Kahnis' disquisition as blasphemy. Yes, blasphemy. Let no one call this expression too strong! For when a pope seeks to strengthen his title of possession by means of the fraudulent Donation of Constantine, we heap contempt upon him. And the Son of the living God is supposed to have committed this same villainy; to have built His exhortation to the disciples on the product of a deceiver devoid of conscience. (134–135)

II.

Fact 3: Dr. Walther insists precisely on "points of doctrine":

The Evangelical Lutheran Church is certain that the doctrine contained in her Symbols is the pure divine truth, because it agrees with the written Word of God in all points. (*True Visible Church,* Thesis XXI A)

When a theologian wants to yield not even in one single point of Christian doctrine, so that there might at last be peace in the Church, then this of course looks to the eyes of reason like intolerable stubbornness, yes, like open malice ... Therefore, blessed be all the faithful warriors, who fought, without asking for human favor, without fearing men, for every point of Christian doctrine! (*Law and Gospel,* Fourth Lecture)

And Walther often cited, with emphasis on the "all," FC SD X 31: "agreed in doctrine and in all its articles."

In the April, 1855 *Lehre und Wehre* Walther approvingly printed Stroebel's reply to a Dr. R. Stier's theses:

> "57) The *'evangelium'* Mr. Stier will no doubt tolerate, but not the *'doctrina evangelii,'* for that is not supposed to be the basis on which the Christian Church can and must rest . . . the Gospel of these people simply is no *doctrina*, but something good for kitchen and cellar."

III.

Fact 4: The "attacking . . . with utmost ferocity" undoubtedly referred to the likes of Pastor Grabau and his Buffalo Synod, who, with incredible hierarchical pretensions, excommunicated the opponents they could not refute, especially Missouri with its "loose," "unchurchly," "democratic" doctrines of the Church and the Ministry.

To compare such malicious calumnies, by implication, with the well-deserved censure of the St. Louis Seminary's aberrations from the very foundations of Biblical, Lutheran theology, is itself grossly calumnious. And to drag in Walther's name is doubly so.

IV.

Fact 5: The accusation of "Biblicism" against Schmucker is not Walther's but Lueker's. Walther would not have dreamt of it. For him Schmucker was not excessively but insufficiently Biblical. What horrified Walther was Schmucker's surrender of Lutheran doctrines like the Real Presence for the sake of unhindered fraternization with the Reformed denominations.

Fact 6: Prominent Missouri "moderates," including seminary professors, have publicly sided with Schmucker, against Walther, by supporting "A Call to Openness and Trust" (January 31, 1970), which held that, among other things, "the definition of the presence of Christ in the Lord's Supper" should not be regarded as church-divisive. This is blatant defiance not of this or that little point in the Lutheran Confessions, but of a vital doctrine to which every single one of the Confessions, except the Tractate, devotes a whole major article or section! To link such treason in any way with the name of that stalwart Lutheran confessor, Dr. Walther, is sheer impudence.

Fact 7: As regards "Biblicism" Dr. Walther was far more rigorous than Schmucker. Apart from Dr. Walther's better known books and addresses, I would refer the reader especially to his much augmented edition of Baier's *Compendium*, and to Vol. XIV of *Lehre und Wehre* (1868), which contains the two magnificent series "What is Theology?" and "The False Props of the Modern Theory of Open Questions."[2]

In the face of all this evidence will anyone dare to claim in all seriousness that Walther's writings give any aid and comfort whatsoever to the position of today's "moderates"? On the contrary: He vigorously insisted on the *factually inerrant* Bible as the *formal principle* of theology; they scorn and deny this ("A Call to Openness and Trust," "Faithful to Our Calling, etc."). ELIM, by the way, find this business so awkward that in recommending an essay by Fred Mayer published by them, they make the astounding admission that it "was edited slightly to eliminate the frequently confusing terms 'formal' and 'material' principles of theology, in order that it might be suitable for congregational use" (*Perspective*, Dec. 24, 1973, p. 4).

Here now are some samples of the real Walther's "Biblicism":

✦ ([This paragraph begins with Walther quoting] Kahnis): "'Protestantism stands and falls with the principle of the sole authority of Scripture. But this principle is independent of the doctrine of inspiration of the old dogmatics. To embrace it again as it was can be done only with a hardening against the truth!' We must confess, when we read these words, we were right heartily frightened by them. Who can go along with a new theology which introduces itself as the further development of the old Lutheran theology, and then deviates from the doctrinal model of our old theology precisely in the doctrine of the principle of theology, of Holy Scripture, viz., of the *ratio formalis scripturae*, of that which makes Holy Scripture what it is?" (*Lehre und Wehre*, 1855, p. 248)

✦ ". . . in the orthodox church freedom may not be granted to deviate even in the smallest point from God's clear Word, be it negatively or positively, directly or indirectly; that such deviation from God's clear Word, even if it consisted merely in the denial that Balaam's ass spoke, requires of the orthodox church that it institute proceedings against this . . . For if the Bible is God's Word, then all affirmations contained in it are decisions of the high divine Majesty Itself. But is it not frightful to declare undecided what the great God has decided? When the great God has spoken, to grant liberty to man to contradict Him?" (*Lehre und Wehre*, 1868, pp. 68–69)

---

2. *Editor's note:* An English translation of the latter is in C. F. W. Walther, *Walther's Works: Church Fellowship* (St. Louis: Concordia Publishing House 2015), 95–140.

◆ "He who imagines that he finds in the Holy Scripture even only one error, believes not in Scripture, but in himself; for even if he accepted everything else as truth, he would believe it not because Scripture says so, but because it agrees with his reason or with his heart. 'Dear fellow,' writes Luther, 'God's Word is God's Word, and won't tolerate much fooling about . . . Look, the circumcision of Abraham is now an old, dead thing, and is now neither necessary nor useful; still, if I were to say: God did not command it at that time, then nothing would help me, even if I believed the Gospel.'" (*ibid.*, p. 101)

◆ "Basically Mr. Nitzsch is far from believing that the whole Bible is God's Word. But because of certain devout little old ladies in his congregation and because of a few other people he doesn't want to come straight out with it. But he gives a hint with the fencepost, as it were. Everything astronomical, physical, geographical, ethnographic, in short everything scientific in the Bible — he says — is by no means revealed." (*Lehre und Wehre*, 1871, p. 40)

[*Editor's note:* Marquart wrote that Christoph Ernst "Luthardt had denied the old doctrine of inspiration, but sensed that modern substitutes were unsatisfactory." Then Marquart quoted Walther as follows concerning Luthardt:]

◆ "But he does not want to go back to the old ship, definitely does not want to go back. He maintains in fact that this ship had been brought down by facts! It is no true ship at all!! Only a kind of Flying Dutchman!!! A construction of dogmatic logic, i.e. of the imagination. — Poor Lutherans, who have been sailing to the haven of salvation in this ship for three hundred years! Have you really arrived? Have you? Of course you have. For your faith, which clung to God's Word, has overcome the world." (*ibid.*, p. 99)

◆ "For he who wholeheartedly believes that the Bible is God's Word cannot believe it to be otherwise than inerrant." (*ibid.*, p. 135)

[*Editor's note:* A quote that Walther cited from Luthardt is omitted here.]

◆ [Walther:] "Until recently the modern-believing theologians treated their doctrine of Holy Scripture, which overturns the foundation of the whole Christian religion, like a secret doctrine for theologians . . . No doubt the gentlemen thought that by now even non-theologians might have progressed far enough to be able to endure an admittedly somewhat glaring light like that that Scripture is full of errors . . .

The most horrifying aspect of the matter by the way is the fact that the new prophets want to make the Lutheran Christian people believe that the doctrine that the Scriptures of the prophets, apostles, and evangelists are really inspired by the Holy Spirit according to content and form, and therefore free from all erroneous material — is not the Lutheran, but the 'pietistic-Reformed'! That is a perfectly ghastly fraud which is being perpetrated on the Lutheran Christian people." (*Lehre und Wehre*, September, 1885, pp. 277–279)

Is this "ghastly fraud" not at the heart of the whole contention in Missouri today, especially at the St. Louis seminary?[3]

Yes, the late Dr. C. S. Meyer put it much more honestly than Dr. Lueker when he admitted, from his "moderate" point of view, that Walther's doctrine of the Word "was not wholly Christocentric but tended toward biblicism" (*CTM* XLIII [April 1972]:262).

Finally, isn't it hypocritical to make a dreadful to-do (falsely yet!) about "common causes with fundamentalists and revivalistic Reformed" while cheerfully cultivating the most cordial fellowship with liberal and existentialist Reformed? Dr. Walther would have cut off his right arm rather than accept an honorary doctorate, as Dr. Tietjen did, from the liberal, Bible-dishonoring Reformed Eden Seminary in St. Louis! Indeed Walther declined, on confessional grounds, just such a doctorate from the nominally Lutheran theological faculty of the University of Goettingen.

V.

Fact 8: Lueker's sentence "True Lutheran doctrine has always been person-centered rather than book-centered" is a classic example of false alternatives. This has always caused a lot of mischief. Hence Melanchthon in the *Apology* urges Socrates' admonition, in making distinctions, "to cut the member at the joint, lest like an unskilled cook he sever the member at the wrong place" (XXIV 16)!

The fact of course is that true Lutheran theology has always been Person (Christ)-*centered* and Book-*based*. Will anyone dare to deny that this is true of Walther's theology, but not of that of the "moderates"? "Faithful to our Calling, etc." is at pains to urge the material principle ("the Gospel") in the place of and to the exclusion of the formal principle (the absolute authority of the inerrant Book). Hence C. S. Meyer's critique of

---

3. *Editor's note:* I take this sentence as indicating that the present article was written before the Walkout. It probably would have been worded somewhat differently if it had been composed later.

Walther. Hence also Lueker's misconception of "true Lutheran doctrine."

It is a pipe-dream of modern-theological ego-tripping that one can honor the Person by dishonoring His Book!

Fact 9: The "moderate" position is "person-centered" indeed, but in the sub-jective, worldly-carnal sense of *man-centered* or *self-centered* (Rom. 16:18).

> Jesus Christ came into the world, not to institute doctrine, but to save people (see Mark 2:27). And when people, bought by the blood of Christ, become expendable for the sake of what may (or may not) be pure doc-trine, Christ's purposes are frustrated and that is sinful. (front page edito-rial in December 3 *Perspective*)

This is exactly the sort of sentimental snivelling for which Walther so despised the "American Lutheranism" of the old General Synod. Let ELIM's "respectable and responsible Christian scholarship" take note of one of Walther's favorite Luther-quotes:

> In short we want to have all articles of Christian doctrine, be they great or small (although for us none is small and trivial), completely pure and certain, and will not yield one tittle in this. And that's the way it must be. For doctrine is our only light, which shines for us, and leads us, and points the way to Heaven ... if we are careless here, love won't help us. We can well be saved without the sacramentarians' love and unity; but not without the pure doctrine and faith ... Therefore one must ... dili-gently separate doctrine from life. Doctrine is Heaven, life is the earth ... But with doctrine it is quite another matter; for it is holy, pure, clear, heavenly, divine: whoever wants to change and falsify it must not be shown either love or mercy ... for one letter, yes one single tittle of Scripture is of vastly greater consequence than heaven and earth." ([Cited in] *True Visible Church*, under Thesis XVII, and Foreword to *Lehre und Wehre*, 1860, p. 13)

And to W. Loehe's complaints about Missouri's narrow-mindedness, especially on chiliasm and church and ministry, Walther replied:

> They accuse the church of hardness because she will not permit them to deviate from God's Word; and they refuse to see that their own hardness with which they cling to their delusion is the sole cause of the fragmenta-tion and dissolution of the church. Should truth yield to error, and not rather error to the truth? (Foreword to *Lehre und Wehre*, 1860, p. 43)

No doubt "respectable and responsible Christian scholarship" can imagine without further assistance what the real Walther would have done with that other terrible Dec. 3 *Perspective* editorial, "Absolute Truth and Love," based, appropriately (?), on a text from that devotee of Hindoo paganism, Gandhi!

VI.

Fact 10: Had Walther shared the easy-going pan-Lutheran ecumania of present day "moderates," he could have spared himself a lifetime of blood, sweat, and tears.

But the fact is that Walther was not impressed by the mere ceremonial acceptance of the Augsburg Confession or even of the whole Book of Concord. That practice was popular then, especially in General Synod circles, and it is nearly universal today.

The General Synod accepted the Augsburg Confession "as a correct exhibition of the fundamental doctrines of the divine Word." This restriction, and the resultant theology and practice, Walther always condemned in the strongest terms. For example, in the April, 1859 issue of *Lehre und Wehre*, he printed a lengthy attack on the General Synod, which, "without much wagging with the fox-tail," used terms like "abomination," "hypocrisy," "dishonesty before God and men," "lazy, false love-spirit," etc.

Fact 11: The St. Louis faculty majority's "subscription" to the Confessions is, if anything, even looser than that of the General Synod: "Our commitment to the Lutheran Confessions means that we adopt their governing theological principles and engage in the theological enterprise in the same way the confessors did" ("Faithful," etc., *Discussion Four*).

And that same faculty faction's house-organ, the *CTM* (the successor of Dr. Walther's no-nonsense *Lehre und Wehre!*) has dared to claim editorially: "It is no part of the doctrinal content of the Lutheran Confessions (which alone is binding) *that they are to be used today as a rule and norm for Christian faith and life*" (XLII [May 1971]:259; *italics in original!*).[4]

Fact 12: Far from being content with mere formal acceptance of the Augsburg Confession, Dr. Walther insisted on full obedience to the entire Christian doctrine in all points — even in those not yet formally fixed in the Confessions!

---

4. *Editor's note:* References above to the *faculty majority* and this *faction's house organ* also indicate that Marquart wrote this analysis before the Walkout.

The Evangelical Lutheran Church accepts the written Word of God (as God's Word) in its entirety, considers nothing contained in it superfluous or trivial, but everything as necessary and important, and also accepts all the doctrines which necessarily follow from the words of Scripture (*True Visible Church*, Thesis XVII).

True Evangelical Lutheran particular or local churches or congregations are only those in which the doctrine of the Evangelical Lutheran Church, as laid down in her Symbols, is not only legally acknowledged, but also holds sway in the public preaching (*ibid.*, XXIII).

The orthodox church has reached finality not only with regard to those articles which are set out in her Symbols, but implicitly with regard to all which are contained in the Word of God (*Lehre und Wehre*, 1860, p. 43).

We cannot regard and treat as an open question any doctrine clearly taught in God's Word or contradicting God's clear Word, no matter how subordinated and far removed from the center of the doctrine of salvation, away in the periphery, it may seem to be or may really be (*Lehre und Wehre*, 1868, p. 66).

But also those grant to the Symbols a false position, who want nothing regarded as Lutheran and churchly except what is explicitly laid down in the Symbols; thereby they do nothing else than that they make the Book of Concord into the Bible of the Lutherans (*Lehre und Wehre*, 1868, p. 194).

On the contrary, it is clear . . . that there are many Lutheran, churchly dogmas which are not contained in the Symbols of our church, and thus not, as they say nowadays, symbolically fixed . . . The assumption that a doctrine becomes a Lutheran, churchly dogma only through its acceptance into our Symbols, but prior to that is an open question, is contradicted finally also by the fact that our church in her Symbols commits herself by no means only to the doctrines which she there, on account of certain circumstances, explicitly mentions, but to the entire Holy Scripture, hence to all doctrines contained in it (*Lehre und Wehre*, 1868, pp. 205, 208).

No man has the freedom, and to no man may be granted the freedom, to believe or teach otherwise than God has revealed in His Word, whether this have to do with . . . fundamental or non-fundamental doctrines, matters of faith or of life, historical or other material subject to the light of nature, important, or seemingly unimportant matters . . .

That those doctrines which are not symbolically fixed are to be reckoned among open questions, militates against the historical origin of the Symbols, as well as against the fact that they do not want to give a complete doctrinal system and at the same time commit themselves to the entire content of Scripture as the object of the church's faith. ("Theses about the Modern Theory of Open Questions," VII and XII, *Lehre und Wehre*, 1868, pp. 318–319)

Fact 13: In practice Dr. Walther and the Missouri Synod implemented these principles, e.g. by refusing fellowship to the Buffalo, Iowa, and Ohio Synods, and to the very conservative General Council, all of which professed subscription not only to the Augsburg Confession, but to all the Symbolical Books. The doctrinal differences were considered church-divisive by the Missouri Synod. And far from despising "theses or statements," Dr. Walther himself wrote dozens of them, to express true Biblical, Confessional unity on various doctrines. It is well known that at the time of the Election Controversy, the Missouri Synod adopted Walther's Thirteen Theses (1881) and insisted on their acceptance as proof of genuine adherence to the Biblical doctrine of Article XI of the Formula of Concord. Church fellowship was refused to those who claimed to accept the Formula of Concord, but rejected the Thirteen Theses.

Fact 14: Dr. Walther wrote a great deal about the Lutheran Church, not about a mere "organization." Why does Dr. Lueker choose that pitiful word? Cannot the "moderates" face Walther's doctrine of the Church? Do they fear its keen dogmatic edge?

Mere organizations can afford to play parliamentary games; a church must believe, teach, and confess — and not on paper only but in practice, and to the point of doctrinal discipline. Walther demanded such confession and doctrinal discipline. His Foreword to the 1860 volume of *Lehre und Wehre* answers W. Loehe's sentimental appeal for "unity" by showing in detail how doctrinal discipline was practiced in the orthodox Lutheran Church after the adoption of the Formula of Concord.

It is not the exercise of doctrinal discipline, but resistance to and evasion of the honest implications of confession, which is "church politics."

Walther had nothing but contempt for the shallow organizational obsessions of the General Synod. In the July, 1859 *Lehre und Wehre* he printed a Missouri observer's scathing report on a convention of the General Synod. Dismissing that synod's claim to "admirable Christian feeling and mutual love," the report notes:

> Up to now also in the battles of the Lutherans the main weapon was: "it is written." In the so-called Lutheran General Synod this weapon is unknown. What people rely on, what is supposed to silence the opponent, is the authority of their notorious General Synod constitution. Among Lu-

therans one submits to the Bible, among the Romans to the Pope, among the General Synodists to the constitution!

Perhaps "respectable and responsible Christian scholarship" will notice the baffling resemblance to current Missouri: the supposed "legalist," President Preus, like his illustrious predecessor [Walther], implements the theological substance of the Church's confession in modern, relevant terms. Meanwhile the "Gospel only" people avoid doctrinal specifics like the plague—when for instance will *Perspective's* discussion of "Faithful, etc." honestly face the theological arguments against it?—and cry "Constitution! Article II!"

While Walther's successors pursue theological faithfulness and honesty, their "evangelical" critics quibble about organizational technicalities, and, amid the most vulgar appeals to the secular prejudices of an absurd permissiveness fomented by the media, threaten law-suits before the civil authorities! These then are the realities behind all the talk about "Law and Gospel."

* * *

Undoctored history plainly will not allow the silly charade of clothing the "moderate" theological nakedness with the prestigious mantle of C. F. W. Walther. Perhaps Dr. Lueker and the editors of *Perspective* really did not know any better—this time. But if the attempt is made again, it will be against better knowledge.

Chapter Six

CHURCH FELLOWSHIP

Editor's note: This is an edited version of a published transcript from a speech that Marquart made to a free conference. The transcript appeared in the conference proceedings under the same title[1] as that of Marquart's ecclesiology book, which was in the process of being finished when the conference took place. While it may be that Marquart had been invited to the conference to discuss the contents of the book in general, he chose to concentrate his remarks specifically on church fellowship.

It is good to have a short treatment by Marquart on church fellowship. His work on this particular subject may well have constituted his single most important contribution to the Missouri Synod's theological stance after he became a seminary professor and especially as a member of the Synod's Commission on Theology and Church Relations for a total of twenty-two years. All the notes to this piece have been provided by the editor.

❧

I want to put before you three particular things, three basic issues to do with church fellowship, then rely on anybody who is interested in detailed documentation to get it when my little effort comes out. It will be entitled, *The Church and Her Fellowship, Ministry and Governance.* So, church fellowship is a large component of the whole business of what the Church really is.

The three points that I wish to discuss are: What is the nature of fellowship? Second, what are the criteria, or what is the basis for fellowship? And third, perhaps one of the most fundamental applications that needs to be made today.

First of all, the nature of fellowship. Here we are victims, of course, of certain cultural pressures that tend to see everything in individualistic, subjective terms. This fundamentally misconceives the nature of church fellowship. The moment we hear the term *fellowship*, we tend to think of togetherness, of camaraderie. For example, after the service people are

---

1. Kurt Marquart, "The Church and Her Fellowship, Ministry and Governance," National Free Conference February 16 & 17, 1990 St Louis Missouri [sic] (Brooklyn Center, Minnesota: N.p., n.d.), 107th through 115th pages (page numbers in this set of proceedings are not sequential).

invited for "fellowship" in the hall, although the real fellowship has just been celebrated at the altar. People have the idea — and our culture reinforces it — that fellowship is something to do with individuals. And then people talk about selecting certain individuals for fellowship, as though it were a matter of you and me picking out this one and that one with whom we might have fellowship. This is really something which students of Christian thought will trace to people like Schleiermacher, not to Luther. Luther was not a subjectivist nor an individualist. Church fellowship is not fundamentally a matter of ethics or morality, not a matter of the law. Church fellowship is first a matter of dogma, of doctrine, because church fellowship is an aspect of the doctrine of the Church. It is not simply a matter of the behavior of individual Christians. Church fellowship makes sense as, and must be seen as an aspect of, the doctrine of the Church.

In the New Testament the word *koinonia*, fellowship, doesn't say everything. But the word does tell us that *koinonia*, fellowship, means fundamentally participating, sharing in something common, in common treasures.

Here we have a great clue from Martin Luther's Ninety-five Theses where he gently corrects the old saying, "The poor are the treasures of the Church." That beautiful saying, you remember, we owe to the martyr St. Lawrence, the great and noble archdeacon of the city of Rome. When his bishop was martyred, the prefect of Rome wanted to collect all the money that he thought the Church was full of. He demanded to see the treasures of the Church. Then Lawrence played this little joke on him. He filled the hall with all the poor and the helpless people and all the people the Church was supporting and then said to him, "See, these are the treasures of the Church." He was beheaded for his troubles. The prefect had no sense of humor. But since then the saying got going that the poor are the treasures of the Church. There is a certain beautiful truth to that.

However, Luther saw even more deeply when he said, "Really the true treasure of the Church, in its most proper sense, is the Gospel. The Gospel, the holy Word and Sacraments, these are the true treasures of the Church, for it is only by these that we become and remain Christians."[2] By these is the Church created and by these she is sustained, and by these also her unity is created, sustained and deepened. So Church fellowship is fundamentally a matter of participation in the treasures of the Church, the saving treasures of the Church. These great treasures which come to a climax in the very blood of Christ shed for the salvation of the whole world, are the holy Gospel and the Sacraments of God.

---

2. See theses 59 to 62, AE 31, 30–31.

All this came to a head in North America in 1961 when our former Synodical Conference was breaking up. It is tragic and at the same time ironic that the Synodical Conference broke up over the same issue on which it was founded. It was founded on the matter of the right, Biblical, Lutheran, Evangelical understanding of church fellowship, the true unity of the Church, of which the Augsburg Confession speaks. The Synodical Conference was founded precisely to give expression to the Biblical, evangelical, orthodox fellowship of the Church of the Augsburg Confession. It was a tremendous treasure and a tremendous boon to the Church which lasted nearly a hundred years. As I say, ironically it broke up over the same issue upon which it had been founded, church fellowship. Unfortunately, at the end of the Synodical Conference there wasn't nearly the clarity about church fellowship on any side of these divides as there was at the beginning.

But one thing stands out, and that is a contribution which, at Dr. [John] Behnken's request, the overseas brethren of our Synod made in a last-ditch effort to save the Synodical Conference. And so, from our sister Synods in England, Germany, Belgium, France, particularly Finland, but also Brazil (which was then a district), and Australia, these people presented to the recessed convention of the Synodical Conference in 1961 some remarkable theses on the Doctrine of Church Fellowship in the context of the Doctrine of the Church and the marks of the Church.

To my mind, that is the high water mark of the discussion of this issue facing the Church. I regard it as tragic that neither the Wisconsin nor the Missouri brethren involved in this discussion paid enough attention to this genuinely Lutheran, Biblical analysis of the matter. It seems to me that if we are going to take up with our Wisconsin and ELS brethren the matters that once divided us, and we ought to, then these Thirteen Theses of 1961 would be an excellent starting point.[3]

So, fellowship is fundamentally pulpit and altar fellowship. It is the public participation in the administration of the treasures of the Church. Therefore you can't mix, for example, private prayer into this question of church fellowship.

---

3. The theses, under the title "Fellowship in Its Necessary Context of the Doctrine of the Church," were appended to Marquart's presentation in the conference proceedings. These theses had also been included as "Appendix B" in Kurt E. Marquart, *Anatomy of an Explosion: Missouri in Lutheran Perspective*, Concordia Seminary Monograph Series Number 3, eds. David P. Scaer and Douglas Judisch (Fort Wayne, Indiana: Concordia Theological Seminary Press, 1977), 145–150.

Pulpit fellowship is always fellowship because the pulpit is the public proclamation of the Church. This is always an action of the Church. There is no such thing as privacy in the pulpit. The altar, too, is not a matter of servicing so many private individual needs of so many people, but the altar is the most public place of the Christian Church where we make the most public confession of the truths of our holy faith and say where we stand, and stand there together. So the altar and the pulpit are the most public places of the Church, including and presupposing of course the baptismal font.

Now some prayer happens of course in public and is therefore a public confession. But when you and I meet over a spaghetti dinner with our dear in-laws or outlaws or whatever and they happen to be of some other church, and we either participate in or endure a prayer or say a common table grace, this, my friends, is not church fellowship. You will find even in the New Testament quite some extraordinary continuation of prayer relationships, for example, Paul's business in the temple.[4] We also see the apostolic Church going to the temple where they could hardly have avoided prayer fellowship with some priests who individually were not Christian believers.[5] But it would have been unthinkable for Paul to have invited one of these temple priests to preach in the church, in any church, or to participate in the Sacrament of the Altar. That would have been unthinkable.[6]

So you see, we've got to make a distinction between that which individuals can do and which is therefore not yet the fellowship of the Church, and the public administration and the joint celebration of the treasures of the Church. Prayer is a response to God's saving activity and isn't a means of grace.

Second, therefore, seeing the nature of church fellowship as fundamentally pulpit and altar fellowship, what is its proper basis? What are the criteria that determine fellowship and also its limits? Here we have a classic formulation which I don't think anybody can improve, and I certainly shan't try to improve it: the text of the Augsburg Confession, our great evangelical *Magna Carta* that has for over four hundred years clearly confessed before all of Christendom.

The genius of the Augsburg Confession is its evangelical nature: the Gospel, the whole Gospel, and nothing but the Gospel. The Tappert

---

4. See Acts 21:17–26.
5. See Acts 3:1 ff.
6. See Hebrews 13:10.

translation omits a very important word which we, especially in our Synod now, ignore to our peril. It omits the word *unanimously, eintrachtiglich:* "it is enough . . . that the Gospel be unanimously preached there according to its pure understanding, and that the Sacraments be administered in accordance to the divine Word."[7] The pure Gospel — in other words, the Truth — must norm and be the basis of unity. We do not begin by look-ing to see how many we can gather together and then seeing how much or little we can agree upon. No, fundamentally what creates the unity of the Church and what norms the public recognition, the public manifestation, the public celebration of the Church's unity, is the same thing which has created the Church in the first place. And that is the prophetic-apostolic foundation: "built upon the foundation of the apostles and prophets, Jesus Christ himself being the chief cornerstone" (Eph. 2:20). Anything built on non-apostolic foundations is a pseudo-church, anti-church, counter-church, a semi-church, what have you. All sorts of combinations are pos-sible. But the Church of Jesus Christ rests upon this Gospel as God Him-self gave it and built His Church on this apostolic-prophetic foundation.

The theological shorthand for this is that pulpit and altar fellowship, the unity of the Church, is entirely governed by the pure marks of the Church, the *notae ecclesiae.* The marks of the Church are those marks and signs by which it can be distinguished. This is a very important notion because it implies that the Church is an article of faith, not of sight. Re-member Luther's great evangelical dictum that the Church is so deeply hidden that no human reason can find her, even if she were to put on all spectacles.[8] It's not the sort of thing that we can detect, least of all through little sociological surveys. The Church is not subject to our manipula-tions. We don't see her; we believe her. As Luther points out, we don't say in the Creed, "I see one, holy Christian Church" (as that gentleman in Rome does); but we say, "I believe one, holy, Christian Church."[9] Strictly speaking, we can see where the Church is but we can't see who the Church is. That's the point because she consists of all true believers in Christ and no man has control of that faith, that mystery. Faith, although it involves some psychological phenomena, is itself a theological mystery which only God can detect, and see because only He has worked it. The effects of it can be counterfeited. There is such a thing as hypocrisy. But God creates faith and only He knows who has it. We can't tell who are the Christians

---

7. AC VII 2. The translation appears to be Marquart's own, from the German.
8. AE 35, 410.
9. AE 39, 220.

and who aren't. Therefore for us the Church remains hidden, a mystery of faith.

But how can we find this thing if it's hidden? There, thank God, the good Lord created the Church in such a way that she can be found even though she is invisible as such. Think of the first messengers of Christmas, the angels who appeared to those dumbfounded shepherds on the plains of Bethlehem. Imagine how silly would have been their message if they had said, "Now be very happy, I announce to you good tidings of great joy which shall be to all the people. Today there is born to you a Savior which is Christ the Lord. Now go and find Him." Where would they have gone? But thank Heaven the angels are not useless messengers. They are sent from God and they carry out their mission properly, so they say: "And this shall be a sign to you. You shall find the baby wrapped in swaddling clothes and lying in a manger" [Luke 2:12]. Without these signs they never would have found Him. And how unlikely it was to find God incarnate in that humble little place!

So also it is with the Church because the Church is the mystical Body and the Bride of Christ. And that Church, too, has signs, marks by which she is found—not legalistic marks that men have invented, but those marks by which she is created. The very seed you see: The sower went out to sow the seed. Walther never tired of saying, "Where do you harvest wheat? Not where you have sown weeds or tomatoes. You look for the wheat where you have sown the grain of wheat."[10] And Walther excoriated the silliness of churchmen who say, "Oh, I don't care very much for the seeding part. I'm just concerned with the harvest." No farmer would be that silly. And yet churchmen fall all over themselves to talk about harvest, harvest, harvest, but are careless about the seed. If you want a good harvest you'd better take care of what seed is sown. This is God's Word, His good wheat that goes into the ground.[11] Not weeds and not dragon's teeth, for heaven's sake!

So it is the truth, the evangelical truth, and nothing but the truth that determines, that shapes, church fellowship. Only where there is agreement in this truth, this Gospel of God, including all the articles of faith, there pulpit and altar fellowship is truthful and God-pleasing.

---

10. See C. F. W. Walther, *Gospel Sermons*, trans. Donald E. Heck (St. Louis: Concordia Publishing House, 2013), 1:297.
11. See Carl Ferdinand Wilhelm Walther, *Law and Gospel: How to Read and Apply the Bible*, trans. Christian C. Tiews, gen. ed. Charles Schaum (St. Louis: Concordia Publishing House, 2010), 25.

There was an interesting exchange about two years ago in *New Blackfriars*, the journal of English Dominicans. An Oxford logic professor took to task some liberal writers in his own Roman Catholic Church. He pointed out that if Jesus did not know anything about the Second Person of the Trinity, or His own Godhead, or the Church, then we can know nothing of the Trinity. Then we cannot know Him to be the Son of God. And then the Church becomes a "distinctly fraudulent institution" and nobody has the right to have complicity with fraud.

But the good professor makes another point. He believes that the Roman Catholic and Eastern Orthodox genius, as distinct from the Reformation, is the paramountcy of unity. On no account, in other words, can you ever break fellowship, no matter how bad things get in the true Church. There you see the limits of this logic, because you cannot at one and the same time say: "What's paramount is unity, not truth," and also say that things are going so badly wrong that the Church is becoming a "fraudulent institution" and you "cannot have complicity with fraud."[12] Well then, there is something more paramount than unity, isn't there? That is truth.

Against the paramountcy of a forced organizational unity, a hierarchical system of men, an enslaving of Christian consciences, against that Luther and the evangelical Reformation asserted the paramountcy of truth — of the Gospel. This is why today you find the Augsburg Confession and Luther's — the Reformation's — understanding of the Church and her unity diametrically opposed to the other chief contender, which is the ecumenical theory of external unity without unity in truth. The difference is very simple once you point it out. That is, you can start in one of two places. You can solve the ecumenical equation either by starting with the Church or by starting with the Gospel. If you start with the Church, if you regard all the established churchdoms and hierarchies as constituting the Church, then the Gospel deduced from that formula will mean some very thin gruel in which all these bureaucracies can agree. Or you can start with Luther at the other end. You begin with the Gospel. The Gospel is the known because for that we have God's revelation in our Holy Scriptures. Then, wherever that is publicly taught, there I know the Church to be present. In other words, I walk by faith rather than by sight.

Technically my time is up; therefore, I shall summarize what I was going to say next and hope that someone will bring out in the question-and-

---

12. Michael Dummet, "A Remarkable Consensus," *New Blackfriars* 809 (October 1987):424–431.

answer period the points that I have in mind. I'd like to say two things. One is this. Sometimes also in our circles one hears careless, unguarded talk about "Gospel reductionism." I suggest there is a good way of talking about it and a bad way.[13]

First, the good way. We certainly must warn against reducing the Gospel of God to something smaller than what He says it is. Those people, for example, who chop out the Sacraments and then call themselves evangelical, are committing theological and logical hara-kari. How is it possible to chop off half the Gospel and call oneself evangelical? "Evangelical" means according to the *evangel*, the Gospel. Baptism and the Lord's Supper are integral parts of the Gospel. When you cut that out you are losing important components of the Gospel itself. So, we are against those who seek to reduce the Gospel to something less than it is and to sacrifice any of the articles of faith.

On the other hand, there is some talk of "Gospel reductionism" that suggests that here is a little Gospel and there is a big Bible. We're told that people are reducing the big Bible to just the little Gospel. That's impossible. There is nothing bigger, there is nothing greater in the holy Scriptures, than the Gospel of the Son of God. Luther says, "In the entire Scripture whether it appears at the face of it or not, Christ is really the point of the whole thing everywhere."[14] Of course, that presupposes the Law. You cannot teach the Gospel correctly if you do not teach the Law correctly first of all. Nevertheless the Law is not the Gospel, and it is not the Law but it is the Gospel that creates the unity of the Church. Pieper said that in a beautiful essay in 1888.[15]

And the last point is this. The major threat to us in the matter of church fellowship is not this, that somebody might manage to snatch the Body of Christ from one of our altars when he is not entitled to it. That is not the ultimate tragedy. The ultimate tragedy is when we ourselves in principle give away the Body of Christ and pretend that this altar is no different from an altar at which there is no Body of Christ, where this is in

---

13. It becomes clear below that by "good" Marquart meant *accurate* and by "bad" he meant *misleading*.

14. Marquart appears to have been paraphrasing statements of Luther like this one from AE 32, 132: "For this much is beyond question, that all the Scriptures point to Christ alone."

15. Francis Pieper, "On Unity in the Faith," in *At Home in the House of My Fathers: Presidential Sermons, Essays, Letters, and Addresses from The Missouri Synod's Greatest Era of Unity and Growth*, ed. Matthew C. Harrison (N.p.: Lutheran Legacy, 2009), 572–599.

fact denied, where even the Trinity is denied or questioned, or, where the Trinity is reinterpreted as some sort of feminist Ashtoreth, some heavenly goddess, but not the Father, Son and Spirit.

Historically, our church has faced the doctrine of fellowship above all, in the matter of union with the Reformed since 1817. To make a long story short, let me simply give you a modern comparison, that of a black hole. A black hole is fundamentally a place where gravity has become well-nigh irresistible and pulls in everything in its vicinity, and nothing, not even light, can escape from there anymore. But it probably doesn't start with much. First there is one atom and then a few more get together and finally we end up with a black hole.

I would like to suggest that our present black hole began with the forced union of Lutheran and Reformed churches in Prussia in the last century. At first it caused quite a disturbance, and led many faithful Lutherans to emigrate to America and to Australia, planting confessional churches there. It was a terrible thing, this forcible surrender of the Lutheran confession and of the Sacrament of the Altar. But gradually church-diplomacy got used to it. The Prussian Union gobbled up more and more churches in Germany, so that shortly after World War II, all the territorial Churches (not the Free Churches) there — Lutheran, Reformed, and Union — merged into one unionistic "EKD," Evangelical Church in Germany. In 1973 the Leuenberg Concord expanded this Lutheran-Reformed Union throughout Europe. In 1977 the Lutheran World Federation adopted "Reconciled Diversity" as its ecumenical plan. The idea was exactly that of the Prussian Union: pulpit and altar fellowship, while each side retains its confession.

Today most of world-Lutheranism has been swallowed up into this anti-confessional "black hole," which mandates pulpit and altar fellowship with Reformed and Union churches. This has not been fully appreciated in our Synod yet. We think of the ELCA as a slightly different Lutheran church, with which we have "not yet" come to an agreement in all points. The fact is that the ELCA, through "interim Eucharistic sharing" with the Episcopal Church, and through altar and pulpit fellowship with Presbyterian and other Reformed churches, agreed to by predecessor bodies of the ELCA (*Invitation to Action*[16]), is not a Lutheran but a Union

---

16. *An Invitation to Action: A Study of Ministry, Sacraments, and Recognition,* The Lutheran-Reformed Dialogue Series III, 1981–1983, James E. Andrews and Joseph A. Burgess, eds. (Philadelphia: Fortress Press, 1984). This volume contained a "common statement and urgent invitation for action" which

Church. There are, of course, Lutheran pastors and people there, but the church as such no longer stands, in its practice of altar fellowship, for the Sacrament of the Altar as confessed in the Book of Concord.

---

urged Lutheran and Reformed churches in the U.S. to "Recognize one another as churches in which the gospel is proclaimed and the sacraments administered according to the ordinance of Christ" and therefore to take steps such as "joint celebrations of the Lord's Supper among congregations, presbyteries, classes, conferences, districts, and synods" and "invitations to the ordained pastors of each tradition to preach in the congregations of the other tradition, and, where local conditions make it necessary or possible, to preside at the Holy Communion of the other tradition" (pp. 1, 4, and 5). It should be noted that the ELCA declared itself to be in full communion with the Presbyterian Church USA, United Church of Christ, and the Reformed Church in America in 1997; the Episcopal Church and the Moravian Church in America in 1999; and the United Methodist Church in 2009.

Chapter Seven

THANKS, LUTHERAN
WITNESS AND LLL!

Editor's note: You might think of this short piece as providing background for the previous essay. It had been published as one of Marquart's regular "Noted in Brief" columns in Affirm (March 1989, 3) about a year before that free conference speech on church fellowship. Cast as a thank-you note, it exemplifies Marquart's practices of giving credit where it was due and of calling attention to faithful Lutheran resources as they became available.

༄

With funds provided by the Lutheran Laymen's League, the *Lutheran Witness* has issued a valuable and attractive booklet consisting of reprints of the C. F. W. Walther anniversary "From the First President" column. . . .[1]

We wish to draw special attention here to the last item (p. 12 of the booklet), which is not strictly speaking a "reprint," since it was not part of the original *Witness* series. Entitled "Altar Fellowship," it consists of Walther's thirteen theses on this subject, which were presented originally before the Western District Convention of our Synod in 1870. The topic is extremely timely, and Walther's crisp formulations provide a welcome antidote to the sentimental confusions now beclouding the issue. Consider his tenth thesis:

> Since the Holy Supper is also a mark of the confession of the faith and doctrine of those with whom one celebrates it, the admission of members of erring communions to the celebration of the Supper within the Lutheran Church militates (a) against Christ's institution, (b) against the mandated unity of the church in the faith and the corresponding confession, (c) against love towards those to whom it is being given, (d) against love towards one's own fellow-believers, especially the weak among them, who are thereby given grave offense, (e) against the prohibition not to become partakers of other people's sins and errors.

---

1. *Lutheran Witness: A Lutheran Witness Reprint* [sic], ed. David L. Mahsman (St. Louis: The Lutheran Church — Missouri Synod), n.d.

Walther was not innovating here, but was expressing what had been self-evident among Christians from the beginning (Acts 2:42; Rom. 16:17; 1 Cor. 10:17; 11:26):

> By his partaking of the Sacrament in a church a Christian declares that the confession of that church is his confession. Since a man cannot at the same time hold two differing confessions, he cannot communicate in two churches of differing confessions. If anyone does this nevertheless, he denies his own confession or has none at all.

So wrote Werner Elert in his classic *Eucharist and Church Fellowship in the First Four Centuries.*[2] Incidentally, [in his seventh chapter] Elert also uses the term "closed communion," as does the Faith and Order classification (Lund, 1952). The term "close communion" means exactly the same thing, because "close" is a synonym of "closed" (see Oxford and Webster dictionaries). The opposite of "close" or "closed" communion is "open" communion — or, in the secular terminology befitting the content, "communion on demand."

Walther's eleventh thesis corrects the fatal misunderstanding that non-admission to the Sacrament amounts to a sentence of excommunication:

> By their exclusion from the celebration of the Holy Supper in communion with the Lutheran Church, members of erring communions are not being excommunicated, much less declared to be heretics and condemned, but they are merely being suspended until they shall have reconciled themselves with the orthodox church by renouncing the false communion (or fellowship) in which they stand.

Here is the ringing conclusion, doubly relevant for our time, in Thesis 13:

> The more unionism and syncretism are the sin and corruption of our time, the more the faithfulness of the orthodox church now requires that the Holy Supper not be misused as a means to an external union without inner unity of faith.

The *Lutheran Witness* introduction rightly points out that "Walther's position continues to be that of the Missouri Synod today." The single-page *Witness* piece could not, of course, reproduce the entire essay of which the theses are a summary. Much of that essay is also very quotable, but we restrict ourselves to one pointed paragraph:

---

2.   Trans. N. E. Nagel (St. Louis: Concordia Publishing House, 1966), 182.

Our tenth thesis is thus aimed squarely against the Union, that grave of the Lutheran Church, and especially also against its devotees and admirers in our church, against the unionistic, syncretistic preachers. We call them all shameful belly-servers, bereft of conscience, who leave it to the conscience of their individual guests at the Lord's Supper, whether and what they believe and confess of this sacrament, and who falsely appeal to the word: "Let a man examine himself," etc. As though this did not apply only to the laity—whereas to the preachers applies the word: "Let everyone consider us . . . as householders over God's mysteries. Now one does not seek more in householders than that they should be found faithful."[3]

By the "Union" Walther meant, of course, the nineteenth century Lutheran-Reformed conglomerates, of which the Prussian Union was the most famous. Meanwhile that Union theology has engulfed nominal world Lutheranism. H. Sasse has written:

> What we cannot do is acknowledge the Church of Sweden as a church of the Unaltered Augsburg Confession when it has altar fellowship with Anglicans and has Anglican bishops, who reject "by faith alone," participate in the consecration of Swedish bishops. The same must be said of other Lutheran churches when they put themselves into a similar situation.[4]

That is now precisely the situation of the "ELCA," which has "interim Eucharistic sharing" with the Episcopal Church, and whose constituent bodies (ALC, LCA, AELC) had, with varying degrees of enthusiasm, accepted pulpit and altar fellowship with Zwingli-Calvinist churches.[5] Altars and pulpits which are in fellowship with non-Lutheran altars and pulpits are no longer Lutheran but are Union altars and Union pulpits.

All in all, the theses on "Altar Fellowship with the Heterodox" are a model of evangelical, confessional integrity in practical theology, and leave us in no doubt about the rather vital difference between "pastoral heart" and pastoral headlessness. The *Witness* and the LLL deserve our Synod's gratitude for this timely publication.

---

3. *Editor's note:* This seems to be Marquart's own translation. For the full essay in translation, see C. F. W. Walther, *Essays for the Church*, vol. 1, *1857–1879* (St. Louis: Concordia Publishing House, 1992), 202–228. The quote cited by Marquart is on page 225. The Bible passages cited within this quote are, respectively, 1 Cor. 11:28 and 1 Cor. 4:1–2.
4. Hermann Sasse, We Confess series, vol. 3, *We Confess the Church* (St. Louis: Concordia Publishing House, 1986), 106.
5. See the last note in the previous essay on "Church Fellowship."

Chapter Eight

FELLOWSHIP OR COMMUNION VS. UNIONISM OR SYNCRETISM

Editor's note: We have included this short essay from early 2003 for the sake of completeness. In it Marquart took note of two then-recent developments. First, the President of the Synod and the CTCR had released the study The Lutheran Understanding of Church Fellowship *in the year 2000. Marquart, then a CTCR member, had been a major proponent of this document. He referred to it in the present paper. Second, near the end, Marquart weighed in briefly on a controversy that arose in the Missouri Synod following the "Prayer for America" service at Yankee Stadium in September of 2001. Here he was going beyond the more standard discussion of church fellowship to take up joint worship services involving officials of different religions.*

෨෯

Churchly fellowship, or ecclesial communion, is a very special association or relationship. Since the church is "not only an association of outward things and rites, like other polities, but is mainly an association of faith and of the Holy Spirit in [people's] hearts" (Apology VII/VIII, 5, my translation), churchly fellowship or communion rests on both *internal* and *external* ties or bonds. The internal bond is faith itself, for it is by grace through faith alone (*sola fide*) that anyone is a member of Christ and therefore of His Body, the Church (John 6:29–50; Eph. 2:8, 19–22; 3:17–19; 4:4–6, 11–16; 5:25–32). Only God can see this internal bond of faith, which binds us securely to Christ and to His Church. We humans can go only by those *external* means (the Gospel in Word and Sacrament) through which alone God Himself works the internal mysteries that, as such, are invisible to us. Therefore churchly fellowship in the outward sense is essentially the mutual acknowledgment of joint participation in the "one Lord, one faith, one baptism" (Eph. 4:5). This means joint confession of "the faith that God has once for all entrusted to the saints" (Jude 3), that is, the apostles' doctrine (Acts 2:42) on which the church is built (Matt. 16:18) and on which her whole life rests (Eph. 2:20).

This life-giving, church-creating divine truth (John 8:31–32) unites and divides. It unites those who confess it rightly, and divides them from those who persistently contradict and oppose it at any point by word or deed. God bids us "beware of false prophets" (Matt. 7:15 KJV), and "avoid [turn away from]" those who cause divisions and offenses "contrary to the doctrine" we have learnt from the apostles (Rom. 16:17 KJV). Particularly severe are St. Paul's warnings against twisted versions of the Gospel in Galatians 1:6–12. False doctrine has no rights in the church.

In 1 Corinthians 5:9–13 St. Paul makes it quite clear what sort of separation is necessary. He does not demand social, commercial, or political separation from all sorts of evil people in this world: "In that case you would have to leave this world" (v. 10 NIV). Rather, it is the evildoer who claims to be a "brother" who must be refused that status, so that he might come to his senses and repent. The church is a spiritual "brotherhood" (1 Pet. 2:17; 5:9, compare Matt. 12:48–50; 23:8). In treating 1 Corinthians 5, Dr. Gregory Lockwood notes that it is here a matter not of all sorts of worldly relationships, but of *"Christian fellowship."* Comments Lockwood: "Paul establishes the Scriptures as the basis for church fellowship. If a person or group refuses to comply with God's Word, fellowship is to be terminated."[1]

That, too, is the meaning of Galatians 2:9, where Sts. James, Peter, and John give to Sts. Paul and Barnabas "the right hand of fellowship." The point was mutual recognition of oneness in faith, doctrine, and confession. Without such agreement, there could be no joint mission work. With it, there is full communion in the church's work and worship — including frank brotherly rebuke of St. Peter's fear-induced lapse into false, hypocritical practice, and this precisely in order that the purity of the Gospel proclamation might be safeguarded. Note, too, that the public offense against the Gospel demanded prompt public correction, not endless secret negotiations.

The best current reference on this topic is *The Lutheran Understanding of Church Fellowship*, commended by our synodical convention in 2001.[2] Far from intending to scuttle or weaken the Missouri Synod's well-known historic position on fellowship and unionism, the *Lutheran Understanding* document actually traced the biblical, confessional, and historical basis for that position. In commending that document, the convention therefore also resolved "That the Synod reaffirm once again its position on joint worship."[3]

---

1. Gregory J. Lockwood, *First Corinthians,* Concordia Commentary (St. Louis: Concordia Publishing House, 2000), 183 (italics original) and 184.
2. *Editor's note:* This document was printed in a booklet, *The Lutheran Understanding of Church Fellowship: Study Materials* (Office of the President and Commission on Theology and Church Relations of The Lutheran Church — Missouri Synod, February, 2000). Hereafter cited in this essay as "CTCR."
3. See Resolution 3-07A, *Convention Proceedings 61st Regular Convention The Lutheran Church — Missouri Synod St. Louis, Mo., July 14–20, 2001* (N.p., n.d.), 137–138.

The great strength of *The Lutheran Understanding of Church Fellowship* is that it anchors everything in the "Marks of the Church," the purely preached Gospel and the rightly administered sacraments (AC VII). Much of the confusion on this issue has been due to a loss of the clear categories "true or orthodox church" and "false or heterodox church." Instead, people were thinking and talking simply about individuals, so-called "other Christians." This led to loose, subjective, sentimental approaches. *Lutheran Understanding* reminds us that fellowship is first of all an aspect of the church. Christians are united with each other not directly, but by way of Christ, the Head (Col. 2:19). When the focus shifts from the church and her Gospel treasures to the individual and his or her personal qualities, the result is either total unionism and permissiveness, or else the exclusive narrowness of certain would-be conservative Lutherans who would forbid even joint table-prayers with family or friends of other synods or other churches!

Since the church is created, fed, united, and preserved only by God through His Gospel (Word and Sacrament), *church fellowship is essentially pulpit and altar fellowship*. Joint proclamation and joint celebration of the sacraments — that is the essence and core of it. Except in emergencies (i.e., danger of death), private, individual Christians do not absolve, baptise, etc. Preaching and administering the sacraments are public, official acts of the church, ordinarily performed through the church's public ministry. But Christians can and do pray in their private lives.

Prayer, though a great gift of God, is not a means of grace. However, from this truth some people appear to draw the conclusion that prayer is not a part of church fellowship and that it is therefore up to everyone's own discretion and whim when, where, and with whom to join in prayer. That is a dangerous illusion. The 1961 theses on "Fellowship in Its Necessary Context of the Doctrine of the Church," favourably cited in *Lutheran Understanding*, conclude with a thesis on prayer:

> 13. Prayer is not one of the marks of the church and should not be co-ordinated with Word and sacraments, as though it were essentially of the same nature as they. As a response to the divine Word, it is an expression of faith and a fruit of faith, and when spoken before others, a profession of faith. As a profession of faith it must be in harmony with and under the control of the marks of the church.

The formulators of the Theses conclude with some statements specifically on joint prayer, citing the following from the Australian Lutheran *Theses of Agreement:*

When joint prayer shows the marks or characteristics of unionism, it must be condemned and avoided. Such marks and characteristics of unionism are

a. failure to confess the whole truth of the divine Word (*in statu confessionis*);

b. failure to reject and denounce every opposing error;

c. assigning to error equal right with truth;

d. creating the impression of unity in faith or of church fellowship where it does not exist.[4]

Clearly, joining with official representatives of heterodox churches (ministers, bishops, etc.) in offering public prayers by turns, and on equal terms, is flagrant unionism. It fails to distinguish between true and false teachings and teachers and is therefore irresponsible. The 1927 *Concordia Cyclopedia* stated that "Religious unionism consists in joint worship and work of those not united in doctrine."[5] Missouri's greatest dogmatician, Francis Pieper, put it like this: "The disobedience against the divine command which forbids Christians [to have] fellowship with false teachers and false doctrine, is called in churchly usage 'unionism,' 'mixing religions,' 'syncretism,' etc."[6] Similarly, the Missouri Synod constitution requires as a condition of membership "Renunciation of unionism and syncretism of every description," such as "b. Taking part in the services and sacramental rites of heterodox congregations or of congregations of mixed confession."[7]

Lutheran Understanding adds two details that may be of interest: (1) It cites Synod's 1977 resolution "[t]hat we expect our pastors and congregations to follow this article with respect to mixed wedding ceremonies."[8] (2) Footnote 64: "'Syncretism' is the older word for mingling confessions, but now usually means joining with non-Christian religions."[9]

---

4. "Fellowship in Its Necessary Context of the Doctrine of the Church," appendix in Kurt E. Marquart, *Anatomy of an Explosion: Missouri in Lutheran Perspective*, Concordia Seminary Monograph Series Number 3 (Fort Wayne: Concordia Theological Seminary Press, 1977), 149, 150.

5. Ludwig Fuerbringer, Theodore Engelder, P. E. Kretzmann, eds.-in-chief, *The Concordia Cyclopedia: A Handbook of Religious Information, with Special Reference to the History, Doctrine, Work, and Usages of the Lutheran Church* (St. Louis: Concordia Publishing House, 1927), s.v. "Unionism."

6. Franz Pieper, *Christliche Dogmatik* (St. Louis: Concordia Publishing House, 1920), 3:490 (author's translation).

7. Quoted in CTCR, 15–16.

8. CTCR, 16.

9. CTCR, 28.

The Lutheran Confessions do not hesitate repeatedly (Tr 41 and FC SD X 22; FC SD X 6) to cite against ecclesial fellowship with the papacy, or even the appearance of it, 2 Corinthians 6:14 NKJV: "Do not be unequally yoked together with unbelievers. For what fellowship has righteousness with lawlessness? And what communion has light with darkness?" Of course our Lutheran fathers were far from denying that there are true children of God in heterodox churches. The point is that misbelief is, to that extent, unbelief. If people who are personally Christians also maintain errors contrary to the revealed truth, these errors are not "Christian" but rather anti-Christian. C. F. W. Walther was right, therefore, to cite also that text under his Thesis XXI C of *The Evangelical Lutheran Church, the True Visible Church of God on Earth*: "The Ev. Lutheran Church rejects all fraternal and churchly fellowship with those who reject its Confession in whole or in part."[10]

But what of "civic events"? Yes, it is quite possible for a faithful Lutheran pastor to offer a prayer at a Right-to-Life dinner, or at the opening of a legislature, at a graduation, etc. Even there, however, he must not allow himself to be drawn into a joint "prayer-service" with official representatives of heterodox churches. It is one thing to offer a prayer, but quite another to make it a part of a "mini-service" on equal terms with official representatives of false doctrine.

Prof. David Adams has written a valuable paper "The Church in the Public Square in a Pluralistic Society." The author shows that "civil" and "religious" are not airtight categories. There are also "civil religious events," governed by the "civil religion" of our pluralistic society, a religion that is inherently "polydox," i.e., idolatrous, syncretistic.[11]

Actually there is nothing really new here. Our Synod has always confronted that issue in the form of Freemasonry. A Masonic Bible states in an introductory essay by H. L. Haywood:

it is the Book of the Old and New Testaments and at the same time represents each of the world's Bibles, and may be replaced by the Koran, the Zend Avesta, the Vedas, etc.; it lies on the Altar and yet does not have possession of it because the Square and Compasses lie on the Altar with it. . . .

---

10. Quoted in CTCR, 14.

11. *Editor's note:* An edited version of this Adams essay was included in David L. Adams and Ken Schurb, eds., *The Anonymous God: The Church Confronts Civil Religion and American Society* (St. Louis: Concordia Publishing House, 2004), 219–249.

There are in the membership of the Fraternity throughout the world Christians, Jews, Theists, Mohammedans, Parsees, Hindus, Confucianists, and many men who believe in God but are not identified with any one religion or Church.[12]

Joint prayers or services on such a basis are clearly in violation of St. Paul's command to flee idolatry (1 Cor. 10:14). And a joint "interfaith" service, with official representatives of various Christian and non-Christian religions taking turns reading from their holy books, giving addresses, and praying, the whole thing bracketed between Christian and non-Christian "invocations" and "benedictions," does not cease to be a service by the mere presence of civic dignitaries or celebrities! The suggestion that such participation has value as "witness" and paves the way for good relations and future mission work must be resisted as Satan's old temptation to religious pragmatism: "All these things I will give You if You will fall down and worship me" (Matt. 4:9 NKJV).

Let me conclude with some words from Dr. Walther's foreword to *Lehre und Wehre* of 1879:

> After all, it was never the pure doctrine in itself which provoked hostility towards its representatives; least of all is that the case in our indifferentist time. Rather taking it seriously, the exclusive holding on to it, the rejection and condemnation of the opposite doctrine, and above all the practical implementation of this doctrinal position, that was what at all times produced hostility. . . . So it is still today. What doctrine isn't one prepared to tolerate in our days, if only it takes its place peacefully next to the others! And just the would-be orthodox achieve the most incredible [feats] in this tolerance. Only observe the harmonious relationship which shows itself in the academic colleges, the peaceful sitting together in pastoral conferences, the tone in the reviews![13]

Lord, have mercy upon us!

---

12. Chicago: The Masonic History Company, 1951, 26, 29.
13. Author's translation from [C. F. W] W[alther], "Vorwort," *Lehre und Wehre* 25 (January 1879):1.

Chapter Nine

THE TROUBLE WITH THE TASK FORCE PROPOSALS

Editor's note: At its 1975 convention, The Lutheran Church—Missouri Synod established a Task Force on Constitution, Bylaws, and Structure. This twnety-one-member group released an initial report to synod in 1977. It submitted its final recommendations to the 1979 convention. Shortly before that meeting, the following article appeared in Affirm 8 (May 31—June 18 1979), with an accompanying note that Affirm's Editorial Group had asked Professor Marquart for an evaluation of the Task Force report. Here, as almost always, Marquart refrained from comment on the practicalities of bylaws and administrative mechanisms. Still, he showed himself much more ready than most theologians to publish theological reflections on and critique of polity proposals.

A noteworthy feature of this article is its ample quotation from a variety of nineteenth- and early twentieth-century Missouri Synod sources. Marquart knew his history, and brought it to bear theologically on present prospects. For the sake of clarity, new section headings have been provided below, replacing those in the original publication.

ళ♥

The final report of the Task Force on Constitution, Bylaws, and Structure of the LCMS and its districts is now open to public inspection in the *Convention Workbook* (1979), pp. 55 ff. There is no doubt that the Task Force has expended an enormous amount of energy, diligence, and expertise on its well-nigh overwhelming assignment. For this the Task Force deserves the genuine and unstinting thanks of Synod.

It is not surprising, however, in view of the nature of the task, that the results raise the most fundamental issues and are thoroughly controversial. And the basic problems are not simply questions of practical wisdom and judgment, but are deeply theological, doctrinal. Oddly enough, the very effort of the Task Force conscientiously to avoid theological problems seems to have created them. The doctrinal dimensions of the synodical union have received insufficient attention, and this has led to serious dislocations and misplacements of emphasis.

One is naturally loath to criticize the work of respected leaders and brethren in Synod. Concern for the church's faith and life, however, demands that the Task Force proposals be examined in all critical candor, without prejudice to the Task Force's good faith, which is not of course in question. The problems are best dealt with under the headings General and Particular.

IN GENERAL

In general the problem is that profound and far-reaching structural changes are being offered without sufficient theological clarification. It is no secret that, as for instance the 1978 Formula of Concord conferences have reminded us, "considerable confusion exists within the Synod on the question of fellowship" (*CTCR* Report, 1979 *CW*, p. 73). There is some uncertainty about questions like "is there a sense in which a synod can be called 'the church'? What is the relationship between a congregation and a synod?" (*Ibid.*, p. 72).

If and as long as this is the case, it is clearly premature to make or even consider fundamental, far-reaching, and possibly irreversible changes in the synodical organization. The first priority must be the restoration, by God's grace, of a clear and confident consensus, under Holy Scripture and the Lutheran Confessions, about the nature of the church as it relates to synods and congregations. Until such time as there is good reason to believe that such a consensus exists among us, Synod must firmly and summarily resist any and all basic structural changes.

To plunge directly into radical reorganization without first making very sure of the doctrinal foundations would be to trifle irresponsibly with sacred matters; "for whatsoever is not of faith is sin," Romans 14:23 [KJV].

IN PARTICULAR

In particular, the Task Force proposals not only fail to provide sufficient theological clarification, but actually imply serious theological defects in the understanding of the doctrines of church and ministry. To take the doctrine of the church first, at least three closely-related and far-reaching features of the proposals are apparent.

Doctrine of the Church

In the first place, the basic premise or starting point significantly misdirects the whole effort along externalistic lines. The Task Force clearly believes that it reflects the traditional Missouri Synod position when it defines "a congregation, a community of believers gathered and organized for worship, nurture, witness, and service," as "the primary fellowship to which God grants certain privileges, etc." and "a Synod" as "a voluntary association of congregations covenanting together etc." (*CW*, p. 57). And at first sight it may indeed appear that this scheme of God-made congregations and man-made synods expresses the historic Lutheran stand of the Missouri Synod. Since the Task Force's reliance on this assumption is the very bedrock of its whole work and recommendation, it should be examined with some care.

Careful analysis shows that the synodical position has in fact been over-simplified, foreshortened, and thereby distorted by the formulations cited. Despite the reference to "believers," the definition proceeds too simply and too quickly to the notion of congregations as "organized" entities. Thereafter the stress remains on this organized aspect, and it is under this aspect that congregations are said to be the "primary" units "to which God grants certain privileges etc." Our synodical fathers were well acquainted with the Biblical, Confessional Lutheran doctrine of the church, and therefore they refused to equate the believers with the "organized" entity in any simple and direct way. They insisted that the believers were one thing (the church in the strict or proper sense of the word) and the outward organization another (the church in the wide or improper sense), inasmuch as the latter includes unbelievers and hypocrites as well.

Nor did the synodical fathers maintain an absolute priority for the local congregation (1 Cor 14:36). They stressed rather that all spiritual power and authority was given by Christ first of all to the one, holy, universal church, His Bride and Mystical Body.[1] Local churches have their authority inasmuch as they are the one church in a given place or places, and then only through and on account of the real members of the one universal church among them, i.e. the believers.[2] And how is the real church, the fellowship of believers to be found locally, if it can only be believed and not seen? The answer is that the church can be located or recognized only by means of the pure marks of Christ's one church, namely the purely preached Gospel (pure doctrine!) and the rightly administered Sacraments. This concentration on evangelical substance is again very different from the Task Force's definition: "organized for worship, nurture, witness, and service." All these words express organized functions, activities, but are in and of themselves neutral in respect of doctrinal substance or content.

But now what about synods? It cannot be denied that the Task Force's scheme of divine congregations and human synods represents a major thrust of the historic Missouri Synod position. But it is not the whole truth and

---

1. C. F. W. Walther, *Kirche und Amt* [*The Voice of our Church in the Question of Church and Ministry*] Thesis VII [on the church]; *Rechte Gestalt* [*The Right Form of an Evangelical Lutheran Local Congregation Independent of the State*], chapter 1, sections 4 and 5.
2. Ibid.

requires important qualifications to avoid a disastrous reductionism. For one thing, the parliamentary-organizational aspects of congregations (constitutions, by-laws, officers, etc.) are no more divinely ordained than similar elements of synodical bodies. What is divinely ordained is the regular life in the pure Gospel and Sacraments administered by the public ministry established and filled by God through His church in each and every place. This means of course that church life is in the very nature of the case local, for this sort of thing cannot be done regionally or nationally. But all the (necessary!) external, organizational and ceremonial "scaffolding" or "infrastructure" which subserves the actual life in the Means of Grace exists by human right alone. Synods, on the other hand, while not divinely commanded as outward organizations with parliamentary structures, officials, etc., do nevertheless express one divinely ordained and commanded element: orthodox church fellowship, in the sense of mutual acknowledgement of confessional (doctrinal) and sacramental unity. Thus Francis Pieper wrote, in his 1916 commentary on Walther's theses on the True Visible Church:

> If there is a church in Australia — and thank God there is a church which agrees with us in the true faith — then we must maintain fellowship of confession and of love also with that church. If we were to deny a body which agrees with us in the faith, that is, which confesses Christ's Name in all points, then we would be denying Christ Himself in such a body. Further: If we would not acknowledge (*nicht bekennen zu*) the Synods of Wisconsin and Minnesota and the Norwegian Lutheran Church, when these are attacked because of their true doctrine, then we would be denying Christ Himself in these synods. And they would be doing the same if they were ashamed of "the Missourians." (*Vortraege*, p. 191)[3]

In this sense the founders of the Missouri Synod did not hesitate to think and speak of Synod as church. To be sure they emphasized, rightly, that the organizational aspect existed by human right alone; yet their major stress was not on Synod as an organization, but on the spiritual, doctrinal, confessional, and thus genuinely churchly fellowship which it represented. This is very clear in the early forms of Synod's constitution. Both the original constitution and the "new" constitutions of 1855 and 1867 begin

---

3. *Editor's note:* The translation above is Marquart's. For the English of the entire work he was citing, see Francis Pieper, *The Church and Her Treasure: Lectures on Justification and the True Visible Church*, trans. O. Marc Tangner (St. Louis: The Luther Academy, 2007). The words quoted by Marquart appear on page 278 of this volume.

with two chapters which contain, except for a rule regarding the use of German, nothing but solidly theological provisions. Then follows a third chapter entitled "external arrangement of the Synod." Clearly the founders thought of Synod as a theological, churchly reality first of all, and as an external organization only secondarily. Walther's first presidential address (1848) was full of references to the church, the servants of the church, and the work of the church, and called the new body a "churchly synod" (*kirchlicher Synodus*). The official "clarifications" attached to the original constitution referred, in connection with the disciplining of pastors, to "the steps of admonition according to Matthew 18:15–17, as well first of all within the congregation, as then also on behalf of the Synod."[4]

Walther himself of course rightly stressed the glory of the local church or congregation, which, as the Bride of Christ in that place, had full spiritual authority independently of any external ecclesiastical bodies elsewhere. Yet Walther was too deeply steeped in the spiritual, objective, Gospel-oriented ecclesiology of Article VII of the Augsburg Confession, to become exclusive or doctrinaire about local congregations. At least once in his major writings Walther cited with approval this definition of universal and particular churches: "The visible church is divided into the *particular*, as that of each house, village, city, diocese, province, nation, realm, empire; and the *universal*, which embraces all the particular [churches] together."[5] Of Synod Walther could unabashedly rhapsodise as follows: "the entire Synod as a true daughter of her mother, namely the Lutheran Church of the Unaltered Augsburg Confession."[6] And the constitution of the Synodical Conference (1872) stated as its "purpose and goal": "Uniting of all Lutheran synods of America into one orthodox American Lutheran Church."

All this seems a far cry from the organizationally oriented "servant structure" which despite gropings for "something more" (*CW*, 267) is the Task Force's controlling conception of Synod (*CW*, 58). The notion of "servant structure" cannot begin to register or to cope with the basic

---

4. *Die Verfassung der deutschen ev.-luth. Synode von Missouri, Ohio und anderen Staaten* (St. Louis: Weber and Olshausen, 1846), 11–12.

5. C. F. W. Walther, *Die Rechte Gestalt ... Evangelisch-Lutherischen Ortsgemeinde* (St. Louis: Concordia, 1890), 4.

6. C. F. W. Walther, "Ueber einige Hauptpflichten welche eine Synode hat wenn sie den Namen einer ev.-lutherischen Synode mit Recht tragen will," *Iowa District Convention Essay*, 1879, 118. *Editor's note:* The translation above is Marquart's. For the English of the entire essay he was citing, see C. F. W. Walther, "Duties of an Evangelical Lutheran Synod," *Walther's Works: Church Fellowship* (St. Louis: Concordia Publishing House, 2015). The words quoted by Marquart appear on page 336.

difference between, say, the Missouri Synod as a confessional *church*, and a discussion-forum like LCUSA, which dare not be *church*, although one suspects that churchly functions are hidden in the phrase "upon a purchase of service basis" (LCUSA Constitution, V g).

So much then for the inadequate anchoring of the Task Force's basic definitions of congregations and synods in the doctrine of the church. This leads, in the second place, to a fateful shift of emphasis from doctrinal, confessional unity to efficiency and effectiveness of operation (see *CW*, 267).

There can be no doubt that for the original Missouri Synod unity and purity of doctrine were absolutely the first priority to which everything else had to be subordinated and if necessary sacrificed. Here are some random samples from presidential addresses or theses of district or synodical essays:

> True church-fellowship, as it finds its most natural expression in the uniting of confessionally faithful congregations into a synod, is a source of rich blessing internally and externally. (California-Oregon District, 1887, p. 7)

> That we preserve the Word and the pure doctrine as our highest good. . . . We have in view here not so much the advantages which the external Synodical connection provides, but much rather the ground on which our Synod is built, the pure doctrine. (Central District, 1891, p. 13)

> Of the blessing of orthodox Synodical fellowship. (Kansas District, 1888, pp. 5 ff.)

> As at that apostolic convention [Acts 15] doctrine was dealt with first of all, so also at our synodical assemblies the main thing have [sic] at all times been doctrinal deliberations. (*Ibid.*, p. 11)

> . . . our Synod was founded mainly for the purpose of taking seriously the pure doctrine of the church and the corresponding practice. (Eastern District, 1888, p. 7)

> True God-pleasing unity is present only where people are one in the faith, i.e. in all the articles of faith. . . . For true church unity is *not* (a) a unionistic, or syncretistic union. . . (b) a hierarchical one or one founded on human laws. . . (c) a constitutionistic one. . . (d) a facultative one. . . (e) a church-political one. (*Ibid.*, pp. 18, 21)

> We do not allow anyone publicly to present a doctrine which is contrary to the confession of our church. Better to die, better to let the Synod be smashed into a million fragments, than to lose the unity of the pure doctrine. If we no longer have that, we have no further right to exist, we are nothing. (Missouri Synod, 1872, p. 56)

Admittedly Synod is much bigger and more complex than it was a hundred years ago. It goes without saying that this requires more detailed rules and regulations than before. But all of these must remain strictly subordinate to the primacy of doctrinal unity and purity. The Task Force proposals, however, while repeatedly referring to confessional unity to be sure, no longer give to this unity the crucial, all-decisive importance it has had and must have. The language surrounding the expression "fellowship of a synodical bond" (*CW*, 58) for example gives no indication that orthodoxy is in any way decisive. The stress is on practical work within the "servant structure," embellished with pious generalities that could be taken this way or that. Certainly "speaking and hearing responsibly to achieve agreement" is a terribly weak and watered-down application of the apostolic example of Acts 15, which the Missouri Synod has always understood as a robust demand for uncompromising, orthodox confession in doctrine and practice.

The very thing of which the historic Missouri Synod "wished to know nothing" (1872 Convention, p. 41), *viz.*, doctrinal decisions by majority vote, is now enshrined as a constitutional principle (*CW*, 59). Worse, the synodical convention cannot make any confession at all, for its doctrinal decisions are without effect unless approved by a referendum among member congregations, with at least half the member congregations voting, and two thirds of them approving (*CW*, 16)! Here Synod has been robbed of its main reason for being, according to the apostolic example of Acts 15 cited in the constitution! Congregations are rightly said to "have the right and duty to test every synodically adopted resolution against the testimony of the Holy Scriptures and the Lutheran Confessions" (*CW*, 58). But nowhere is it suggested that if such congregations or their pastors find themselves in disagreement with Synod's doctrinal position, they must finally go their separate ways. That of course was taken for granted in "old Missouri." ("This doctrinal discipline, sometimes also called Synodical discipline, is not a sort of medieval inquisition, but a procedure required in God's Word in order to guard and preserve the unity in the pure doctrine and to cleanse and rid the church of what is harmful and destructive for her" — Pastor R. Koehler in an essay about the "first six paragraphs of the second chapter of our Synodical constitution," *Minnesota and Dakota District Convention*, 1906, 26.)

The new model of the Task Force seems to envision independentistic churches differing about doctrine and fellowship but held together by the organizational glue of the "servant structure" and of a voluntaristic "covenanting."

In the third place, the misplaced stress on the organizational function-ing of the "servant structure" at the expense of unity and purity of doc-trine, culminates quite logically and with a vengeance as it were in the concept of a "Synodical Assembly." The trouble with this Assembly is not that it is an executive power between conventions, but that it is a second legislature! The resultant mischief and disaster are easy to foresee. The only real power would be held by an entrenched bureaucracy upon which the Assembly would depend well-nigh absolutely.

It is all very well to reserve "doctrine and fellowship matters" to the relatively infrequent conventions — and then only subject to approval by referendum, and with the communications media not under convention control. If, however, another body, *viz.*, the Assembly, has the enormous power not only to "determine programs, . . . allocate resources," but also to appoint and control practically the entire personnel responsible for the implementation of synodical policies, the convention is in practice reduced to the status of an impotent figure-head. What is to prevent the conven-tion's doctrine and confession from merely "reigning" — as a dead letter on patient paper—while the pragmatically-oriented Assembly actually rules? This deliberate hiatus between doctrine and implementation, principle and practice, constitutes an invitation to theological shipwreck. It is the same trend which has destroyed other American churches:

> the Church was becoming increasingly responsive to everything that made for effectiveness of action, and correspondingly allergic to any theoretical considerations that might hamper its vigorous activism. . . . Following the dominant patterns of American life, there was an increasing tendency to think of the Church as a kind of business corporation chartered to do the Lord's work. The subordination of questions of truth — though only of those regarded as "unessential" — to efficiency of operation carries a recognizable suggestion of pragmatism. . . . the Church was moving simultaneously to-ward administrative centralization and theological decentralization.[7]

This is a formula not for a "synodical bond" but for synodical bondage.

Doctrine of the Ministry

Closely bound up with the doctrine of the church is that of the ministerial office. The difference between Synod's historic understanding of the ministerial office and that of the Task Force becomes dramatically evident

---

7. Lefferts A. Loetscher, *The Broadening Church* (Philadelphia: University of Pennsylvania Press, 1954), 8, 59, 151.

in the latter's proposals regarding the franchise. Historically member congregations had two votes at Synods and district conventions, one pastoral and one lay—with other pastors, professors, and called (male) parish school teachers as non-voting advisory delegates. The Task Force proposes that congregations be given the right to choose as their non-lay representative either a pastor or a "certified teacher in the full-time service of a congregation" (CW, 59), possibly a woman. This equation of the ministerial office with other offices in church or school, as if they were all interchangeable, was totally foreign to the synodical founders. Nor is the Task Force correct in suggesting that the whole question of franchise is purely an external, organizational one, without theological implications (CW, p. 266).

In point of fact, the Missouri Synod in the past based its practice in this regard at least in part on theological considerations. A few quotations from past official reports will illustrate the traditional approach. The 1874 Convention of Synod decided:

> Whereas teachers must appear at the Synodical sessions for their own persons as representatives of the school-office (*Schulamt*), and the pastors as representatives of the ministry (*Predigtamt*) of the congregations; whereas furthermore, every congregation is obligated to be represented by a delegate from its midst who is neither a pastor nor a teacher;
>
> Resolved, that in future no District Synod is to be allowed to recognize at any of its synodical meetings a teacher of a parish school or an educational institution of our Synod as a delegate of a congregation. (1874, p. 79)

The matter arose again, and was settled with a deliberate refusal to initiate constitutional changes in this regard (1887 Convention, p. 85).

In 1893 Synod again resolved that teachers could be recognized as congregational representatives neither at district nor at synodical conventions. The reasoning was: "Since the teachers, like the advisory pastors, are already represented elsewhere at the Synod, they cannot appear again as representatives from among the hearers (*Hoererschaft*)" (1893, p. 126). Most instructive is the reasoning of the 1907 synodical convention:

> The question whether in the absence of the pastor the teacher of the congregation might not be able to exercise the former's franchise in Synodical assemblies, was answered: The official actions of the pastor, preaching, baptising, giving the sacrament, are done by authority (*im Auftrag*) of the congregation. He holds his office as representative (*Vertreter*) of the congregation, and so also he appears at Synodical assemblies not as represen-

tative of the teaching order (*Lehrstand*) but of the congregation ex officio. The teacher, however, has been given (*uebertragen*) only a certain branch of the office, the instruction in the divine Word in the school, and therefore he cannot represent the pastor *ex officio*; but should this custom be introduced, that he exercise the franchise in place of the pastor, then such a decision belongs solely to the General Synod. (1907, pp. 14–15)

In his presentation to the 1863 synodical convention, incidentally, C. F. W. Walther made the point that a congregation which already had a pastor had no right unilaterally to call an additional pastor. And: "If a congregation elects an auxiliary preacher without its pastor, the election is likewise null and void" (1863, p. 37). In other words, congregations do not have boundless freedom to do what they like as regards offices, but are bound by the divinely established office of the public ministry.

It may be of interest, in conclusion, to note that at least the synodical constitutions of 1855 and 1867 provided under "rights and duties of the General President":

> The general President shall take over a pastorate (*Pfarramt*), in order that he might more easily be preserved from a one-sided mentality (*Geistesrichtung*). But he shall have an assistant (*Adjunct*) in office. Assistants shall, where necessary, also be given the District presidents, so that they might regularly undertake the visitations which are so important.

And the 1874 Synod held:

> The professors at the practical seminary should also simultaneously have the ministry (*Predigtamt*) in a congregation. Only when that is the case will they be preserved in the right competence to educate future servants of the Word. (p. 21)

Let our dear Synod occupy itself deeply and thoroughly with the glorious evangelical realities of church and ministry, according to God's Word and the Lutheran Confession, before entertaining any questions of basic reorganization.

Chapter Ten

ELCA ECUMENICAL DECISIONS

Editor's note: In 1998 The Lutheran Church—Missouri Synod encouraged continuing discussions with the Evangelical Lutheran Church in America. It desired that "these discussions address such theological issues as the doctrine of justification, the Lord's Supper, the nature of Lutheran identity, and the appropriate relationships with churches of other theological traditions . . ." (Resolution 3-08A, 1998 Convention Proceedings, 117). One of the representatives appointed by President A. L. Barry for discussion with the ELCA at the church body level was Professor Kurt Marquart.

The paper below was delivered to a discussion session involving Missouri Synod and ELCA representatives in Chicago on June 14, 1999. In view of then-recent ELCA ecumenical decisions, the very points raised by the Synod bulked large in Marquart's presentation.

❧

It is not to be expected that my modest efforts today can do more than set out some key features of the decisions in question, as they would typically appear to churches like the Missouri Synod, which, for all their faults, seek intentionally and conscientiously to maintain the doctrine solemnly confessed in the Book of Concord. To this end I propose to divide the assigned topic as follows: (1) The ELCA-Roman Catholic *Joint Declaration on the Doctrine of Justification*; (2) ELCA-Reformed altar and pulpit fellowship; (3) ELCA-Episcopal relations; (4) The *"Zen effect"* in ecumenical dialogues: loss of core Christian contents to historical relativism; (5) What does this mean? Deploying the *ecclesial criteria* of the Evangelical Lutheran Church.

Since my colleagues in both St. Louis and Fort Wayne have recently gone over much of this ground, I shall rely shamelessly on their work.[1]

---

1. Department of Systematic Theology, Concordia Theological Seminary, Fort Wayne, "Joint Lutheran/Roman Catholic Declaration on Justification: A Response," and "A Formula of Agreement: A Theological Assessment," *Concordia Theological Quarterly* 62 (April 1998), 83–124. *The Porvoo Declaration in Confessional Perspective.* A Joint Report by the Departments of Systematic Theology of Concordia Theological Seminary, Fort Wayne, Indiana, and Concordia Seminary, St. Louis, Missouri (St. Louis: Office of the President, The Lutheran Church — Missouri Synod, 1997).

THE ELCA-ROMAN CATHOLIC JOINT
DECLARATION ON THE
DOCTRINE OF JUSTIFICATION

Although the overall thrust of the language is decidedly more evangelical than that of the Council of Trent, careful formulation ensures that no substantive provision of Trent is actually given up. From the Lutheran point of view, however, four main areas of concern emerge.

In the first place, there is the matter of sin remaining after Baptism. The crucial nature of this issue is explained by Hubert Jedin, the great Roman Catholic historian of the Council of Trent:

> The Council was now brought up against the very basis of the Lutheran teaching on justification, and one of the most difficult points of controversy, because Luther's view seemingly found support in St. Paul and St. Augustine. . . . The teaching of canon 5 on concupiscence laid the foundation of the subsequent decree on justification.[2]

Contrary to both St. Paul and St. Augustine, who regarded the inborn concupiscence or inclination to sin, which remains after Baptism, as really and truly sin, Trent decreed:

> This concupiscence, which at times the Apostle calls sin [Rom. 6:12 ff.] the holy Synod declares that the Catholic Church has never understood to be called sin, as truly and properly sin in those born again, but because it is from sin and inclines to sin. But if anyone is of the contrary opinion, let him be anathema.[3]

Paragraph 30 of the *Joint Declaration* asserts that the Catholic party "do not see this inclination as sin in an authentic sense." It is difficult to see how this inclination could be "in contradiction to God," yet not really be sin. Since sin and justification are correlatives, any agreement on justification is illusory, if it involves such a fundamental disagreement about the nature of sin. Compare what the Evangelical Lutheran Church confesses in AC and Ap II and FC I.

Second, although the term "grace" is used throughout, no definition of it is given. This makes for some considerable equivocation, since in terms

---

2. Hubert Jedin, *A History of the Council of Trent* (London: Thomas Nelson, 1961), 2:145, 162.
3. *Editor's note:* Marquart cited these words from Trent via Denzinger. A slightly different translation is in Martin Chemnitz, *Examination I*, 335.

of the Reformation conflict, everything depends on whether "grace" is understood as the undeserved favour of God (*favor Dei*), or as the works-producing energy in us (*gratia infusa*). If grace is the former, then, as St. Paul argues, grace and works are mutually exclusive in justification (Rom. 4:4; 11:6). If the latter, then the more it is by grace, the more it is by works; "grace" is simply code for "works." Equivocation in the understanding of such a fundamental term should be unthinkable in a joint statement on the subject.

Third, as already in the U.S. dialogue's *Justification by Faith,*[4] so also here the Lutherans simply abandon their confessional claim that justification is forgiveness (Ap IV 76, compare FC III), and not also the internal transformation producing love and good works. *Joint Declaration,* 4.2 "Justification as Forgiveness of Sins and Making Righteous," lumps both of these together in the Tridentine manner. The famous point number 72 of Ap IV, incidentally, does not say what it is often taken to say, i.e., that justification may be taken either as forensic or as transformational. The "being made righteous" here refers not to the new obedience, etc., but to the reality of God's imputation. This is clear both from the context, where the "both faith and works" notion of justification is expressly rejected (71), and from the wording: "faith alone makes a righteous man out of an unrighteous one, *that is, that it receives the forgiveness of sins*" (my emphases). The only "making righteous" in justification happens by the forgiveness of sins.

Perhaps this nonchalance about the non-transformational character of justification is due to the fact that much current Luther-scholarship, including regrettably the invaluable contribution of the Helsinki school regarding Luther and *theosis,* gives the impression that Luther himself was careless about the distinction between what FC III calls "imputed" and "inherent" righteousness. On the contrary, it is precisely in the introduction to his great 1535 Galatians commentary (which contains the "star witness" to Luther's understanding of *theosis* [deification]: *in ipsa fide Christus adest*) that Luther insists without letup on the utter difference between the passive righteousness of faith, by which alone we are justified, and all forms of *active* righteousness, including that which results from the inner renewal, which make no contribution to justification.[5]

---

4. H. George Anderson, T. Austin Murphy, and Joseph A. Burgess, eds., *Justification by Faith: Lutherans and Catholics in Dialogue VII* (Minneapolis: Augsburg Publishing House, 1985).

5. AE 26, 4–12

Fourth, there is the matter of justification as "criterion" in paragraph 18. Originally the German LWF contingent had successfully proposed the insertion of language to the effect that the truth of justification be recognized "as criterion which constantly serves to orient all the teaching and practice of our churches to Christ." However, Cardinal Ratzinger's Sacred Congregation for the Doctrine of the Faith over-ruled Cardinal Cassidy's Pontifical Council for Promoting Christian Unity, and allowed to justification the status only of "an indispensable criterion," not that of exclusive criterion as such. So Eberhard Juengel.[6]

According to the Lutheran understanding justification is indeed the criterion for everything else: "Where this single article remains pure, Christendom will remain pure, in beautiful harmony, and without any schisms. But where it does not remain pure, it is impossible to repel any error or heretical spirit" (FC SD III 6). Hence the whole approach to adiaphora in FC X! But mixed with such other criteria as papal infallibility and Mariological tradition, justification as criterion becomes simply meaningless. The implications had been fully spelt out in *Justification by Faith*, #153, under the heading, "Use of the Criterion":

> Catholics and Lutherans, for example, traditionally differ on purgatory, the papacy and the cult of saints. . . . Lutherans, however, do not exclude the possibility that such teachings can be understood and used in ways consistent with justification by faith; if such teachings are preached and practised in accord with this doctrine, they need not, from this Lutheran perspective, divide the churches even though Lutherans do not accept them.[7]

On the other hand (#118): "Catholics on their side, are wary of using any one doctrine as the absolute principle by which to purify from outside, so to speak, the catholic heritage."[8]

In sum, acceptance of the *Joint Declaration on the Doctrine of Justification* is incompatible with the Lutheran Confession in general, and with Smalcald Articles II i 5 in particular: "Nothing in this article can be given up or compromised, even if heaven and earth and things temporal should be destroyed."

---

6. "Um Gottes willen — Klarheit!" *Zeitschrift fuer Theologie und Kirche* 94 (1997):394–406.
7. *Justification by Faith*, 69.
8. *Justification by Faith*, 56.

ELCA-REFORMED ALTAR AND PULPIT FELLOWSHIP

The strongest language of *A Formula of Agreement*—and it is not very strong—is that quoted from the *Leuenberg Concord:* "In the Lord's Supper the risen Jesus Christ imparts himself in his body and blood, given up for all, through his word of promise with bread and wine" (the second citation of this language under "The Presence of Christ" in *A Formula* appears to be faulty).

The main trouble here appears to be two-fold. In the first place, the whole argument, especially in the thoroughly relativistic *A Common Calling*, is not really that a difficult disagreement has now finally been resolved, but rather that it has now been found that the past division had been unnecessary all along. Past differences have not been resolved. On the contrary, it is expressly acknowledged that it has not been possible to reconcile the confessional formulations from the sixteenth century with a "common language . . . which could do justice to all the insights, convictions, and concerns of our ancestors in the faith."[9] Instead, it was decided to regard the differences as complementary, rather than contradictory. What changed then was not the differences but the perspective.

Second, it is assumed throughout that, as an appendix to *An Invitation To Action* puts it, "those churches that have subscribed to the Reformed Confessions have always taught and still teach the real presence of Christ in the Eucharist."[10] Therefore the difference is not about the "fact" but only about the "mode" or the "how" of the Real Presence, which then should not be church-divisive. Even the independent and often boldly critical *Forum Letter* (July 1996) muted its opposition to *A Formula of Agreement* in response to a letter from United Church of Christ Professor Gabriel Fackre:

> Dr. Fackre is the sort of Reformed theologian with whom we'd rejoice to be in official communion and were his views more widely shared, we'd jump at the opportunity. He ably represents the "high" Reformed tradition of the sacraments . . . and makes the case, alluded to in his letter, that the "mode" of Christ's presence in the Eucharist is a theological dispute that should not be church-dividing.

---

9. *A Common Calling: The Witness of Our Reformation Churches in North America Today*, eds. Keith F. Nickle and Timothy F. Lull (Minneapolis: Augsburg Fortress, 1993), 49.

10. *An Invitation to Action: A Study of Ministry, Sacraments, and Recognition*, eds. James E. Andrews and Joseph A. Burgess, The Lutheran-Reformed Dialogue Series III: 1981–1983 (Philadelphia: Fortress Press, 1984), 114.

All this presupposes that the Lutheran Confession excludes "low" Zwinglianism but not "high" Calvinism. That assumption directly contradicts the Formula of Concord, which in the introductory paragraphs of Article VII disavows the rather misleading rhetoric of Calvinism more energetically than the plain and pedestrian denials of Zwingli. The FC throughout regards the dispute as being about the *fact* of the bodily presence in the Sacrament, not about the "mode" or the "how." To distinguish bona fide confession of this presence from mere sound-alike rhetoric, the FC, as is well known, defines three criteria: sacramental union, oral reception, and reception on the part of the unworthy.

Today's agreed formulas generally operate with a mere personal presence, which of course neither Zwingli nor Calvin ever denied. If "most contemporary exegesis" indeed interprets "the words 'body' and 'blood' ... increasingly not as substances but as saving event," then this closely parallels Calvin's habit of resolving *body* and *blood* into *fruits and benefits of the body and blood*.[11]

The *Leuenberg Concord* language, quoted in *A Formula of Agreement*, does not pass the muster of the FC's three criteria of authenticity. The verbal buffering between "body and blood" and "bread and wine" further weakens the already weak connective, "with." The Small Catechism uses the word "under": "It is the true body and blood of our Lord Jesus Christ under the bread and wine . . . ." And the Smalcald Articles drop the prepositions altogether: "We hold that the bread and the wine in the Supper are the true body and blood of Christ and that these are given and received not only by godly but also by wicked Christians" (SA III vi 1).

Leuenberg neither intends to confess all this, nor does it do so. To accept such ambiguities as adequate grounds for full communion is to equate Lutheran altars with sacramentarian altars and thus to give up the Sacrament of the Altar as confessed and understood by the Evangelical Lutheran Church in the Book of Concord. (See especially FC SD VII 32 and 33.)

Furthermore, *A Formula of Agreement* must be seen in its global historical context. Hermann Sasse's classic *Here We Stand* traces a certain chronology of shame for our Lutheran Church. He begins with the conversion of Elector John Sigismund to the Reformed Church in 1613, and ends with the transformation of the German Evangelical Church Federation into the German Evangelical Church in 1933. Later he came to see the formation of the Evangelical Church in Germany (EKD) in 1948 as the extension of the Prussian Union to all of Germany, and the *Leuenberg*

---

11. Lutheran-Episcopal dialogue, as quoted in *An Invitation to Action*, 123.

Concord as the extension of that Union to a Europe-wide level in 1973. The global sway of the Union was accepted by "world Lutheranism" in 1977 at Dar-es-Salaam, where the Lutheran World Federation committed itself to the ecumenical scheme of "Reconciled Diversity." This called for "genuine church fellowship" among the various churches, including the Roman Catholic, while at the same time granting "the legitimacy of the confessional differences and therefore the need to preserve them." *A Common Calling* and *A Formula of Agreement* are thoroughly in tune with this paradigm and echo its language.

ELCA-EPISCOPAL RELATIONS

Since I am not certain of the final form of the proposed instrument for bringing about full communion between the ELCA and the Episcopal Church, I am able to offer only a few brief general comments.

There are deep cultural and theological bonds between the Anglican and the Lutheran communions, which go back to the Reformation. Although the Anglican Church is historically a Reformed church, some of its early leadership was decidedly Lutheran. It is the least Reformed of all the Reformed churches, and is the only other liturgical Protestant church, beside the Lutheran — although the latter seems to be losing its grip on this treasure.

Since the Anglican Church is Reformed in origin and history, the Sacramental Presence will be the litmus-test. The 1981 report of the Lutheran-Episcopal dialogue carries the following agreed statements:

> Both communions affirm the real presence of Christ's Body and Blood in the Lord's Supper, but they express this faith somewhat differently. Lutherans (especially strongly confessional Lutheranism as represented by the Missouri Synod) tend to assert the Real Presence by doctrinal statement, as in the classical affirmations of *manducatio impiorum* and *manducatio oralis*. Although Article XXIX refers to these questions, and takes a somewhat different stand on them from that of classical Lutheranism, Anglicans today have no interest in these particular doctrinal affirmations. Rather, they tend to express their belief in the Real Presence in ceremonial action, by the reverence with which they treat the consecrated elements outside of Communion.
>
> Lutherans defended the Real Presence of Christ's body and blood "in, with, and under" the forms of bread and wine in order to make the christological affirmation that God meets us in the humanity as well as the divinity of Christ in this means of grace. For them, this implied a two-

fold eating of the sacrament, spiritually and orally (Formula of Concord, Solid Declaration VII:60–61). Anglicans, on the other hand, followed the Reformed emphasis on the spiritual eating by faith, thus denying that the wicked and unbelievers partake of Christ. (Articles of Religion 28–29)[12]

There follow some claims about "convergences," but there is no clear confession of the Sacramental Presence in the sense of the Book of Concord.

Regarding the "historic episcopate" and "apostolic succession," the essential point was made by Archbishop Söderblom and the Church of Sweden in response to the Lambeth Conference's overture of 1920:

> God has instituted *ministerium docendi evangelii et porrigendi sacramenta* — our Church cannot recognize any essential difference, *de jure divino*, of aim and authority between the two or three Orders into which the ministry of grace may have been divided, *jure humano*, for the benefit and convenience of the Church.[13]

Given the essential latitudinarianism of the Anglican Communion today, it is difficult to see much point in lengthy negotiations about the "historic episcopate" as a "sign" of apostolic unity and continuity, when it is the substance of that apostolicity which is so largely and scandalously absent. If ecclesial communion, as the true unity of the church, rests on a consensus in the apostolic-evangelical doctrine and sacraments, how can such a consensus possibly be established with a non-doctrinal, latitudinarian church? What would such a consensus mean?

THE "ZEN EFFECT" IN ECUMENICAL DIALOGUES
Loss of Core Christian Contents to Historical Relativism

No one can fail to be grateful for the dramatic openness to Luther's Reformation among many post–Vatican II Roman Catholic scholars. One thinks of Peter Manns, or of honourable Council speeches like Leon-Arthur Elchinger's, then Coadjutor Bishop of Strasbourg.[14] Then there is the outstanding recent study of Luther's theology of the cross, *Luther's Kreuzestheologie*, done by Hubertus Blaumeiser in Rome. Yet it must be borne in mind that the real intention of Vatican II was openness not to

---

12. *The Report of the Lutheran-Episcopal Dialogue Second Series 1976–1980* (Cincinnati: Forward Movement Publications, 1981), 16–17, 25–26.
13. Vilmos Vajta, ed., *Church in Fellowship: Lutheran Interchurch Agreements and Practices* (Minneapolis: Augsburg, 1963), 183.
14. Yves Congar, Hans Kueng, and Daniel O'Hanlon, eds., *Council Speeches of Vatican II* (London: Sheed and Ward, 1964), 143–146.

the Gospel, but to the world, indeed as *"apertura a sinistra"* — "opening to the Left." There is, thank God, no limiting the divine grace which signally touches a few and thereby blesses many. Yet when it comes to the organisational-institutional basis and ideology of the global ecumenical establishment, a sober realism is in order.

There is a depth-dimension to the modern ecumenical dialogue enterprise which cannot be left out of account without completely misleading consequences. To ignore that underlying feature is to limit the understanding of mainstream ecumenical discourse to a quite innocuous, superficial level. That will predictably result in complacently attributing conventional meanings to formulations often intended quite unconventionally and anti-conventionally.

Gottfried Martens' brilliant monograph on the various contemporary dialogues about justification identifies the common thread that runs through them all: "the axiomatisation of 'historicity' ['*Geschichtlichkeit*'] as ecumenical method" (182).[15] Martens finds the Malta Report, summing up LWF-Vatican "break-through" dialogues on justification between 1967 and 1971, particularly vitiated by this approach. That means, for example, that the notion of "doctrine" is virtually given up. With it goes the differentiation in principle between true and false doctrine. The place of the *consensus de doctrina* is taken by a joint "understanding" and "realization" (*Verwirklichung*) of the Gospel (181). Dogmatical and theological statements have their historical place and are therefore "time-conditioned" and "relative." The relativity of statements of the past is due to changed "world-views" and the corresponding "structures of thought" (183). The antagonism between true and false doctrine is replaced by the contrast of Yesterday and Today, or of "dogmatical" and "historical" method (184). This involves in effect the old saw, *finitum non capax infiniti*: the Gospel in its concrete historical form can never be adequately grasped or stated (191). That the Spirit has bound Himself to the Word of Scripture is given up. Instead there is the Roman Catholic theory of the development of dogma (193). A "multiplicity of theological conceptions" are said to exist within Scripture itself (195), which then leads to the notion of "centre of the Gospel," a Roman Catholic category, to be resolved in terms of Vatican II's "hierarchy of truths" (197). An important aim, foreshadowed already by

15. Gottfried Martens, *Die Rechtfertigung des Suenders — Rettungshandeln Gottes oder historisches Interpretament?* Forschungen zur systematischen und oekumenischen Theologie, ed. Wolfhart Pannenberg and Reinhard Slenczka, vol. 64 (Goettingen: Vandenhoeck & Ruprecht, 1992). Page numbers in parentheses in this section refer to this volume.

the Helsinki debacle of 1963, is to see justification as an impulse and entree to (political) "world-service" on the part of the church — in contrast to the Lutheran two-realms approach (211).

Summing up, instead of seeking a consensus resting on joint hearing of the Word of God and expressed in genuine liturgical (*gottesdienstlich*) confession,

> agreement is sought and found in the joint recognition of the historical relativity of theological and dogmatical statements, in the joint acknowledgment and the joint use of certain methods and in joint efforts at mediation towards the world. . . . The cultural-historical process and the action of the church then jointly supply a new foundation of unity. (213)

There comes to mind Johann Georg Hamann's keen observation "that all philosophers are enthusiasts, and vice versa, without knowing it."[16]

The Joint Declaration expressly states that it is "not a new independent presentation alongside the dialogue reports and documents to date, let alone a replacement of them" (#6). It clearly builds on the other dialogue results, including the "break-through" Malta Report, although there appears to be no express reference to that. There is, however, express reliance on the U.S. dialogue report of 1983 (#3). This report made much of new theological approaches among both Roman Catholics and Lutherans. It was noted that at the 1963 Lutheran World Federation meeting in Helsinki,

> problems were posed for traditional Lutheran understandings . . . by historical study of the Bible, the "greater variety and diversity among the biblical writers" which "we now see," erosion of theological terms, changes in cultural climate (including a more anthropocentric emphasis and the loss of eschatology) and the fact that "the gospel can be proclaimed without . . . the word justification." (#83)

For instance, "These themes from contemporary Catholic political theology and liberation theology converge . . . with the stress on corporate service in certain recent Lutheran theologies of justification" (#81). In short, "Theology in both churches is influenced by modern scriptural studies and intellectual developments in the humanities, social studies and the natural sciences" (#151).

---

16. Cited in Oswald Bayer, *Autoritaet und Kritik: Zu Hermeneutik und Wissenschaftstheorie* (Tuebingen: J.C.B. Mohr [Paul Siebeck], 1991), 104, n. 92.

As also Martens notes (260), the deployment of the historical-critical ideology resulted in full accommodation of the Council of Trent—a "transformist view" is just as good as the forensic one (#158)—whilst it is recognised that the crucial joint formulation "is not fully equivalent to the Reformation teaching on justification according to which God accepts sinners as righteous for Christ's sake on the basis of faith alone" (#157). The two quite different doctrines (Trent's and the Reformation's) are simply treated "as divergent linguistic ways of presenting the same thing, which rest on different conceptual models, and in which divergent but complementary concerns come to expression" (Martens, 254).

The *Leuenberg Concord* (1973), foundational for *A Formula of Agreement*, also relies on historical relativism. The definitive study here is Tuomo Mannermaa's "attempt . . . to examine the Leuenberg Concord 'historically-critically.'"[17] According to Mannermaa the decisive breakthrough came with the new conceptual scheme proposed by Wenzel Lohff. Earlier Gerhard Ebeling had distinguished between "justifying faith" (*fides justificans*) and "dogmatical faith" (*fides dogmatica*), and argued that only the former, not the latter, is necessary for the true unity of the church. He admitted, however, that he was parting company with the actual historical self-understanding of Augsburg Confession VII.[18] Wenzel Lohff pressed essentially the same distinction, but with this new justification in terms of AC VII: Justifying faith is God-given, but doctrine is "man-made," and therefore belongs to the "ceremonies, instituted by men," uniformity in which is not necessary for the true unity of the church. There is thus a divine "ground" which is "enough" for the true unity of the church, and a human, theological "expression," which can vary without violating the "ground."[19]

Marc Lienhard regards as a decisive factor for Leuenberg "the historical-critical method, which determines our relation to Scripture, and has also changed it in contrast to the sixteenth century."[20] This involves recognising "the plurality of biblical testimonies," such that "If the question

---

17. Tuomo Mannermaa, *Von Preussen nach Leuenberg: Hintergrund und Entwicklung der theologischen Methode in der Leuenberger Konkordie*, Arbeiten zur Geschichte und Theologie des Luthertums. Neue Folge, vol. I (Hamburg: Lutherisches Verlagshaus, 1981), 9.

18. Mannermaa, 45–50.

19. Mannermaa, 54–79.

20. Marc Lienhard, *Lutherisch-Reformierte Kirchengemeinschaft Heute*. Oekumenische Perspektiven Nr. 2 (Frankfurt: Verlag Otto Lembeck, Verlag Josef Knecht, 1972), 51.

about the elements had been put—which it is not!—then the Palestinian would have answered 'Reformedly,' the Hellenist 'Lutheranly'" (E. Schweitzer).[21] This is worlds apart from the Lutheran Church's conviction that her teaching "rests on a unique, firm, immovable, and indubitable rock of truth in the words of institution recorded in the holy Word of God and so understood, taught, and transmitted by the holy evangelists and apostles, and by their disciples and hearers in turn" (FC SD VII 42).[22]

But beyond leading to mutual understanding and agreement, says Lienhard, the historical-critical approach also created "new problems, unknown to the sixteenth century, as became evident for example in Arnoldshain [a precursor to Leuenberg], where it was no longer possible to connect the institution of the Lord's Supper with the night in which he was betrayed."[23] And by the "collapse of traditional thought forms" (*Leuenberg Concord*, #22), Lienhard tells us, is meant the alleged collapse "of the two-natures doctrine and of the doctrine of the communication of attributes."[24]

A Common Calling, the direct theological base of *A Formula of Agreement*, also abounds in the language of historical relativism. The ELCA's confessional paragraph, for instance, relegates all the other Lutheran confessions besides the Augsburg Confession to the category of "further valid interpretations of the faith of the Church." This is said to "block any claim to requiring their language and thought forms as the exclusive expression of the fundamental truth of the gospel in the life of the church."[25] Lutheran and Reformed confessions are accepted as equally valid: "We affirm the common commitment of all these traditions, Lutheran and Reformed, to the Reformation heritage that we share. We recognize our need of mutual edification and correction in the area of confessional hermeneutics."[26] Or:

> all of the divergent assertions and rejections among Lutheran and Reformed theologians of the classical age have a right to be heard and affirmed, but these interpretations are not uncritically received as definitive. Seen in the light of the beginnings, they are inclusive of each other, not exclusive, each of them necessary to express the fullness of the biblical witness and its patristic appropriation.

21. Lienhard, 54.
22. Tappert, 576.
23. Lienhard, 54.
24. Lienhard, 107.
25. *A Common Calling*, 34.
26. *A Common Calling*, 30.

[Historic creeds and confessions in the United Church of Christ] are understood as "testimonies" rather than tests of the faith. They function as nonbinding but authoritative norms. . . . It seems that today, more than in the past, this role of creeds and confessions has close parallels in the actual life of other Reformed as well as Lutheran churches. . . . We all are conscious of the passage of the "age of orthodoxy," of nineteenth-century debates about authority and infallible sources, and even of neo-orthodox "biblical theology." The politics of modern democracies, equal opportunity, and globalisation have altered the traditional authority structures within which our forebears ordered the world. . . . The impact of religious experience and rationalism on biblical interpretation, the rise of literary, sociological, and historical criticism, and the long-standing co-operation of biblical scholars across national and denominational lines have created a new environment for the application of the biblical norm.[27]

On this basis *A Formula for Agreement* asserts "the complementarity of affirmation and admonition as the basic principle for entering into full communion."

The Anglican-Lutheran dialogues are likewise steeped in historical relativism. An early conversation at the international level reported: "Within both Churches different attitudes exist concerning the nature of inspiration and the ways and means of interpreting the Scriptures, and these attitudes run across the denominational boundaries."[28] The U.S. dialogue was much more explicit in referring to

a renewed emphasis on the pluralism of the biblical witness and the time-conditioned character of its language and conceptuality (cf. Ernst Kaesemann among Lutherans and Dennis Nineham among Anglicans). Exegetes, however, are beginning to see again that the one gospel is proclaimed in, with and through these pluralistic, time-conditioned human expressions.[29]

One final quotation must suffice:

To some Lutherans it may seem strange that limited agreement on controverted dogmatic *loci* should be thought adequate for some degree of ecclesial relationship, when the classical Lutheran position has been that

---

27. *A Common Calling*, 48, 61–62.
28. *Anglican-Lutheran International Conversations*. The Report of the Conversations 1970–1972 authorized by the Lambeth Conference and the Lutheran World Federation (London: SPCK, 1973), 9.
29. *Lutheran-Episcopal Dialogue*, 18.

the complete confessional agreement is essential for union. However, Dr. Rusch reports some change here in some recent Lutheran thinking. This is evident in two documents put out by the Lutheran World Federation entitled "More than Church Unity" and "Guidelines for Ecumenical Encounter." Here there is recognition for the first time of the possibility of multiple expressions of doctrine. A model of church unity for much of recent Lutheran theology is that of a fellowship in which confessional peculiarities are not blended but reconciled as legitimate pluralism. In such a pattern joint statements would represent an essential core of dogmatic agreement within a wider pluralism.[30]

Just how wide are the bounds of the "wider pluralism"? Lienhard's hints at some Christological implications are disturbing. One of the clearest indications of what is at stake comes from Thomas Sheehan, a well-known philosopher at Loyola University in Chicago. In *The New York Review of Books* for 14 June 1984 Sheehan wrote, approvingly, that there was a developing "liberal consensus" among Roman Catholic biblical scholars, presumably in this country, "that Jesus of Nazareth did not assert any of the divine or messianic claims the Gospels attribute to him and that he died without believing he was Christ or the Son of God."

In North American Lutheranism the Christological import of the "wider pluralism" is not unknown.[31] The extent and significance of the problem is best gauged from one of the final efforts of the former LCUSA's Division of Theological Studies. In 1981 that Division was assigned "as a matter of urgency" the topic of the "'far-reaching implications of historical criticism, as practiced in U.S. Lutheranism' for (a) the central, Christological-Trinitarian core of the Gospel; (b) the very possibility of confessional subscription; and (c) the preamble of LCUSA's constitution, according to which 'the participating Lutheran church bodies . . . see in the three Ecumenical Creeds and in the Confessions of the Lu-

---

30. *Lutheran-Episcopal Dialogue*, 19–20.
31. See for example, *Who Can This Be? Studies in Christology* (New York: Division of Theological Studies, Lutheran Council in the U.S.A., 1968). The materials "will allow men to take a variety of positions and hopefully contribute to an openness of faith and thought . . ." (7). For instance: "So the gospels clearly give us a picture of one who, like the rest of us, was groping through each new situation to find some clear indication of what the Father's will might be. . . . Likely he was even unaware of the resurrection that lay beyond the criminal's death" (25). But: "The chapters of this handbook reflect the conviction that biblical criticism is here to stay" (10).

theran Church . . . a pure exposition of the Word of God.'" Five years later the Division issued a six-page leaflet, *Statement on Historical Criticism*, reporting that it had "not dealt with the implications of historical criticism for Christology, justification, and confessional subscription. . . . Time has not permitted us to do this." But, concluded the Division, despite some "mutual misunderstanding" and even "sharp disagreement," these "did not destroy our sense of oneness in Christ."

No academic work today, certainly not theology, and certainly not ecumenical discussion, can be carried on in isolation, apart from the global context. And since theology is above all interested in the life of the church, and not simply in abstruse philosophical abstractions, theologians must not flinch from facing up to the sometimes grotesque eruptions in practice of what may look like reasonable principles. Here is a case in point, from the Evangelische Kirche in Deutschland, a mix of "Lutheran," Reformed, and Union churches in Germany, and incidentally the main ecclesiastical source and base of the *Leuenberg Concord*. At this very time, in the middle of June, the EKD is holding its *Kirchentag*, a sort of church fair, in Stuttgart. *Die Welt online* of 1 June 1999 carried an article on it by Dr. Gerhard Besier, professor of church history in the University of Heidelberg. The "festival communions" are to employ "prayers and symbols of non-Christian religions," presumably in the interests of "inter-religious dialogue." But on "theological and historical grounds" the EKD "rejects a mission among Jews." Asks Besier:

> Does the withholding of mission refer only to Judaism? How intensively does the evangelical church still bear witness, among non-believers, to salvation in Jesus Christ? It is evident that missionary activities would have a disturbing effect on the creation of a multi-confessional "religion of peace," and under this goal-setting it is also understandable if it is desired to lead Christians towards a Muslim prayer-rug, a Buddhist wheel, a Hindu idol and a Jewish menorah as new liturgical symbols of this super-religion. A little annoying in these happenings is only the stereotypical claim that now as ever all this remains on Reformational ground. After all, what is involved is a gentle transformation from the Reformational church into the all-the-world's-church (Allerweltskirche).

Given this global context (the Lutheran component bodies of EKD belong to the Lutheran World Federation, of course), one must face the fact that the "wider pluralism" pre-supposed by the ideology of historical-critical relativism has no clearly definable bounds. Dialogue results from such premises cannot have any stable, certain meanings, and should be considered as allowing anything not expressly excluded. But the average reader needs to be forewarned of this feature, which, with only a modest flight of fancy, I have dubbed the "*Zen* effect."

But let us leave exotic examples. Take the matter-of-fact assertion in the Lutheran-Episcopal Dialogue: "In most contemporary exegesis the words 'body' and 'blood' are interpreted increasingly not as substances but as saving event (*Heilsereignis*)."[32] This is referenced, with evident approval, in the Lutheran-Reformed dialogue, *An Invitation To Action*.[33] How many average members in participating churches will ever see or understand this "fine print"? But if traditional believers are allowed to assume that traditional words in inter-church agreements mean traditional things, is this not "by good words and fair speeches" to "deceive the hearts of the simple" (Rom. 16:18)? If doctrinal truth has become the victim of ecumenical rhetoric, now swirling between the critical acids of modernity and post-modernity's willful vacuity, perhaps an ode in celebration of truth and fact is in order, this one by Sir John Betjeman, late poet laureate of England:

> And is it true? And is it true,
> This most tremendous tale of all,
> Seen in a stained-glass window's hue,
> A Baby in an ox's stall?
> The Maker of the stars and sea
> Become a Child on earth for me?
> And is it true? For if it is,
> No loving fingers tying strings
> Around those treasured fripperies,
> The sweet and silly Christmas things,
> Bath salts and inexpensive scent
> And hideous tie so kindly meant,
> No love that in a family dwells
> No carolling in frosty air,
> Nor all the steeple-shaking bells
> Can with this single truth compare —
> That God was Man in Palestine
> And lives today in Bread and Wine.[34]

---

32. *Lutheran-Episcopal Dialogue*, 17.
33. *An Invitation to Action*, 123.
34. Cited in B. A. Santamaria, "Christmas . . . the mystery of faith," *News Weekly* [Australia], 13 December 1997, 24.

WHAT DOES THIS MEAN?
Deploying the Ecclesial Criteria
of the Evangelical Lutheran Church

Not quite half a century ago, President Franklin Clark Fry of the ULCA declared:

> Insistence upon agreement in doctrine as a precondition for church fellowship is the distinguishing mark of Lutherans among all Protestants and should never be relaxed. . . . Lutherans unanimously affirm that a wide and deep consensus of doctrine must underlie church union. For our own ULCA, this includes not only the Word of God and the ecumenical creeds, but also "the confessions which have always been regarded as the standards of Evangelical Lutheran doctrine."[35]

I do not know whether President Fry would have regarded the present ecumenical commitments of the ELCA as in fact documenting "a wide and deep consensus of doctrine." However, he stated the confessional principle itself with admirable clarity. The ecclesial standards or criteria of the Evangelical Lutheran Church self-evidently are those set out in the official creeds and confessions of that Church, as contained in the Book of Concord of 1580.

The classic Lutheran ecumenical platform is set down in AC VII:

> Therefore this is enough for the true unity of the Christian church, that the Gospel be harmoniously preached there according to its pure understanding and the sacraments be dispensed in accord with the divine Word.[36]

By the same token, what is "not necessary for the true unity of the Christian church" is that "ceremonies, instituted by men, should be observed uniformly in all places."

---

35. "Franklin Clark Fry's Presentation of the United Lutheran Attitude, 1956," *Documents of Lutheran Unity in America*, ed. Richard C. Wolf, (Philadelphia: Fortress Press, 1966), 547, 553.

36. AC VII 2 and 3, German. The translation of this article in Tappert, 32, is seriously flawed. First, it simply ignores the German *"eintraechtiglich"* (unanimously or harmoniously). Second, it wrongly introduces an indefinite article (*"a* pure understanding"). This mistranslation has actually been used to argue that there are several pure understandings of the Gospel, not just one! To be consistent, the Tappert version should have rendered the grammatically parallel *"zu wahrer Einigkeit"* as "for *a* true unity of the Christian church."

Three clarifications need to be stated but obviously cannot be argued at length here: In the first place, the contrast in AC VII is not between "the Gospel" and "other kinds of doctrine," but between the (rightly preached and administered) Gospel and sacraments on the one hand, and "ceremonies, instituted by men," that is, adiaphora, on the other. Second, the "Gospel" here, precisely in its narrow sense, that is, in opposition to the Law (FC V) means not an isolated "article of justification," but all the articles of faith. Note the Large Catechism's contrast between the Ten Commandments as Law, and the Creed (not just the Second Article!) as Gospel. Third, the Gospel preached "according to its pure understanding" or the agreement "about the teaching of the Gospel" (AC VII 2) is therefore precisely equivalent to the agreement "in the doctrine and in all its articles" of FC SD X 31.

Here is ecumenical generosity at its best: the church-creating divine givens are quite enough — but they are of course also necessary. No dispensation from or suspension of these givens, however temporary or "provisional," is possible or tolerable. By contrast, Rome and Geneva — as well as Constantinople and Canterbury — are not satisfied with dogmatical-sacramental consensus in the biblical Gospel as such. They demand submission also to "ceremonies" or adiaphora, such as papal or conciliar authority, Calvin's allegedly biblical offices and church-structures, and the notion of "apostolic succession" by way of the "historic episcopate." The Anglican-influenced "ecumenical" formula "Faith and Order" clearly implies that these human accretions are as necessary for the true unity of the church as is her evangelical-sacramental fullness.[37] Our Lutheran confession is fully satisfied with agreement in the *Faith*, including of course the holy sacraments (Eph. 4:5). Anything "more" than that is less (Gal. 2:5).

Oneness in the Gospel and sacraments therefore is oneness in the church, or church fellowship. Conversely, ecclesial communion or fellowship professes unity in doctrine and sacraments.[38] From the Lutheran point of view, therefore, two churches become one church not when they merge their administrative structures, but when they profess doctrinal

---

37. See Ruth Rouse and Stephen Charles Neill, eds., *A History of the Ecumenical Movement 1517–1948* (London: S.P.C.K., 1967), 264–266, 405 ff.

38. Lutheran Church of Australia: ". . . Church fellowship, that is, mutual recognition as brethren, altar and pulpit fellowship and resultant co-operation in the preaching of the Gospel and the administration of the Sacraments, presupposes unanimity in the pure doctrine of the Gospel and in the right administration of the Sacraments. . . . We declare that wherever continued cooperation in the preaching of the Gospel and the administration of the

unity or altar and pulpit fellowship — i.e., unity in the divine givens of Gospel-preaching and sacramental practice. Buchrucker's splendid monograph on the subject puts it tersely and well:

> to accede to (*einwilligen*) the doctrine of the other, that is church fellowship. For church-fellowship is doctrinal fellowship, which exists for Luther only where equality (*aequitas*) of doctrine obtains.[39]

The conventional contrast between "communion in sacred things [*in sacris*]" and "co-operation in externals [*in externis*]" therefore must not be misconstrued as though external, outward things as such were nonessential or "un-sacred" or "unspiritual." The opposite of "spiritual" is not "external" — unless one is a Platonist, opposed to incarnational-sacramental realism — but "unspiritual"! The real contrast is not between "spiritual" and "external" things, but between *divine* and *human* externals. The Gospel and sacraments, and ecclesial communion in them, are as utterly outward, external, and observable as is the famous tip of the iceberg. But nothing can be more *spiritual*, and therefore essential to the true unity of the church, as are these blessed divine "externals." What is not essential to the church and her true unity are man-made, "indifferent," adiaphorous externals, e.g., confessionally neutral rites and ceremonies, all sorts of legal, purely administrative-bureaucratic trappings, and the like.

Sacraments and worship exists, there we have a witness to the world of unity in the faith and a profession of Church fellowship" (*Theses of Agreement* [1966], V, 26. 28). American Lutheran Conference: ". . . according to the Word of God and our Confessions, church fellowship, that is, mutual recognition, altar and pulpit fellowship, and eventually co-operation in the strictly essential work of the Church, presupposes unanimity in the pure doctrine of the Gospel and in the confession of the same in word and deed. Where the establishment and maintenance of church fellowship ignores present doctrinal differences or declares them a matter of indifference, there is unionism, pretense of union which does not exist. . . . [The Iowa, Ohio, and Buffalo Synods] agree that the rule, 'Lutheran pulpits for Lutheran pastors only, and Lutheran altars for Lutheran communicants only,' is not only in full accord with, but necessarily implied in, the teachings of the divine Word and the Confessions of the evangelical Lutheran Church. This rule, implying the rejection of all unionism and syncretism, must be observed as setting forth a principle elementary to sound and conservative Lutheranism" ("Minneapolis Theses" [1925, 1930], III, in Wolf, 146).

39. Armin-Ernst Buchrucker, *Wort, Kirche und Abendmahl bei Luther* (Bremen: Verlag Stelten & Co., 1972), 175, n. 70.

If the purely preached Gospel and the rightly administered sacraments are the marks of the church (*notae ecclesiae*, Ap VII/VIII 20), then the Book of Concord, which spells out these marks most concretely, is the mark *par excellence* ("*nota notarum*"). The Lutheran Confession defines itself primarily against two fronts, Rome and Zurich/Geneva: The Augsburg Confession "distinguishes our reformed churches from the papacy and from other condemned sects and heresies."[40] As for the Small and Large Catechisms,

> [t]he pure churches and schools have everywhere recognized these publicly and generally accepted documents as the sum and pattern of the doctrine which Dr. Luther of blessed memory clearly set forth in his writings on the basis of God's Word and conclusively established against the papacy and other sects.[41]

The Lutheran Confession, moreover, is not content with lip-service.[42] Nor is it content with the status of a treasured ethnic heirloom or a highly valued piece of "loyalty to heritage."[43] It claims rather to be a humble but deliberate confession of the divine truth, as "a public and certain testimony not only among our contemporaries, but also among our posterity," of "what our churches' unanimous position and judgment in respect of the controverted articles is and shall remain."[44] The point of the Confession, in the face of contradictory views such that "the opinions of the erring party cannot be tolerated in the church of God, much less be excused and defended," is to function as concrete doctrinal standard and umpire, i.e., as "a single, universally accepted, certain, and common form of doc-

---

40. FC SD Rule and Norm 5 (Tappert, 504).
41. FC SD Rule and Norm, 9 (Tappert, 505).
42. The Lutheran Church of Australia insists "that there be some real consonance between the formal acceptance of the Confessions as documented in the Church's constitution and the actual teaching and ecclesiastical life of the Church concerned. A basic discrepancy at this point would mean that the Church was not actually what it claimed to be. The LCA does not intend to take God's place and judge other Churches. At the same time it cannot close its eyes to an obvious hiatus between saying and doing which in effect cancels out the formal confession and veils the truth of the Gospel (cf. Peter in Galatians 2). Here judgment in truth and love is demanded" (1968 and 1972 General Convention, Lutheran Church of Australia). The prime test of whether a church's confession is being put into practice is whether that confession is allowed to define the basis and limits of church fellowship.
43. *A Common Calling*, 18.
44. FC SD Rule and Norm 16 (author's translation); compare Tappert, 507.

trine which all our Evangelical churches subscribe, and from which and according to which, because it is drawn from the Word of God, all other writings are to be approved and accepted, judged and regulated."[45] The Confession, in other words, defines the basis and boundaries of church fellowship, or it is no confession.

Since the chief difference with the papacy is over the article of justification ("On this article rests all that we teach and practice against the pope, the devil, and the world")[46] and the central point at issue with the sacramentarians is the true bodily presence in the Sacrament, not surprisingly these two articles — the second of them the most concentrated concretisation of the former—constitute the two foci 'round which everything else in the Book of Concord revolves.[47] This corresponds remarkably to the two occurrences of solemn "traditioning" language in St. Paul's First Epistle to the Corinthians (11:23; 15:3).

Contrary to a certain "Evangelical Catholic" romanticism, the confessional border of ecclesial communion in the direction of the papacy is definitely closed:

> Moreover the true doctrine and church [*die rechte Lehre und Kirche*] is often so thoroughly suppressed and lost, as happened under the papacy, as though there were no church, and it often looks as though she had quite perished.[48]

> Although our opponents arrogate to themselves the name of the church, therefore, we know that the church of Christ is among those who teach the Gospel of Christ, not among those who defend wicked opinions against the Gospel, as the Lord says, "My sheep hear my voice." (John 10:27)[49]

> We should forsake wicked teachers because they no longer function in the place of Christ, but are antichrists. Christ says (Matt. 7:15), "Beware of false prophets"; Paul says (Gal. 1:9), "If anyone is preaching to you a gospel contrary to that which you received, let him be accursed."[50]

> [Enthusiasm] is the source, strength, and power of all heresy, including that of the papacy and Mohammedanism.[51]

---

45. FC SD Preface 10 (Tappert, 503); FC SD Rule and Norm 10 (Tappert, 506).
46. SA II i 5 (Tappert, 292).
47. In the Formula of Concord, for instance, Arts. I–VI and X centre in justification and are directed against Romanising errors, whilst Arts. VII–IX and XI are anti-sacramentarian.
48. Ap VII/VIII 9, German (author's translation).
49. Ap IV 400 (Tappert, 168).
50. Ap VII/VIII 48 (Tappert, 177).
51. SA III viii 9 (Tappert, 313).

All Christians ought to beware of becoming participants in the impious doctrines, blasphemies, and unjust cruelties of the pope. They ought rather to abandon and execrate the pope and his adherents as the kingdom of the Antichrist. Christ commanded, "Beware of false prophets" (Matt. 7:15). Paul also commanded that ungodly teachers should be shunned and execrated as accursed. . . .

To dissent from the consensus of so many nations and to be called schismatics is a serious matter. But divine authority commands us all not to be associated with and not to support impiety and unjust cruelty. . . .

The errors of the pope are manifest, and they are not trifling. . . . Those who agree with the pope and defend his doctrines and forms of worship defile themselves with idolatry and blasphemous opinions . . . detract from the glory of God, and hinder the welfare of the church by so strengthening errors and other crimes as to impose them on all posterity.[52]

[In the Smalcald Articles and the Treatise of the Power and Primacy of the Pope] the grounds and reasons are set forth at necessary length for renouncing the papistic errors and idolatries, for having no communion with the papists, and for neither expecting nor planning to come to an understanding with the pope about these matters.[53]

Nor do we include among truly free adiaphora or things indifferent those ceremonies which give or (to avoid persecution) are designed to give the impression that our religion does not differ greatly from that of the papists, or that we are not seriously opposed to it. Nor are such rites matters of indifference when these ceremonies are intended to create the illusion (or are demanded or agreed to with that intention) that these two opposing religions have been brought into agreement and become one body, or that a return to the papacy and an apostasy from the pure doctrine of the Gospel and from true religion has taken place or will allegedly result little by little from these ceremonies.[54]

With particular reference to the article of justification the Evangelical Lutheran Confession holds:

Nothing in this article can be given up or compromised, even if heaven and earth and things temporal should be destroyed. . . . On this article rests all that we teach and practice against the pope, the devil, and the world. Therefore we must be quite certain and have no doubts about it.

---

52. Tr 41, 42, 58, 59 (Tappert, 327–328, 330).
53. FC SD Rule and Norm 7 (Tappert, 505).
54. FC SD X 5 (Tappert, 611).

Otherwise all is lost, and the pope, the devil, and all our adversaries will gain the victory.[55]

In light of all the above, subscription to the *Joint Declaration on the Doctrine of Justification* is in no way compatible with the official doctrine of the Church of the Augsburg Confession.

As for the Bodily Presence of Christ in the Holy Sacrament of the Altar, the evangelical Lutheran confession is quite unambiguous:

> Dr. Luther, who understood the true intention of the Augsburg Confession better than any one else, remained by it steadfastly and defended it constantly until he died. Shortly before his death, in his last confession, he repeated his faith in this article with great fervor and wrote as follows: "I reckon them all as belonging together (that is, as Sacramentarians and enthusiasts), for that is what they are who will not believe that the Lord's bread in the Supper is his true, natural body, which the godless or Judas receive orally as well as St. Peter and all the saints. Whoever, I say, will not believe this, will please let me alone and expect no fellowship from me. This is final."
>
> From these statements and especially from the exposition of Dr. Luther, as the chief teacher of the Augsburg Confession, every intelligent person who loves truth and peace can understand beyond all doubt what the Augsburg Confession's real meaning and intention in this article have always been.[56]

The real claim of the ELCA-Reformed *A Formula of Agreement*, however, is not that the historic differences between the Lutheran and the Reformed confessions on the Holy Supper have been resolved. Rather, the claim is that they do not now justify a rupture in church fellowship, and really did not justify it then. A basic premise, as has been shown above, is that Calvinism is basically acceptable, though outright Zwinglianism is not. This radically contradicts the Lutheran confession. The introductory paragraphs of Formula of Concord Article VII are at pains to reject precisely Calvin's more slippery rhetoric, and not simply Zwingli's quite straightforward denial of the Sacramental Presence.[57]

In urging adoption of the previous stage of Reformed-Lutheran union (*An Invitation to Action*, now incorporated into *A Formula of Agreement*),

---

55. SA II i 5 (Tappert, 292).
56. FC SD VII 33–34 (Tappert, 575).
57. FC SD VII 1–8 (Tappert, 569–570).

the then Lutheran Church in America's Bishop Perry was only being honest when he "calmly and explicitly repudiated Article Seven of the Formula" [of Concord] (*Forum Letter,* 16 September 1986). Likewise Harding Meyer, of the Lutheran World Federation's Institute for Ecumenical Studies in Strasbourg, argued that adoption of the *Leuenberg Concord* (also approved in the decisive formulations by *A Formula of Agreement*) signaled a major change in "Lutheran confessionality." Adoption of *Leuenberg* "can only mean that both churches no longer hold to the same position on certain points which had for a long time been considered important." Specifically, it means that the Altered Augsburg Confession (*Variata,* 1540) "can be considered again as a legitimate possibility of Lutheran understanding of the eucharist," in contrast to "the previous Lutheran insistence on the Unaltered Augsburg Confession."[58]

A church which accedes to *A Formula of Agreement* thereby grants equal status and legitimacy to Reformed altars and confessions and so renounces the Lutheran Confession. Such a church proclaims itself a union church rather than a church of the Augsburg Confession.

Taking into account also the projected ecclesial coalescence with the totally latitudinarian Episcopal Church (think of Bishop Shelby Spong of New Jersey), the global implications are melancholy from a Lutheran standpoint:

> With justification out of the way as a stumbling-block to reunion with Rome, and the sacramental presence re-negotiated with Canterbury and then Geneva, the way will be clear for "full communion" everywhere, and whatever anyone may choose to make of the Gospel and sacraments, it will all be fully warranted as apostolic by the "sign" of a joint episcopate.[59]

---

58. Harding Meyer, "The LWF and Its Role in the Ecumenical Movement," *Lutheran World* 20 (1973):23–31.
59. *The Porvoo Declaration In Confessional Perspective,* 19.

Chapter Eleven

RESPONSE TO CARDINAL
CASSIDY'S ADDRESS

Editor's note: Marquart had a major hand in writing a response to the Lutheran-Roman Cath-olic Joint Declaration on the Doctrine of Justification *for the Department of Systematic Theology of Concordia Theological Seminary, published in CTQ 62 (April 1998):83–106. This analysis frankly stated: "The* Joint Declaration *fails not simply in this or that detail of justifi-cation, but in terms of the 'big picture'." At roughly the same time (April, 1998), the seminary in Fort Wayne hosted an open dialog between Lutherans and Roman Catholics. Marquart was a key participant. Here is his simultaneously gracious and tenacious response to an address de-livered on that occasion by Cardinal Edward I. Cassidy, a promoter of the* Joint Declaration.

ॐ

We are indeed honoured by the presence in our midst of His Eminence, Cardinal Cassidy, and it is a particular privilege for me to respond to his wide-ranging and thoughtful address.

Allow me to arrange my brief remarks under three heads: the gift of ec-umenism, the task of ecumenism, and a foremost obstacle to ecumenism.

Although our little corner of the Lord's Vineyard is not known for its ecumenical enthusiasm, also we must freely acknowledge that the Ecu-menical Movement has brought about profound changes for the better, so far as the attitudes of Christians of various confessions towards one another are concerned. One cannot today hear without horror the ac-counts within living memory, of unbecoming and even shocking hostili-ties among members of different churches. There never was in the New Testament any basis or excuse for such personal animosity. The Paschal Mysteries we have just celebrated do not allow us to treat even our worst enemies — let alone people of divergent convictions — with anything but charity and compassion! That there is now generally a climate of mutual respect and friendship among members of the various churches, for that one can only be deeply grateful to Almighty God.

Nor is it merely a matter of gingerly toleration. In the conflict with the forces of secularist oppression and inhumanity in this terrible century now ending, millions of Christians have enjoyed the benefits of what is fondly called "grass-roots ecumenism." Without any compromise of their

convictions, people of good will have found ways and means to act together effectively for the well-being of society, and especially for the protection
of its most helpless members. In this country, for example. Dr. Bernard
Nathanson, a former mass-abortionist, was drawn from agnosticism to
Christianity simply through encountering so many men and women of
faith, hope, and charity in the pro-life movement.

In view of His Eminence's own Australian background, I may perhaps
be permitted to share a personal recollection. Early last month there took
place in Melbourne's Roman Catholic cathedral the state funeral of a most
remarkable Christian, Mr. B. A. Santamaria. In life this man of firmly
traditionalist Roman Catholic beliefs had often been regarded as divisive
and extremist, but in death he was honoured by lords spiritual and temporal, the prime minister and the state premier being among those in at-
tendance, and this despite the fact that Santamaria himself had not been
a political office-holder. One former opponent said that Santamaria's had
been the best political mind in Australia. His friend the late Malcolm
Muggeridge would have concurred.

Although I had met Mr. Santamaria personally on only one or two
occasions, I found his cause utterly admirable and worthy of unhesitating
support. Throughout the Cold War years, Santamaria intelligently and
effectively exposed the barbarities, the conspiratorial intentions, and the
various deceits and beguilements of the Marxist slave empire. Vindicated
by the collapse of the Soviet Union a thousand years after the Baptism
of Russia on Easter Sunday of 988 A.D., Santamaria raised the banner of
social responsibility in the face of a Western world decaying into cultural
barbarism and an untrammeled cut-throat capitalism indifferent to human dignity and suffering. One of Santamaria's most significant achievements was to have enacted into Australian law, after a century of fierce
struggle over the issue, the principle that parents as taxpayers have the
right to public support for the schools of their own choice, rather than
having public funding restricted to a monopoly of government schools.
Whether it was communism, or economic chaos and injustice, or abortion, or the whole suicidal anti-family agenda of current fashion, Santamaria was able to galvanise effective opposition to the corrosive public
malignancies of our time. I thank God for this humble, modest, but brave
and resourceful soldier in the church militant—yes, he tangled also with
ecclesiastics! — and I count it an honour to have had however small a part
with so many others in this particular bit of "grass-roots ecumenism,"
that is, plain service to humanity in the public, civil realm, inspired by a
common love of Christ.

But of course ecumenism is not really about temporal friendship and civil collaboration, although they are important. What is at stake in ecumenism, as His Eminence has pointed out in his address, is the very nature of the one holy catholic and apostolic Church of Christ. And that far transcends any social or political issues of the day.

The great primal given about the Church is that as the Bride or the Mystical Body of Christ, she is indivisibly one. This is ontologically so, regardless of church political huffings and puffings or the lack of them. All the major confessions to-day accept in one way or another that this great reality of the Church exists also beyond their own organisational bounds. If there is only one Lord, one Faith, and one Baptism (Eph. 4:5), and if Christians have a share in this indissoluble unity only by the gift and mercy of God, it follows that all Christians as such, that is, to the extent that they are Christians at all, have exactly one and the same Lord, faith, and baptism — even if the psychological and historical implications are not yet apparent, and perhaps cannot become fully apparent in this present age. After all, the divine, supernatural life of Christians is safely hid with Christ in God, as St. Paul teaches in Colossians 3:3. In light of this primal gift and fact, what is ecumenism's major task?

Quite some years ago there came to this town the great Russian theologian, Alexander Schmemann, who has since died. He had been asked by the inter-confessional council of churches here to address the issue of ecumenism. Father Schmemann began by expressing appreciation for the introductory stages of ecumenical activity, in which people got to know and respect one another, and to take pleasure in the beauties of one another's Easter customs and other such ethnic traditions. But now, he said, it was time to move beyond what he called "greeting card ecumenism," and to face the hard issues of truth, of Christian dogma. That, he said, was the real challenge of ecumenical work, and could be deferred no longer.

Some were disturbed, even annoyed, by this rather straightforward message, but many of us were deeply thankful that the basal note of truth had been sounded. We are thankful again tonight to be reminded by His Eminence, on the basis of the Encyclical Letter of Pope John Paul II, *Ut Unum Sint*, of the paramount issue of truth in the pursuit of Christian re-union. "Truth" here of course does not refer to any qualities or achievements of our own poor fickle, fallen human nature. "Yea let God be true and every man a liar!" (Rom. 3:4). It refers rather to that truth which alone can make us free, the truth as it is in Jesus, our divine-human Saviour, Who is Himself the Way, the Truth, and the Life. That life-giving truth is the one thing needful, the only genuine way and key to the ultimate ecumenical goal of visible unity in full communion.

If I now turn to some concrete particulars, then not with the intention of lecturing His Eminence, who is well versed in these matters. There is upon us, however, an ecumenical obligation to the dear people of God in all our churches, whose right and duty it is to be as clear as they can be in their own minds and consciences about just what unites us, and what divides us, and why.

Those of us whose convictions on the subject are given voice in the ecumenical manifesto of the Augsburg Confession of 1530 are accustomed to speak of the *purely preached Gospel* and the *rightly administered sacraments* as pivotal for everything in the Church's life. Here we may be confident of the authentic and life-giving Voice of the Church's one true Shepherd (St. John 10). Other things, even beautiful ancient customs and traditions that arose within the Church in the course of time, may not be put on a par with the dogmatic-sacramental fullness with which the Lord Himself has endowed His Church by His gift and institution. It is for this reason that we for our part cannot consider that binary ecumenical formula, Faith and Order, a very happy one. For it suggests that issues of human, historical order and structure in the church are as decisive for unity as are the divinely given faith and sacraments. In practice the "structure" issue then tends to overshadow everything else, as for instance in the Lima Statement, *Baptism, Eucharist, Ministry*, produced in 1982 by the Faith and Order Commission of the World Council of Churches. This document devotes by far the greatest attention to traditional structures of ministry, while the decisive issues of truth and dogma in the sacraments are left unresolved. Does Holy Baptism work regeneration in babies or not? Are the Lord's body and blood truly present and distributed to all communicants, or not? The Lima document would suggest that the churches may answer these questions variously, to their own satisfaction, so long as they conform outwardly to uniform traditional structures of ministry! Something has clearly gone ecumenically awry here.

Of the Roman Catholic-Lutheran dialogues it must be said with gratitude that they have advanced a good bit beyond Father Schmemann's "greeting card ecumenism." Even the crucial issue of justification has been tackled painstakingly. While there has been considerable progress in mutual understanding here, and even some convergence, it must be said in all candour that the fundamental gap between justification as imputation, or the forgiveness of sins, and justification as inner transformation, has not been bridged. Yet one must hope that whatever common ground has been gained will mark not the end of the line, but only a milestone on the way to the goal of actual consensus in doctrine. So far as I know, no modern dialogue has brought the two parties as close again on the matter of justification as they were at the Colloquy in Regensburg or Ratisbon, in 1541. Perhaps that Colloquy is worth revisiting together.

On the other hand, the Church of the Augsburg Confession is conscious of sharing with the Church of Rome, but not with that of Zurich and Geneva, the confession of the true bodily presence of Christ in the sacramental elements. Pressed with the finer philosophical details of transubstantiation, which he did not accept, Luther quipped in characteristic fashion that given that choice, he'd rather drink only the Blood of Christ with the Pope than only wine with Zwingli! Anyone holding the faith of the Augsburg Confession must regard it as nothing short of calamitous that much of nominal Lutheranism in the world to-day finds it easy to enter into full communion with the tradition of Zwingli and Calvin, which despite the diplomatic formulas really means giving up the Sacrament of the Altar in the sense of the Lutheran Confessions. Surely genuine ecumenicity, like genuine love, "rejoices in the truth" (1 Cor. 13:6), and takes no pleasure in compromise.

The task of facing up to, understanding, specifying, and defining the exact matters at issue among the major confessions, in order then to adjudicate them by the revealed Word of God, is indeed an immensely daunting one — but by God's grace not a hopeless one. It is for us to pursue and press towards the divine truth to the very conscientious best of our ability. The outcome, however, lies not in our hands, but in His without Whom the builders build in vain. To Him be all our humble ecumenical efforts commended.

Finally, I should be shirking my duty in this response were I to fail to name what I consider to be the single most intractable obstacle to genuine ecumenical progress. I take this up not to sabotage but to promote and encourage real and realistic dialogue. The Spirit of God is the Spirit of truth, and since we must depend on His help utterly, we dare not yield to illusions which would cloud our judgments and dissipate our efforts.

I am referring to the historical-critical ideology, which surfaces with particular clarity for instance in the so-called "Protestant Principle" popularised by the late Paul Tillich. According to this alleged "Protestant Principle," there are no fixed truths of dogma, no absolutes, no permanent creeds, no infallible authorities of any kind. Instead, everything is subject to constant historical flux and criticism, revision, and change. The divine Scriptures, too, are systematically immersed in these acids of scepticism and relativism, till nothing is left but pointless, bloodless abstractions. But how does this relate to ecumenism? Countless examples could be given, but I shall cite only two to illustrate the problem.

Marc Lienhard, of the Lutheran World Federation's Ecumenical Institute in Strasbourg, has written an illuminating account of the origin and meaning of the Leuenberg Concord of 1973, which was intended to legitimate full communion between the Lutheran and Reformed churches of Europe. Having pointed out that the new, historical-critical approach to Holy Scripture had been a major factor in producing the formula of agreement, Lienhard continued that this also produced new problems unknown in the sixteenth century, "as became apparent, for example at Amoldshain [a predecessor agreement of 1957], where it was no longer possible to connect the institution of the Lord's Supper with the night in which he was betrayed."[1] What does this mean? Simply that leading New Testament scholars do not believe that the historical Jesus actually said and did what the Gospels attribute to Him. Instead, they think, many of these things were thought up much later and were then ascribed to Him! But what possible theological or ecumenical value, let alone integrity, can a Communion agreement have, if the question of who actually established this Sacrament cannot be answered?

For my second and last example I refer, with your indulgence, to the English Dominican journal, *New Blackfriars*, for October, 1987. Here Michael Dummet, a professor of logic in the University of Oxford, takes issue with Thomas Sheehan, a well-known philosophy professor of Loyola University in Chicago. In reviewing a book by Hans Kueng in *The New York Review* for 14 June 1984, Sheehan had claimed a developing "liberal consensus" among leading Roman Catholic biblical scholars to the effect "that Jesus of Nazareth did not assert any of the divine or messianic claims the Gospels attribute to him and that he died without believing he was Christ or the Son of God." To this Dummet replied with irrefutable logic that if Jesus

> did not believe himself divine, then we have no ground to do so, and hence commit idolatry in praying to him. If he knew nothing of the Trinity, then we know nothing of the Trinity, and have no warrant whatever for supposing that there is a Trinity. If he intended to found no community, then the church has no standing and is an impostor institution.

---

1. Mark Lienhard, *Lutherisch-Reformierte Kirchengemeinschaft Heute*. Oekumenische Perspektiven Nr. 2 (Frankfurt am Main: Lembeck, Knecht, 1972), 54.

Since many well-meaning Christians have been lulled into complacency with the soothing assurance that biblical criticism involves only obscure technical squabbles among scholarly experts, I should like to cite Thomas Sheehan's conclusion from his book *The First Coming: How the Kingdom of God Became Christianity:*

> The crisis in Christianity is about its origins, its founding story, but not in the sense that its doctrines have been found to be myths (all religious doctrines are mythical) or to be totally lacking in truth (they are presumably as true, and as false, as any other decent religion's) or that they have no more meaning in the sophisticated modem world. Rather, the crisis is that at last Christianity is discovering what it always was about: not God or Christ or Jesus of Nazareth, but the endless, unresolvable mystery inscribed at the heart of being human.[2]

Such fantasies do not and cannot build the church. They destroy it. And whatever cannot build the church cannot advance genuine ecumenism either. It is not dogma, the dogma of the Holy Gospel of Christ, but the absence and the dissolution of dogma, that stands in the way of true, God-pleasing ecumenicity. And without the full authority of the divine revelation in His inscripturated Word, there are no criteria whatever, and the Gospel cannot then be distinguished from all sorts of human conceits and counterfeits.

The ecumenical dogma of the divine inspiration of Holy Scripture enshrined in the Nicene Creed's "Who spoke by the prophets," was never in dispute between our two churches. It would, in my humble opinion, be an event of enormous ecumenical significance, if that ancient consensus could be spelt out once more for our time. For the inviolate, indissoluble sacramentality of Holy Scripture as God's Word defines the divine and apostolic constitution of the church, and is therefore the very Magna Charta of all authentic ecumenical labours.

In conclusion may I greet you with some lines by Sir John Betjeman, a former English poet laureate. This poem was cited in Mr. Santamaria's last column, which appeared in *News Weekly*'s Christmas issue for 1997. The transition and application to Easter, celebrating the Church's founding Fact, is easily made:

---

2. Thomas Sheehan, *The First Coming: How the Kingdom of God Became Christianity* (New York: Random House, 1986), 226–227.

And is it true? For if it is,
No loving fingers tying strings
Around those treasured fripperies.
The sweet and silly Christmas things,
Bath salts and inexpensive scent
And hideous tie so kindly meant,
No love that in a family dwells
No caroling in frosty air,
Nor all the steeple-chasing bells
Can with this single Truth compare —
That God was Man in Palestine
And lives today in Bread and Wine.[3]

---

3. Cited in B. A. Santamaria, "Christmas . . . the mystery of faith," *News Weekly* [Australia], 13 December 1997, 24.

Chapter Twelve

WAR

Editor's note: After Marquart delivered a short paper at a conference of the International Council on Biblical Inerrancy in 1982 ("A Response to Adequacy of Language and Accommodation," in the previous volume in this series), he was invited to make a major address on the subject "War" at next such meeting, December 10–13, 1986. At this same meeting Robert Preus delivered the lead essay, "The Living God," a version of which appeared in volume one of this series.

This essay on War gives readers a glimpse into Marquart's ethical thought, in which he engaged only after the relevant doctrinal issues had been sorted out. It was originally published in Kenneth S. Kantzer, ed., Applying the Scriptures: Papers from ICBI Summit III *(Grand Rapids: Academie Books [Zondervan], 1987), 361–376. The essay appears here by permission of the Alliance of Confessing Evangelicals, which holds the copyright on ICBI materials.*

۶♦

The divine commands not to kill and to turn the other cheek are quite straightforward and not the least bit obscure. Nor is there any doubt about the deadly potential of nuclear weapons. Given this rare clarity on both the question of law and the question of fact, the case seems open and shut: the very existence of nuclear weapons, not to mention any possible use of them, is an affront to Christian morality. This perception has become practically self-evident for many of our contemporaries both inside and outside the churches. Yet its appealing simplicity is thoroughly misleading. Such plausible perceptions habitually short-circuit real moral reasoning for they are charged with the powerful, primal currents of popular culture, which in our time and place includes goodly doses of utopianism and sentimentality.[1] A valid transition from biblical teaching to the nuclear-weapons issue is, in fact, far from direct or obvious. I propose first to examine some reasons why this should be so, and then to see whether and how biblical ethics offers any guidance in respect of nuclear weapons.

---

1. Bernice Martin, "Invisible Religion, Popular Culture and Anti-nuclear Sentiment," *Unholy Warfare: The Church and the Bomb,* eds. David Martin and Peter Mullen (Oxford: Blackwell, 1983), 108–40.

BIBLICAL DISTINCTIONS

Our Lord rejects out of hand any resort to self-serving distinctions and technicalities designed to evade the clear claims of moral duty (Matt. 23:16–22). This does not mean, however, that moral distinctions as such are wrong. On the contrary, if we are to "stop judging by mere appearances, and make a right judgment" (John 7:24), moral distinctions are indispensable. Distaste for such moral "discrimination" owes more to modern cultural egalitarianism than to the Savior, who said that "from everyone who has been given much, much will be demanded" (Luke 12:48), and that on Judgment Day Sodom and Gomorrah would fare better than those who had despised the messengers of the Son of God Incarnate (Matt. 10:15). Circumstances do alter cases. It is wrong, for instance, to take one's own life (e.g., Judas). But giving it up for the sake of others is admirable not only in a military code of honor but in Christian ethics itself (John 15:13).

A most important question about every biblical command is: "To whom is this addressed?" One cannot simply add a "Go and do thou likewise" to every divine command in Scripture. So, for instance, Abraham but no one else was told to sacrifice his son. And the genocidal commands of Deuteronomy 20:16–17 were given to ancient Israel, not to us — nor to the modern Zionist state, for that matter.

It is also possible that quite opposite commands are addressed to the same persons but in different capacities or roles. Under the Pentateuch legislation, for example, murder— that is, the taking of human life by private individuals at their own discretion —was of course strictly forbidden. On the other hand, it was a public duty to impose and carry out the death penalty for a whole catalogue of capital crimes (Lev. 20). This private/public dichotomy is by no means abolished in the New Testament. As a human being, particularly as a Christian, I must love and forgive those who wrong me. Yet as a citizen, policeman, judge, juror, prison guard, or executioner, I am duty-bound to help catch, convict, punish, and sometimes even execute criminals — regardless of my personal feelings about them (Rom. 13:1–5). Pacifism risks moral incoherence by collapsing this vital distinction between private and public duty or between person and office.[2]

Important as the differences between the Old and New Testaments are, they do not amount to a moral evolution. It is not true, for instance, that Old Testament morality required "an eye for an eye" and that Christ

---

2. A valuable treatment of the issue is John Helgeland, Robert J. Daly, and J. Patout Burns, *Christians and the Military: The Early Experience* (Philadelphia: Fortress, 1985).

upgraded ethics from this primitive level by his command to turn the other cheek (Matt. 5:38–39). The contrast in Matthew 5 is not between the Old and the New Testaments but between traditional misinterpretations of the Old Testament (see Matt. 5:43) and its genuine authentic sense (Matt. 5:17). The "eye for an eye" maxim is civil, not moral law in the Old Testament (Exod. 21:24; Lev. 24:20; Deut. 19:21) and is in principle endorsed by Christ (Matt. 26:52; cf. Gen. 9:6). The basic moral law, also in the Old Testament, is not "an eye for an eye" but "Love your neighbor as yourself" (Lev. 19:18; Matt. 22:39). The Ten Commandments themselves cannot simply be identified with the moral law—that is, with the ethical duties of all men everywhere. Since the Ten Commandments in their original form (Ex. 20; Deut. 5) include elements of the ceremonial law and are embedded in the civil, theocratic code of ancient Israel, they must pass through the "filter" of their proper, New Testament interpretation (Matt. 5; Col. 2:16–17) in order to function as moral law today. Most important of all for our purposes is the radical "separation of powers" instituted by the New Testament. In Christ the provisional Old Testament theocracy is fulfilled, transcended, and abolished. The church, the true Israel (Rom 2:28; 9:6–9; Eph. 2:19–22), is truly universal now, no longer tied to or bounded by national, geographic, racial, or political particularities of any kind. Christ's kingdom is not of this world (John 18:36), and the church's weapons and warfare are entirely spiritual, not political or military (Eph. 6:10–18). Civil and spiritual authority, therefore, are strictly distinct. The church is sent to transmit to lost mankind that supernatural, divine life and salvation which "is in his Son" (1 Jn. 5:11). This transmission happens through the faith-creating gospel, including baptism and the Holy Supper (Matt. 28:19–20; Rom. 1:16; 1 Jn. 5:8). While the state, or civil society, too, is God's servant, God rules in that realm not through the revealed gospel of his grace but through reason, conscience, natural law (Rom. 2:14–15), and a coercive power based on these (Rom. 13:1–5).

Although some established churches in Europe manage to dodder on better than others, the real challenge today is to shake off entirely the fateful Constantinian state/church embrace as a "kind of collective experience of the far country in which the prodigal spent his inheritance with harlots."[3] Freed of these illusions, we may catch a glimpse again of the New Testament vision of the church as the humble bride of Christ, gloriously endowed by her divine Bridegroom with all the treasures of salvation. The caricature of the church as a moral policewoman patroling the

---

3. Fr. Robert Adolfs, quoted by Bishop Graham Leonard in *Unholy Warfare,* 192.

public square arises ultimately out of an alien abyss (Rev. 17:8). The New Testament church meets in public assembly for the solemn transaction of the salvific, evangelical "mysteries of God" (1 Cor. 4:1; 10:16–17; 11:23 ff.), not to conduct pep rallies for social causes, however worthy.

The Savior himself refused to act as arbiter of social justice (Luke 12:14) and solved a moral dilemma about controversial taxes by differentiating sharply between God and Caesar (Matt. 22:21). As the promised messianic King he offered liberation from sin, death, and hell. Preferring something more practical, official Jerusalem got the crowds to shout instead for the Liberation Front terrorist Barabbas (Matt. 27:21). The same political frenzy agitates contemporary churches as they huff and puff against social, military, economic, nuclear, and all other temporal oppressions.[4] The agendas of modern church conventions, ever anxious to be "relevant," compete with the United Nations Organization in concerning themselves with everything from Afghanistan to Zambia.[5] The apostolic church's agenda in Acts 15 seems modest, even petty, by comparison. Ignoring all the grave social ills then bedeviling the Roman Empire, the Jerusalem Council debated and settled the implications of the gospel for circumcision and Jewish dietary regulation! Concentrating all its energies on the alone-saving gospel of Christ (Gal. 1), the apostolic church had not yet made the category mistake which seemed so self-evident to the World Council of Churches in Amsterdam (1948) when it spoke in the report on "The Church and the Disorder of Society" of "the responsible society" as "the goal for which the churches in all lands must work."

The church's marching orders are to make disciples of all nations by baptism and Christian instruction (Matt. 28:19–20). As the reference to baptism shows, the church's teaching function is controlled entirely by her missionary command. There is no God-given basis for civics lessons on the side. The object of the church's teaching mission is not general uplift but that "repentance and forgiveness of sins [be] preached in his name to all nations, beginning at Jerusalem" (Luke 24:47). States can neither repent nor believe nor receive forgiveness; nor, thank Heaven, are they capable of eternal life. Therefore, while the church indeed addresses all mankind with the message of God's judgment against sin and his mercy in Christ, the church as church has nothing at all to say to any state as

---

4. Edward Norman, *Christianity and the World Order* (Oxford: Oxford University Press, 1979).

5. For a perspective discussion of this fatal "relevance," see James Turner, *Without God, Without: The Origins of Unbelief in America* (Baltimore: Johns Hopkins University Press, 1985).

state. That legally incorporated bodies called "churches" may make use of their civil and social standing to express some public concerns of their members as citizens is another matter altogether and has no direct basis in the church's mission as such. The concerted action of Christians as citizens should not be called even a "secondary" duty or function of the church, as if Christ had said: "My kingdom is not *primarily* of this world."

Has Christian ethics then any guidance at all to offer the Christian citizen or public official? Yes, of course it has. But in light of the foregoing we can now appreciate the full import of the question with which we began: "To whom is this addressed?" If the nuclear-weapons discussion among Christians is to be rescued from the flaccid moral murkiness in which at present it largely flounders, then some such delimiting preliminaries as the following must be nailed down first:

1. The Bible is not a handbook for all and sundry on good behavior, but it is the book about Jesus Christ (Luke 24:44–45; John 5:39).

2. To unbelievers and believers alike the church preaches the law in order that the knowledge of sin (Rom. 3:19–20; 7:7) might prepare the way for the gospel of the Savior.

3. To Christian believers the church explains the law also as a guide — though not the motive power (Rom. 12:1) — for the good works which flow out of a genuine life in Christ and which cannot exist apart from him (John 15). Biblical ethics addresses Christians.

4. To unbelievers the church has in principle nothing to say except: "Repent and believe the gospel." Apart from this evangelical mission the church has no warrant to prescribe the behavior of non-Christians (1 Cor. 5:12), be they government officials, basketball players, or candlestick makers.

5. Since the Old Testament theocracy has been abolished, no country today is or can be in the special position of ancient Israel. States and civil societies are to be ruled not with the written Word of God —which offers no divine blueprint of statecraft— but with the justice and common sense resting on natural law (Rom. 2:14–15; 13:1–5).

6. While there are Christian politicians, farmers, chemists, and the like, there is no such thing as Christian politics, biblical farming, or evangelical chemistry. Laws can be just or unjust, furrows can be straight or crooked, and laboratory procedures can be competent or incompetent, but it is a category mistake to replace such

terms with the words "Christian" or "non-Christian." Civil society is to be "humanized" not "Christianized."

7. Christians must be taught that it is their duty to employ also their political, social, and economic power and influence in the best interests of their fellow human beings. But how such goals are best implemented in practice, i.e., prudential judgment, must be left to the conscience of individual Christians themselves in their various callings. Ministers of the Word exceed their authority and competence when they make pronouncements beyond the scope of the written Word of God. As citizens of course they are entitled to their own opinions like everyone else.

NUCLEAR WEAPONS: MORAL DIMENSIONS

One's first impulse is to say that Christian ethics is opposed to all weapons. Such a pronouncement, however, would reflect secular sentimentality more than Christian morality. Optimistic Utopians (including Marxists) see evil as residing not in human nature but in unjust systems, institutions, and structures, which, when smashed, will release humanity's native goodness. Also, contemporary cultural relativism is loath to speak of "good" and "evil" in relation to "alternative lifestyles." It is easier to focus on symptoms and to crusade against "violence," guns, and bombs generally. Thus there arises the utterly amoral perception that guns in the hands of the police and in the hands of the criminal "community" are somehow equivalent. Christianity, on the other hand, knows that good and evil reside not in things but in persons — that is, in the wills of moral agents. Biblical ethics therefore focuses on the moral nature of purposes and actions, not on weapons as such, which are simply a function of a morally neutral technology. Barring devices designed for senseless cruelty (e.g., dumdum bullets), modern weapons are inherently no worse than swords and spears. And once it is admitted that killing is ethically permissible in some circumstances, then a weapon's capacity for killing more people does not in and of itself render it immoral. Otherwise, jumbo-jets would be much more immoral than oxcarts because they place many more lives at risk.

Paradoxically, biblical ethics has less to say about nuclear bombs than about swords, and this not for the trivial reason that bombs are only a recent invention. The point is rather that unlike swords, nuclear bombs are, for the present at least, the prerogative of states, not of private individuals. Nuclear weapons thus virtually by definition comply with one of the traditional criteria of a just war — namely, that it is to be started and prosecuted by lawful authority and not at the whim of private persons. The main point of biblical ethics concerning swords is that private individuals should not wield them (Gen. 9:6). States, on the other hand, must wield the sword (Rom. 13:4), and this largely to insure that individuals do not. When the state's sword-bearers are Christians, they must, of course, be motivated by love and therefore seek genuine justice, mitigate severity, protect the weak, and the like. But there is no specifically Christian way of governing a state or of fighting a war.

The crux of the nuclear-weapons issue today is not nuclear war but nuclear deterrence. No one advocates nuclear war. The main question is whether, given the danger of nuclear war, it is ethically acceptable to prevent nuclear war by threatening potential nuclear aggressors with nuclear retaliation. (I accept the distinction urged in this connection by the Anglican Bishop of London, Graham Leonard, between the morally acceptable and the morally good.[6] The latter sounds too much like approving something as ideal. In the real world statesmen often face non-ideal options, *e.g.*, terrorists holding hostages. The operative moral principle here is to minimize harm and evil, not to expound abstractly good non-options.)

Most American churches which have spoken to the issue grudgingly allow deterrence,[7] the Roman Catholic bishops more grudgingly than their West European counterparts.[8] The World Council of Churches, with Iron Curtain participation, takes the purist view that nuclear deterrence "is to be rejected as morally unacceptable and as incapable of safeguarding peace and security in the long term."[9]

The usual argument against the morality of deterrence is that if it is wrong to do something, then it is also wrong to threaten to do it. Although this sounds plausible in the abstract, it fails to take account of the fact that if injustice or bloodshed can be averted by a judicious use of bluff, then such bluffing is the morally indicated policy. In any case the alleged principle is refuted by a celebrated biblical counterexample: King Solomon's threat to cut a baby in half could not have been carried out ethically. But since the threat issued happily in justice being done, it has

---

6. Graham Leonard, "The Morality of Nuclear Deterrence," *Unholy Warfare*, 186. This of course is the old distinction between the good and the right.
7. Donald L. Davidson, *Nuclear Weapons and the American Churches: Ethical Positions on Modern Warfare* (Boulder, CO: Westview, 1983), 203–4 and passim.
8. At least the French and the German bishops were much more concerned with justice.
9. Paul Abrecht and Ninan Koshy, eds., *Before It's Too Late: The Challenge of Nuclear Disarmament* (Geneva: World Council of Churches, 1983), 384.

always been taken as evidence that Solomon "had wisdom from God to administer justice" (1 Kings 3:28 [NIV]). Thus "wisdom is proved right by her actions" (Matt. 11:19).

What is remarkable about the whole case against nuclear deterrence is that it is short on moral argument and long on political and ideological judgments — surely not what one would expect from churches. How does the WCC's central committee know, for instance, that nuclear deterrence is "incapable of safeguarding peace and security in the long term" and that its own prescriptions, such as renunciation of the "first use" option and disarmament efforts, including "unilateral initiatives leading to the relaxation of tensions and building of mutual confidence," are likely to have the desired effects? Most of the ecclesiastical pronouncements, in fact, seem to assume that disarmament is the basic key to peace. Edward Norman put it very charitably when he pointed out that Christian leaders "tend to amateurism" in the political realm and "are permanently liable to absorb seemingly any account of world conditions which exploits their generosity."[10]

The fact is, of course, that responsible decisions about how to keep World War III at bay involve many hard questions about military, historical, technological, political, and other matters about which it is simply inappropriate for churches to pontificate. Let the churches tell their statesmen and citizen members that it is their duty to prevent nuclear war if possible. But the statesmen and citizens must decide for themselves, in light of the best information available to them, what actual policies can most realistically be expected to achieve the desired results. It is in fact arrogant and unethical to suggest that those who on prudential grounds favor disarmament as the best way to avoid war are for peace, while those who seek the same end by means of deterrence are for war.

It is refreshing therefore to see books like Jerram Barrs's *Who Are the Peacemakers?* (1983) and the splendid symposium by Francis Schaeffer, Vladimir Bukovsky, and James Hitchcock entitled *Who Is For Peace?* (1983). These very titles challenge the disarmament advocates' exclusive claims to the "peace" banner. Both Barrs and Schaeffer show that biblical morality requires the responsible use of force in the civil realm and that to shrink from this use is to abandon the weak to the tender mercies of the Hitlers and Stalins of this world. Love for the neighbor requires our best efforts in his behalf against his oppressors.

Schaeffer quotes Jacques Ellul to the effect that in the era leading up to World War II "the Christians, full of good intentions, were thinking only

---

10. Norman, 18–19.

of peace and were loudly proclaiming pacifism! In matters of that kind, Christian good intentions are often disastrous."[11] No less an authority on strategic analysis than Captain Basil Liddell Hart has concluded that one of the main causes of World War II was the long period of Western complacency which encouraged Hitler's aggressiveness.[12] Korea and the Falklands provide perhaps even clearer examples of wars brought about directly by a perceived unwillingness to defend the areas in question. On January 12, 1950, United States Secretary of State Dean Acheson had given a speech in which he had forgotten to mention Korea in defining the American defense perimeter. Later Acheson recalled

> that he had actually been rebuked by the then Soviet Ambassador to the UN for delivering a speech which permitted the Soviet Union to deduce that Korea did not matter to the United States, then changing his mind and, by reason of this blunder, involving both nations in a war which neither wanted.[13]

Likewise, Argentina's ex-President Galtieri has stated that Argentina would never have attacked the Falkland Islands had a minimal deterrent force there made clear Britain's intention to defend the Falklands.[14]

I am not suggesting that the World Council of Churches, having taken to heart these lessons, should now reverse itself and urge nuclear deterrence as the best way to avoid nuclear war. The point is rather that churches are not competent to determine just what sort of measures are most likely to prevent war. Nor is that the function of biblical ethics. That is why it would have been better, in my view, had Barrs's valuable little book mentioned above been subtitled "The Moral Deterrence." There simply is no "Christian case" either for or against deterrence. While the Christian citizen will be motivated differently from his non-Christian neighbor, he will reason about nuclear deterrence very much like any other person of good will and common sense.

Ethics supplies the principles, but valid applications depend on correct and realistic perceptions of the facts of the case. In this respect ethics is like a computer: put garbage in, and you get garbage out. The finest principles can, if the facts are misread, result in gross miscarriages of justice.

---

11. Francis Schaeffer, Vladimir Bukovsky, and James Hitchcock, *Who Is for Peace?* (New York: Thomas Nelson, 1983), p. 28.
12. *News Weekly* (Australia), 12 January 1983, 6.
13. Ibid.
14. Ibid., 12.

It is therefore the Christian statesman's supreme ethical duty to know as many of the relevant facts as well as he possibly can. It would be an unethical and fanatical illusion on his part to believe that his Christian faith itself provides him with privileged information about statecraft or that his good Christian intentions excuse him from the rigors of attaining competent understanding. Biblical ethics does not seek to impose on the conscience of the Christian citizen or statesman a set of ready-made case law, or of one-dimensional idealisms. Instead it seeks to discipline that conscience to pursue the freedom and responsibility innate in the utmost sobriety and realism, for the neighbor's need requires nothing less. (Given the biblical realism about human sin, it is strange to read in Chaplain [Major] Davidson's rather fair analysis of the major American churches' attitudes to nuclear weapons that, unlike governments, "Churches tend to be optimistic in their views of human nature".)[15]

In this context the constant clamor for "negotiations" as an alternative to effective weapons needs to be seen as spurious — that is, pseudo-ethical. Diplomacy has been defined as the art of saying "nice doggie" while one is reaching for a stick. It is fatuous to suggest that it is the Christian diplomat's duty to throw away his stick in order to say "nice doggie" more sincerely! Negotiations and force are not alternatives in the sense that the former could work by itself without the latter. Bishop Leonard provides a good discussion of the point and states:

> Not only does the power remain [in negotiations], even if hid in the velvet glove. It may be that negotiation has only become possible because the existence of that power has previously been made evident in an exemplary and limited way.[16]

It might be thought that the nuclear-arms discussion is so sobering that the participants in this discussion need not reality therapy but a strengthening of their ideals. It is useful, therefore, to remind ourselves of just what is being urged by some in the name of Christian duty. The following sentences are taken from a contribution to a recent British symposium by Lord MacLeod (The Very Reverend Doctor George Fielden MacLeod, M.C.):

> Is the Christian Church never to trust her enemy? Is Christ's commandment that we must trust them something for us to disregard? . . . I trust

---

15. Davidson, 186.
16. Leonard, *Unholy Warfare*, 189.

Russia. . . . There is sufficient evidence of the constancy with which they
have tried to convince America and the West of their efforts to prove the
sincerity of their desire for peace.[17]

Lord MacLeod gives a glowing report of the 1982 "World Conference:
Religious Workers for Saving the Sacred Gift of Life from Nuclear
Tragedy" in Moscow, in which he participated. "Five hundred and ninety
eminent representatives of Buddhism, Christianity, Hinduism, Islam,
Judaism, Sikhism, Shintoism and Zoroastrianism met to discuss" how
to erect "an insurmountable barrier on the road to nuclear war." He
concludes, "Is it conceivable that all this could take place in Moscow if
the hierarchy [sic] was secretly opposed to peace and disarmament? No!"

Few would articulate this position in as clear-headed and candid a
manner as did Lord MacLeod. Similar assumptions, however, influence
the whole discussion in various degrees. The moral duty of geopolitical
sobriety requires Christian citizens, before endorsing naive "peace" efforts, to assess the strategic aims of the Soviet Union. How do the Soviets
themselves understand "peaceful coexistence," and how do they regard
treaties and international law?[18] What are the implications of the Soviet
Strategic Plan and its "aim of 'global peace' following final Soviet victory," as described in detail by the former chief-of-staff of the Czech Communist minister of defense?[19] Is it true, as former Soviet U.N. diplomat
Arkady N. Schevchenko writes, that "There is no disagreement among
Soviet leaders — political or military, young or old — as far as their ultimate goals are concerned"?[20] And not only citizens but church leaders
must prick up their ears at the report that Boris Ponomaryov himself, an
alternate member of the Politburo and chief orchestrator of "peace" cam-
paigns for the Soviet Union globally, "urged Communist parties to work
more closely with religious organizations."[21] This took place a few months
before Lord MacLeod's antinuclear "peace" conference in Moscow.

17. Lord MacLeod, "But What About Russia?" *Unholy Warfare*, 224.
18. Bernard A. Ramundo, *Peaceful Coexistence: International Law in the Building of Communism* (Baltimore: Johns Hopkins Press, 1967).
19. Jan Sejna, *We Will Bury You* (London: Sidgwick and Jackson, 1982), 103. For the classic Red Chinese strategic analysis see Lin Piao, "Long Live the Victory of People's War!" *Peking Review* (3 September 1965), 9–30.
20. Arkady N. Schevchenko, *Breaking with Moscow* (New York: Knopf, 1985), 369.
21. Michael Binyon *The Times* [London], 8 November 1981, cited in B. A. Santa-maria, "Fighting for Peace — Moscow Style," *News Weekly*, 28 April 1982.

The moral justification of deterrence policies, then, must rest largely on considerations of the prudential, strategic sort. And the proper forum for that sort of discussion is not the church but the political arena. This leaves unsettled the question whether Christians could ever regard the actual use of nuclear weapons as morally acceptable. Although the mind boggles at the potential for destruction, it would be irresponsible to strike an ostrich pose and pretend that nuclear war is simply unthinkable.

We may begin with an observation by Bishop Leonard. He notes that just when the general trend is to recognize ever fewer moral absolutes, the prohibition of nuclear weapons is being made into such an unqualified moral absolute. This simply sweeps aside the competing moral claims of other legitimate human values, such as liberty, truth, and human dignity. Bishop Leonard continues:

> It is, I believe, not consistent with the moral nature of man to proclaim one principle of such moral rigidity that these other fundamental moral issues become secondary. Nor do I believe that for a Christian who believes that man is made for eternal communion with the living God who is just and holy can the principle of survival take precedence over all other moral claims.[22]

If there were, as pacifists maintain there is, one single biblical maxim directly applicable to war and, therefore, to nuclear war, the case would be simple. But there is no such single directly applicable maxim. To guide Christian office-bearers in their civil duties, the Christian love ethic must be "refracted" through a complex grid of social and political interdependences. Human goods and moral obligations are many and various, and their claims often appear in the hurly-burly of life in a fallen world to compete in such a way that while self-sacrificing love for the neighbor is always the overarching duty, the exact apportionment of this duty among conflicting claims and claimants is by no means always clear. Simplistic panaceas like "nonviolence," therefore, are bound to be false. As Paul Ramsey put it, "Jesus did not teach that his disciples should lift up the face of another oppressed man to be struck again on the other cheek."[23] Pacifism and holy war are simply two sides of the same false coin, that of the confusion of the church with civil society. (Lord MacLeod's impres-

22. *Unholy Warfare,* 187–88.
23. Paul Ramsey, "The Case for Making 'Just War' Possible," in John C. Bennett, ed., *Nuclear Weapons and the Conflict of Conscience* (New York: Scribner, 1962), 145.

sion, quoted above, that the "Christian Church" has "Christ's command-ment that we must trust" the communist enemy, goes well beyond the common confusion in forgetting that not even within the church itself is it the duty of shepherds to bring up their lambs to trust wolves [John 10:12].)

Since neither holy war nor holy peace is an authentic biblical directive for politics, what is left? What is left is precisely the traditional just-war doctrine. Adapted by Saint Augustine and others from pre-Christian con-siderations of natural justice, the just-war concept establishes constraints which decent people must observe in waging war. It must be noted, how-ever, that these moral limitations on war, as Paul Ramsey has said so well,

> arose not from autonomous natural reason asserting its sovereignty over determinations of right and wrong (and threatening to lead Christian faith and love, which are and should be free, into bondage to alien principles), but from a quite humble moral reason subjecting itself to the sovereignty of God and the Lordship of Christ, as Christian men felt themselves im-pelled out of love to justify war and by love severely to limit war.[24]

Given this nature of the just-war doctrine refracted through many-sid-ed civil obligation, and given that in the realm of civil power love expresses itself as justice, it is clear that the just-war "doctrine" is not a singular mea-suring rod but a bundle of criteria with variable relative weightings. For instance, in the past much was made of the necessity of a formal declara-tion of war—something which in some imaginable circumstances, given modern military technology, might well be an unaffordable luxury. But surely a formal declaration of war cannot as a criterion of ethical warfare have the same weight as, for instance, the importance of avoiding unnec-essary civilian casualties. Just-war doctrine then is not a rigid monolith, but a mosaic taking into account several different goods. It is even more important not to treat the just-war criteria as if they were pedantic bu-reaucratic regulations or scholastic subtleties. Legality, when separated from morality, decays into legalism, as Solzhenitsyn reminded us in his Harvard speech.[25] And nothing is more unjust than a legalistic insistence

---

24. Paul Ramsey, *War and the Christian Conscience* (Duke University Press, 1961), 59, quoted in Colin Fletcher, *Banning the Bomb? An Argument from the "Just War" Position* (Bramcote, Notts.: Grove, 1982), 13–14.

25. A. Solzhenitsyn, *A World Split Apart* (New York: Harper and Row, 1978), 15–19.

on the letter of the law against its spirit. To pursue justice is to seek real equity—not abstract formalisms—and this cannot be done without attending to those significant moral features and their unique "mix," which distinguish one case from another.

Hard cases make bad law, and nuclear war is so hard that many take it to be beyond all law, including the law of just war. Paul Ramsey in particular is noted for having argued credibly for some, strictly limited, resort to nuclear weapons as justifiable within the just war framework.[26] It cannot be our purpose here to review the several just war criteria in detail. Some concluding observations may be in order, however, regarding the two criteria — (1) discriminating combatants from noncombatants and (2) proportionality — which are widely held to prohibit the use of any nuclear weapons outright.

Discrimination between combatants and noncombatants rests ultimately on the moral principle that not even lawful authorities have the right to punish the innocent (Exod. 23:7; Rom. 13:3). In war, of course, it is usually not possible to prevent all civilian deaths. The moral requirement means not that civilian casualties must be avoided at all costs — else even peacetime automobile traffic would have to be forbidden since a statistically predictable number of people die every week in road mishaps — but the destruction of civilians may not be directly intended. Civilian deaths may occur as a foreseen and unavoidable consequence of justified attacks on military targets. This means that (1) it is immoral to attack civilian populations even with "conventional" bombs, and (2) it may be moral to attack an enemy's nuclear arsenals, say, with minimum all-out weapons like the neutron bomb.

Just war doctrine therefore condemns obliteration bombing like that of Dresden in World War II, in which perhaps more people died than in Hiroshima. Hiroshima, however, was the military headquarters for southern Japan and may therefore be regarded as a proper military target. This cannot be said about Nagasaki, however, which was bombed because the primary target, Kokura, happened to be covered by clouds on August 9, 1945. The official British observer of the Nagasaki bombing, Group Captain Leonard Cheshire, VC, makes a persuasive case that this second bombing was justified and, indeed, that the scourge of world war "was buried there forever."[27] The action saved millions of lives, both Japanese

---

26. See the good historical overview in Davidson, 1–67.
27. Leonard Cheshire, "How the Bomb Brought Peace," *The Sunday Times*, 4 August 1985.

and American, which would have been lost had the war continued, and was necessary to break the Japanese war cabinet's five-to-one determination, even after Hiroshima, to continue the war. Under just war doctrine, however, saving many combatants' lives by directly and deliberately killing fewer non-combatants is not as such defensible and smacks rather of terrorism. The same would be true of massive retaliatory obliterations of civilian populations, as envisioned in the old policy of "Mutual Assured Destruction." It is virtually certain, however, that Hiroshima and Nagasaki could happen only because Japan lacked the capability of nuclear retaliation against, say, San Francisco and Kansas City.

On the other hand, the present counter-force rather than counter-people nuclear strategy would be defensible in just war terms if the weapons and target selection were designed only to cripple the enemy's military capabilities while minimizing his civilian losses. What is odd is that some Christian spokesmen actually prefer "Mutual Assured Destruction" to the new emphasis on limited weapons and strategies.[28] Given that "slogans and [e]motive imagery are at times substituted for factual data"[29] by churchmen in this context, Christian ethicists cannot be indifferent to the possibility that should the slogans and emotive imagery succeed in creating a public mood hostile to the development of effective nuclear weapons and defense strategies, the result may well be nuclear war. That is one implication of the chilling scenario projected by the "father" of the neutron bomb, physicist Sam Cohen,[30] on the basis of the known reliance of Soviet military doctrine on surprise, deception, and a massive first strike.[31]

Finally, there is the principle of proportionality: that the evil of a war must not outweigh the good which can reasonably be expected from it. This principle of weighing anticipated benefits and damages is basic to the very idea of equity but is very difficult to apply because, like apples and oranges, different public goods are difficult to compare. (For example, if one of two major presidential contenders took a good stand on abortion but advocated disastrous policies on national security, while the other was good on national security but wrong on abortion, for whom would it be the conscientious Christian citizen's duty to vote?) The church's real task

---

28. Davidson, 121–22.
29. Ibid., 142.
30. Sam Cohen, *We Can Prevent World War III* (Ottawa, Ill.: Jameson, 1985).
31. Viktor Suvorov, *Inside the Soviet Army* (New York: Macmillan, 1982), *Inside Soviet Military Intelligence* (New York: Macmillan, 1984).

here is to form good Christian consciences in those who will later face moral dilemmas but not to bind their consciences to particular solutions without a clear Word of God. Ethicists should not rush to where conscientious judges and generals fear to tread. By the same token, of course, if a Christian citizen is convinced that his government's directives to him are morally wrong, he must obey God rather than men (Acts 4:19; 5:29).

Nuclear pacifists argue that nothing, not even Soviet domination, could be worse than nuclear war itself and that such war must therefore be avoided at all costs. This may well be true, but it cannot be assumed in advance without a tough-minded moral appraisal of many complex human factors. A disturbing feature of much supposedly Christian sentiment on this subject is the unseemly haste with which all moral issues are simply smothered under what looks like an atavistic obsession with physical survival. In a veritable zoo of obscene mockeries of the Creator's purposes, is The Bomb really convincing as the *summum malum?* The pitiless official indifference of Western Christendom to the unspeakable torments of the Marxist inferno, and the compulsive anxiety to stifle the cries of the oppressed lest they irritate the oppressors and prevent "relaxation of tensions," suggest not Christian compassion and morality as the real engines of nuclear "peacemaking" but rather the essentially secular urgencies of self-indulgence. And clearly something other than morality is at work when Stalinist international socialism is, however, subtly, painted as ethically superior to Hitlerite national socialism.[32] Apart from a serious moral misjudgment of communism, based perhaps on wishful thinking, it is difficult to account for the hostility of many Western churchmen toward their own governments, combined with the same churchmen's relatively benign evaluation of Soviet policies and intentions.[33]

The "even-handedness" which treats the West and the Soviets as moral equals because both are guilty of ultimate evil in possessing nuclear weapons rests on a shallow, bureaucratic "conflict management techniques" model. A genuinely ethical model would, with Solzhenitsyn, assert the radical moral asymmetry of the two systems without in the least glossing over the serious flaws in Western society.[34] It is not only political but moral nonsense to play "global village" while shutting one's eyes to all evi-

---

32. "But the changes in the Soviet Union may lead us to judge that it is in the long term not as absolutely destructive of all values as Nazism was with its gas chambers. . ." (Bennett, ed., 117).
33. Davidson, 142, 182–83, passim.
34. See A. Solzhenitsyn, *A World Split Apart.*

dence suggesting that half the "village" is an armed concentration camp scheming to subdue the rest.

Especially if one takes into account the hopes and aspirations of the millions of innocent victims languishing in the Gulag,[35] it is by no means self-evident, under the principle of proportionality, that the defense of Western civilization's values of freedom, justice, and human dignity—however flawed, necessarily, in application by and to sinful human beings—is not worth the risk even of nuclear war as a last resort. Much depends on whether one holds to Bertrand Russell's "Better Red than Dead," or to Solzhenitsyn's reply: "Better to be dead than a scoundrel. In this horrible expression of Bertrand Russell's there is an absence of all moral criteria."[36]

Not to fear those who can kill only the body is a prime imperative of biblical ethics (Luke 12:4). What of the cosmic fear of the grand medieval *dies irae?*

> Day of wrath, O day of mourning!
> See fulfilled the prophet's warning.
> Heaven and earth in ashes burning.

Physical destruction is not the worst of it:

> Oh, what fear man's bosom rendeth
> When from heaven the Judge descendeth
> On whose sentence all dependeth!

Here no ethics, not even biblical ethics, can help, but only the biblical evangel: "Thanks be to God! He gives us the victory through our Lord Jesus Christ"! (1 Cor. 15:57 [NIV])

---

35. See Julius Epstein, Operation Keelhaul: *The Story of Forced Repatriation* (Old Greenwich: Devin-Adair, 1973), for an insight into the attitude of many Soviet citizens toward their regime. And among South East Asian refugees today hardly anyone would support the view that the present "peace" in their countries is preferable to the Vietnam War, which so distressed the Western intelligentsia.

36. A. Solzhenitsyn, *Warning to the West* (New York: Farrar, Straus, and Giroux, 1976), 119.

Chapter Thirteen

ABORTION AND LUTHER'S TWO KINGDOMS THEOLOGY

Editor's note: Marquart took abortion quite seriously indeed. No attempt to represent his interests and his efforts could afford to omit this subject. For years, while teaching in Fort Wayne, he also took on the chairmanship of the Allen County Right to Life organization. This previously unpublished essay, delivered at Concordia University Wisconsin in 2002 and edited for the present volume, sums up a great deal of his thinking on abortion. As the title indicates, this piece also deals with Luther's theology of "two kingdoms," a subject of perennial importance.

❧

WHAT IS MEANT BY THE "TWO KINGDOMS"?

William Barclay (1971) made the astonishing claim that "Luther's ethic of church and state was the greatest disaster in all the history of ethics, for it opened the way for a kind of Christianity which allowed the state to do terrible things. . . ." (188). Indeed, this two-realms ethic ultimately "allowed Hitler to come to power and begat Belsen and Dachau" (187). This judgment essentially repeats the 1945 war-time hysteria of P. Wiener, "a third-rate pamphleteer" (Stephenson, 321), who described Luther as "Hitler's spiritual ancestor."

These sorts of allegations about the two-realms theology really have in view not Luther's actual teachings, but the pathology of so-called "Lutheran" churches, exhibiting the deadly effects of four centuries of church-state embrace. That embrace resulted in a nearly total spineless-ness — quite contrary to the real intent of the Two Realms doctrine. Take for example the sycophancy of the "Ansbach Proposal," the supposedly Lutheran response to the Barmen Declaration of 1934:

> . . . as faithful Christians we give thanks to God the Lord for bestowing the Führer (i.e. Adolf Hitler) as "a pious and faithful chief of state" upon our people in their time of need, just as we thank God for desiring to grant us "good government," a government with "discipline and honor," in the form of the National-Socialist state.

For this reason, we recognize that we are held responsible before God to assist the Führer in his work through our respective vocations and professions. (Hertz, 190–191)

It is this sort of self-confessed bankruptcy which has given the Two Realms doctrine its bad name. The real Luther is very different. Let us start with a possibly surprising passage, from Luther's 1538 Preface to the *Smalcald Articles*, designed for presentation to the Council convoked by Pope Paul III:

In addition to such necessary concerns of the church, there are also countless important matters in worldly affairs that need improvement. There is disunity among the princes and the estates. Greed and usury have burst in like a great flood and have attained a semblance of legality. Wantonness, lewdness, extravagant dress, gluttony, gambling, conspicuous consumption with all kinds of vice and wickedness, disobedience — of subjects, servants, laborers — extortion by all the artisans and the peasants (who can list everything?) have so gained the upper hand that a person could not set things right again with ten councils and twenty imperial diets. If participants in the council were to deal with the chief concerns in the spiritual and secular estates that are opposed to God, then their hands would be so full that they would forget all about the child's games and fool's play of long robes, great tonsures, broad cinctures, bishop's and cardinal's hats, crosiers, and similar clowning around. If we had already been following God's command and precept in the spiritual and secular estates, then we would have found the spare time to reform food, vestments, tonsures, and chasubles. But if we swallow such camels and strain out gnats or let logs stand and dispute about specks, then we might just as well be satisfied with such a council.

I, therefore, have provided only a few articles, because in any case we already have received from God so many mandates to carry out in the church, in the government, and in the home that we can never fulfill them. (K-W, 299–300)

Moral issues in "worldly affairs," "secular estates," and "mandates" for "government" — are these really proper subjects for consideration at an ecclesiastical council or synod, according to Luther? Yes, because the distinction between the two realms does not at all amount to the same thing as the American principle of the separation of church and state. Distinction remains one thing, separation another!

Yet this does not mean that the distinction between the two realms and the separation of church and state stand in conflict with each other.

On the contrary, the Lutheran distinction turns out much more compatible with the American separation of church and state than with the traditional European mingling of them. Likewise, given the multi-cultural American setting, the clear distinction between spiritual and political realms is by far the most realistic and promising account of the relations that ought to obtain between Christians or churches on the one hand and society or the general public on the other.

One of the finest brief treatments of Luther's thought to this point is John Stephenson's 1981 piece in the *Scottish Journal of Theology*. Stephenson points out that the term "two kingdoms" can mean two quite different things. First, it can mean the contrast between the realms of good and evil, God and Satan. That was the great duality stressed in St. Augustine's classic *City of God*, and sometimes it was what Luther meant by the term. However, what he usually meant by the "Two Kingdoms" is something else, namely, the two realms or governments by which *God* rules His world. He has a spiritual rule or government by which He distributes life and salvation through preaching and the sacraments, then He has also a temporal, political rule (Rom. 13:4) through which He maintains basic order even among fallen mankind by means of law, reason, and force. Stephenson notes incisively that Luther's recognition of divine benevolence behind the institution of the state did not lead him to utopian fantasies:

> The business of government at all levels is to patch up and preserve a non-ideal reality, and were its task to be compared with that of the modern hospital, then it might more properly be likened to the casualty department than to that of plastic surgery. (324)

Without forcible constraints, sinful humanity cannot be kept in order. Pacifist sentimentalities make for fatuous illusions:

> To rule the world with the gospel would ... be like a shepherd putting wolves, lions, eagles and sheep all together in the same fold. In blissful naivete the shepherd bids these creatures of disparate temperament enjoy their fodder in peace unhindered by the coercion of dogs or clubs. The sheep, surmises the Reformer, will indeed follow the ways of peace, but not for long. (324–325)

The *Augsburg Confession* itself concludes that

> one should not mix or confuse the two authorities, the spiritual and the secular. For spiritual power has its command to preach the gospel and to

administer the sacraments. It should not invade an alien office. It should not set up and depose kings. It should not annul or disrupt secular law and obedience to political authority. It should not make or prescribe laws for the secular power concerning secular affairs. . . .

In this way our people distinguish the offices of the two authorities and powers and direct that both be honored as the highest gifts of God on earth. (AC XXVIII 12–13, 18; K-W, 92)

But this does not mean unconditional obedience to the human representatives of either power. Ministers of the Gospel are bound to the divine Scriptures as the revealed Word of God. And the state may not command violations of the Moral Law. "But if a command of the political authority cannot be followed without sin, one must obey God rather than any human being (Acts 5[:29])" (AC XVI 7; K-W, 50). Luther says the same:

> Should it transpire, as is in fact often the case, that secular authority . . . should try to persuade a subject to act contrary to God's commands or to prevent him from keeping them, then his obedience is at an end and his duty is abrogated. We must here echo St. Peter's statement to the Jewish rulers: "We must obey God more than men." (Stephenson, 332, quoting WA 6, 265)

In a 1542 letter, Luther urges the soldier who finds himself trapped in an unjust war to "run . . . from the field [and] save his soul" (WA Br 10, 36).

Of course, Luther did not invent the distinction between the two powers or "kingdoms." It is clearly taught in the New Testament itself. Our Lord bids us "render unto Caesar the things that are Caesar's, and unto God the things that are God's" (Matt. 22:21). He confesses before Pontius Pilate: "My Kingdom is not of this world" (John 18:36). Accordingly, the first Christian Council (Acts 15) occupied itself not with the social and political problems of the decaying Roman Empire but only with theological issues that needed to be settled within the church. The integrity of the Gospel was at stake. These matters would have struck a secular reporter as simply trivial.

The strict differentiation between spiritual and temporal power in fact distinguishes Christianity from the other so-called "religions of the Book," Judaism and Islam. Both of the latter are essentially theocratic, that is, they mingle religion and politics in principle. On the other hand, when Christians have done so — e.g., in the Inquisition — they have acted in flagrant violation of their own deepest principles. The so-called "Lutheran" two-kingdoms distinction abides as part and parcel of consistent

Christianity. It ultimately forms but an aspect of the all-important differentiation between Law and Gospel, which is the real key to a proper understanding of Holy Scripture.

Probably the most controversial feature of the two-realms distinction is the idea that the state must be governed by reason and common sense, not by the Bible. Thus, for instance, Francis Pieper wrote in his *Christian Dogmatics:* "the State cannot and should not be ruled with the Word of God, but should be organized and ruled according to natural reason (common sense)" (Pieper, 418). But this is anathema to "Christian Reconstructionists," for example, who maintain: "The Bible, the whole Bible, is our final standard for every area of life. Everything is under Christ's Lordship" (DeMar, 22). Such biblicistic sentiments are probably widespread among the so-called "Religious Right," yet liberals and leftists of all descriptions have been more successful still in imposing their views in the name of religion. Thus the whole World Council of Churches, at its founding meeting in 1948, accepted the principle that the "responsible society of which we have spoken represents . . . the goal for which the churches in all lands must work. . . ." (World Council of Churches, 205).

In his 1978 BBC Reith Lectures on *Christianity and the World Order,* Dr. Edward Norman, a historian in the University of Cambridge severely criticised the political activism of the churches. He said that in politics church leaders "tend to amateurism" and "are permanently liable to absorb seemingly any account of world conditions which exploits their generosity" (18–19). The tragedy is, he said, that the real divisions among Christians to-day are not over truth and doctrine, "but over sharply defined political beliefs" (58). Indeed, the preoccupation with "the just society has shifted the whole centre of Christianity, so that it is now becoming defined in terms of precise political morality" (59). This has led to ludicrous spectacles, which are actually more blatant than the pro-Nazi "Ansbach Proposal" quoted earlier, yet are dutifully applauded by the leftist media. Here is a scene from the 1978 Spring Assembly of the British Council of Churches:

> The Reverend (Miss) Lee Ching Chee (of Hong Kong) contrasted the many Churches in Hong Kong with the lack of them in China: she asked whether the people of Hong Kong were any more Christian than those of China. The Reverend Dr. John Fleming underlined this when he asserted that God still lives in China to-day, not because there are Christians there, but because He is at work there, confronting us with what He is doing through non-Christians, through science, through political leaders. (12)

The point of course is not whether churches ought to pursue leftist or rightist politics, but whether they should pursue politics at all. The New Testament offers no social, economic, or political blueprints for society in general. In light of its missionary command, the church has nothing to say to unbelievers except: "Repent, and believe the Gospel." She has no mandate to make unbelievers behave properly or to impose on them a "just society." But this is speaking about the church as church. *Christians* live under both governments, however. And as citizens they clearly have the duty to seek their neighbours' welfare by all available means, or, as Luther says, to be "little Christs" to them. Naturally the Table of Duties must be preached to all Christians, including government officials — hence the propriety of dealing with urgent moral issues at Christian councils or synods. But while the motivation is Christian (i.e., Divine, Self-giving Love), the political details must be hammered out on the anvil of reason. It is wrongheaded to try to use the machinery of government to force people to behave according to biblical principles. Besides, the First Amendment forbids that in this country! Such attempts misrepresent and libel God, the Church, and the Bible to unbelievers, and thus undercut the church's real missionary work.

But is reason adequate to this task? We today tend to think of reason simply as the ability to calculate. For Luther, on the other hand, reason, even in fallen humans, has an important *moral* component. This reflects what St. Paul says in Romans 2:15 [RSV]: The Gentiles, which do not have the revealed Law, nevertheless "show that what the law requires is written on their hearts, while their conscience also bears witness and their conflicting thoughts accuse or perhaps excuse them." The average human being, regardless of his religion, knows perfectly well that it is wrong to murder, to rob, to steal, to slander, etc. This moral compass was built into humanity at creation, and its main features are still clearly discernible in the human conscience. Hence at the end of his work *On Secular Authority — To What Extent We Owe It Obedience* (WA 11:245 ff.), Luther refers to "the natural law, of which all reason is full" (see AE 45, 128).

We are now ready to see how this profoundly Christian and sensible approach can handle the crucial life-and-death issue of abortion.

ABORTION AND THE SPIRITUAL REALM

The church is the realm not of force or coercion but of grace. She comes into being and is constantly renewed and preserved not by reason or by the Law, but by the Gospel (in Word and Sacrament) alone. Yet the proclamation of the Law is always presupposed, the way a diagnosis is presupposed by the cure or remedy in medical practice. Also, believers receive from the Gospel the desire and the power to serve and please God, namely according to His revealed will or Law. This is the so-called "third use of the Law." In the matter of abortion, the revealed will of God is perfectly clear, and must be taught in the church in no uncertain terms.

The decisive moral truth here is twofold: (1) Human beings are such from conception, and (2) it is wrong to shed innocent human blood. The first truth is evident from texts like Psalms 51:5; 139:13–17; Job 10:10–11; and Jeramiah 1:5. The object of conception here is "me," not some amorphous entity which later developed into "me"! The late Mother Theresa was fond of pointing out that the unborn St. John the Baptist was the first human to welcome our Lord to earth, while Christ Himself was as yet unborn! (See the account of the Visitation in Luke 1:39 ff.) The church celebrates the Miracle of the Incarnation exactly nine months before the Nativity, on the twenty-fifth of March. It would be monstrous to declare either our Lord Himself or St. John to have been somehow pre-human, non-human, or sub-human prior to birth — and therefore freely abortable!

The second truth comes across with equal clarity from texts like Genesis 4:10 and Numbers 35:33. Shedding innocent blood is not simply an "ordinary" sin, if indeed there is such a thing. Rather, the words suggested by Genesis 4, it is a "heaven-crying" sin. (So are sodomy, Gen. 18:20–21; withholding just wages from workers, Jas 5:4; and oppression of the helpless generally, Ex. 3:7–9; 22:21–24.) In view of King Herod's brutal slaughter of the babies of Bethlehem (Matt. 2:16), the ancient church called abortion "Herodism."

It is true that abortion as such is not expressly dealt with in the New Testament. Some scholars believe, however, that when lists of vices refer to "murder" in close proximity to "immorality" and "witchcraft," abortion is meant. (See Rev. 9:21; 21:8; 22:15.) *"Pharmakia/pharmakon"* ("sorcery/ sorcerer") included the preparation and administration of abortifacients. Further, Strack and Billerbeck point out the real meaning of John 18:28 [RSV], where the Jewish leaders "themselves did not enter the praetorium, so that they might not be defiled, but might eat the passover." When one entered a house where a dead body had been, one contracted the defilement of having touched a dead body (Num. 19:14). Gentile houses were considered to be places defiled by the dead bodies of aborted babies unless a particular house was vouched for by a Jewish slave or woman who had observed it in this regard (838).

Attempts have been made to write off the opposition to abortion simply as a "sectarian," which in this case is to say Roman Catholic, issue.

Pro-abortion forces engaged in this deliberate strategy during the early 1970s, according to then-insider Bernard Nathanson (1983, 177 ff.). For that reason it is important that the public and the media regularly encounter "Lutherans for Life," "Baptists for Life," etc. Ironically, however, although the Roman Catholic Church is undoubtedly the major champion of the pro-life cause among Western churches today, it was not so in the sixteenth century. According to the 1978 *Encyclopedia of Bioethics*, the

> reformers [Luther, Melanchthon, and Calvin are meant] insisted upon the full humanity of the fetus from the time of conception... The major reformers, then, were rigorously opposed to abortion at any stage of pregnancy. Moreover, they had significantly enhanced the fetal status for reasons more basically doctrinal than for ethical reasons against abortion. Regarding fetal status, they were more conservative than the sixteenth-century Roman Catholic Church, which still maintained the Septuagint's distinction between the "unformed" and the "formed" fetus, and with it a consequent distinction in the gravity of abortion, depending upon its timing. (1:14)

The real authority behind this false distinction was Aristotle, who held that "ensoulment" or "quickening" happens in the case of males forty days after conception, and eighty days after it in the case of females.

Highly suggestive, too, is the connexion between the words for "womb" and "mercy" in several languages. In Hebrew the word for each is *racham*. The German *Barmherzigkeit* (mercy) literally means "womb-heartedness." I understand that the same is true in the case of the related Dutch language. Perhaps the reason for this odd linguistic link is that nothing expresses compassion better than the tender solicitude which expectant mothers feel for their pre-born babies. No asylum on earth should be safer or more inviolate than that sacred refuge which nurtures a developing baby beneath the mother's heart during the first nine months of life. To invade and destroy this refuge is to destroy human mercy at its very source. It is part and parcel of the progressive brutalization of human life, as documented daily in the news media.

Mercy stands at the heart of the Christian faith. Having received God's radical mercy in His Son, we are then to be merciful towards one another. Justice is not enough; compassion must reign among Christians. Our Lord therefore places a high premium on mutual forgiveness, even teaching us to pray that we should not be forgiven if we do not forgive those who trespass against us. The reason for this is explained in the parable of the unmerciful servant (Matt. 18:23–35). The psychological monstrosity of this situation dramatises the truth that to refuse to forgive is not to believe oneself forgiven. If one truly believes oneself forgiven by God in Christ, one cannot possibly refuse forgiveness to another. Persistent refusal to do so therefore constitutes a clear confession of unbelief.

The Gospel of God's mercy must also shape the church's handling of the abortion issue. It goes without saying that abortion must not be presented as the one unforgivable sin. The Lord welcomes all penitent sinners. Christian preaching, unlike mere social crusading, dare never forget this Good News.

Two anecdotes illustrate different facets of the problem. A good friend and colleague of mine in Australia had opened a pregnancy crisis centre in Adelaide. One day a fifteen-year old girl came in, thinking she could get an abortion there. My friend showed her the ghastly reality of abortion, and she decided to keep her baby. A few days later her enraged father came in, fulminating: "I am an elder at such-and-such a church. Don't you realise how I shall be disgraced if she has this illegitimate child? How dare you tell her *not* to have an abortion?" It would be difficult to imagine a more repulsive instance of unmerciful Pharisaic cruelty! How can a father be so obsessed with appearances as to wish to burden his own daughter's soul with the sin of murder? Yet here is the oppressive power of the false god Respectability, which has disfigured so much "church" culture!

The other example I heard some years ago from one of the leaders of "Women Exploited." These are women who had been misled into having abortions, then came to have lifelong regret. This lady told us that she had believed the propaganda that the fetus was simply a mass of cells. How horrified she had been when she saw the clearly human shape of the being she had killed! In her guilt and despair she went to her pastor and confessed her sin. But the pastor made light of it and said, "It's OK, don't worry about it!" That, she said, did not help her at all. She knew that it was not "OK," and that she had done evil. What she needed was absolution, forgiveness, not excuses!

In concrete pastoral care, the full weight of the Law's condemnation must fall not on the poor, troubled woman or girl who had an abortion and regretted ever after, but on callous "Christian" doctors and nurses who habitually do abortion "procedures" without any emotional confusion or pressure, but simply for money. They need to be told that until they repent, they cannot receive the Holy Sacrament (1 Jn. 3:15). Those who shed innocent blood may not partake of the sacred cup of the Lord's blood!

These are the sorts of things which Christians ought to be saying to one another in the spiritual realm, in Christ's holy church. Finally, the public teachers of the church especially are not doing their full duty in this matter if they neglect to tell their hearers that it is their solemn responsibility to use such economic and political "clout" as they have to restore the protection of the law to the unborn. That is not "politics," but a basic decency required by the Fifth Commandment:

> Likewise, if you see anyone who is [innocently] condemned to death or in similar peril and do not save him although you have means and ways to do so, you have killed him. It will be of no help for you to use the excuse that you did not assist their deaths by word or deed, for you have withheld your love from them and robbed them of the kindness by means of which their lives might have been saved.
>
> Therefore God rightly calls all persons murderers who do not offer counsel or assistance to those in need and peril of body and life. . . . What else is this but to call these people murderous and bloodthirsty? For although you have not actually committed all these crimes, as far as you are concerned, you have nevertheless permitted your neighbors to languish and perish in their misfortune. (LC I 190–192; K-W, 412)

ABORTION AND THE PUBLIC SQUARE
Medicine, Science

At the heart of the U.S. Supreme Court's *Roe v. Wade* decision of January 22, 1973 lies a strange evasiveness bordering on the disingenuous. On the one hand the court quoted the 1859 report to the American Medical Association of the latter's Committee on Criminal Abortion, regarding the three causes "of this general demoralization":

> The first of these causes is a wide-spread popular ignorance of the true character of the crime — a belief, even among mothers themselves, that the foetus is not alive till after the period of quickening.
>
> The second of the agents alluded to is the fact that the profession themselves are frequently supposed careless of foetal life. . . .
>
> The third reason of the frightful extent of this crime is found in the grave defects of our laws, both common and statute, as regards the independent and actual existence of the child before birth, as a living being. These errors, which are sufficient in most instances to prevent conviction, are based, and only based, upon mistaken and exploded medical dogmas. With strange inconsistency, the law fully acknowledges the foetus in utero and its inher-

ent rights, for civil purposes; while personally and as criminally affected, it fails to recognize it, and to its life as yet denies all protection.

On this basis the American Medical Association officially protested "against such unwarrantable destruction of human life," and demanded full legal protection for the unborn (Supreme Court of the United States, 1921).

Having stated this crucial medical and historical evidence, the majority then tried in various ways to evade and minimise its significance. For instance: "Gradually, in the middle and late nineteenth century the quickening distinction disappeared from the statutory law of most States and the degree of the offense and the penalties were increased" (Supreme Court, 1920). Then the AMA's action was introduced like this: "The anti-abortion mood prevalent in this country in the late nineteenth century was shared by the medical profession. Indeed, the attitude of the profession may have played a significant role in the enactment of stringent criminal abortion legislation during that period" (Supreme Court, 1921).

So, the "quickening distinction" disappeared for some reason at that time, and the medical profession shared the prevalent anti-abortion "mood"! The reason for the disappearance of the "quickening distinction" was the advancing medical-scientific understanding of human reproduction. Not a "mood," but the newly discovered scientific facts compelled the medical profession to abandon the traditional fantasies about "quickening" or "ensoulment" *a la* Aristotle, and to demand legal protection for what were now understood to be real, living human beings.

The court's majority cited three reasons which "have been advanced to explain historically the enactment of criminal abortion laws in the nineteenth century and to justify their continued existence" (Supreme Court, 1922). First, it had been suggested that these laws arose out of "a Victorian social concern to discourage illicit sexual conduct" (Supreme Court, 1922). This was deemed irrelevant in the present case. Yet the mere mention of it no doubt helped to create an emotional antipathy to laws even remotely associated with alleged Victorian prudery! The second reason given was that "when most criminal abortion laws were first enacted, the procedure was a hazardous one for the woman" (Supreme Court, 1923). The real concern of these laws, then, was "to protect the pregnant woman," not the fetus. A great deal of credence was given to this point by the Court's majority, which pointed out that "Modern medical techniques have altered this situation" (Supreme Court, 1923). Yet this claim flatly contradicted the crucial evidence cited from the AMA, where the concern was precisely for the unborn baby. And the court had already admitted the "significant role" of the medical profession! Finally, the third reason was "the State's interest— some phrase it in terms of duty— in protecting prenatal life" (Supreme Court, 1923). But this was dismissed at once: "Some of the argument for this justification rests on the theory that a new human life is present from the moment of conception" (Supreme Court, 1923). At the mention of "theory," one searches in vain for a reference to the medical profession, which embraced precisely this "theory"! Instead, references were made to contemporary pro-life literature by way of documentation!

The medical profession said in 1859 that antiquated laws failed to recognise "the independent and actual existence of the child before birth, as a living being," and that this wrong legal position was "based, and only based, upon mistaken and exploded medical dogmas" (Supreme Court, 1921). A century later the Court dismissed as a mere "theory" the medical, scientific facts, which had replaced the "mistaken and exploded medical dogmas"! Did the high court then wish to return to abandoned unscientific superstitions, or give them "equal rights" with the scientific facts? The majority waffled piously: "We need not resolve the difficult question of when life begins. When those trained in the respective disciplines of medicine, philosophy, and theology are unable to arrive at any consensus, the judiciary, at this point in the development of man's knowledge, is not in a position to speculate as to the answer" (Supreme Court, 1926).

So if the court could not answer the fundamental question on which the whole case turned, then why did it overturn most of the states' laws to this point, by "an exercise of raw judicial power," as Mr. Justice White called it in his dissent? Why not let the democratic process work itself out in this matter? Wrote Mr. Justice White: "The upshot is that the people and the legislatures of the fifty States are constitutionally disentitled to weigh the relative importance of the continued existence and development of the fetus on the one hand against a spectrum of possible impacts on the mother on the other hand" (quoted in Hutchinson, 368–369).

The court was tragically mistaken in its claim that there is any medical doubt or ambiguity about "when life begins." And why did it even mention philosophy and theology, as though it would have taken serious notice of them? A cover story in *Time* (6 April 1981) included a piece that began: "When does a human being begin to exist? That question is at the very heart of the abortion debate, yet it is far from susceptible to a sure answer." Yet the very next sentence said, "This much is beyond serious dispute: biological life begins at fertilization, when the female's egg is united with the male's sperm." And then there followed various views about why the fertilized egg should not be considered a human life. Here was pure sophistry. If no serious dispute exists about when "biological life" begins, how can there be a dispute about when "human life" begins? Given the refutation, by the discovery of DNA, of Darwin's fantasies about the embryo undergoing "pre-human" stages, it is clear that the fertilized ovum is a living being. Since it has a full complement of human DNA, it is a living human being. Yet the *Time* piece had been entitled "The Unresolvable Question."

Life also had a 1981 cover story about the unborn. It was entitled, "A Special Poll—How Women Feel About Abortion—When Does Life Really Begin?" (November). Various percentages were dutifully reported on how people "feel" about this and that. Then three experts were quoted, one for and two against the true humanity of the fetus. Dr. Christopher Tietze, senior consultant, Population Council of New York, said: "Biological life of the individual begins at the union of ovum and sperm; but at what point does this life deserve the respect and protection that we accord people?" (52). Dr. Leon Rosenberg, chairman of the department of human genetics at Yale University School of Medicine, opined: "This is such a metaphysical concept. Of course, a new life is generated when the egg is fertilized by the sperm." Yet then he went on to argue that "humanness" is as complex as "love, faith or trust," and is therefore beyond the competence of science! One would have thought that in an age that prides itself on its enlightened, scientific realism, "human life" would simply be shorthand for "the biological life of a human being." The only possible reason for all the waffling, posturing, and sophistry in the face of clear scientific facts is that the Moloch of abortion has become an untouchable sacred cow for the cultural elites irrevocably committed to the "Sexual Revolution."

One should not underestimate the power of photographic evidence in this regard. The development of sophisticated medical technology for intra-uterine surgery has had an enormous impact on the public perception of the fetus. See, for instance, the cover story in *Life* for April, 1983: "Treating the Unborn—Surgical Miracles Inside the Womb." It was just this development that forced Dr. Bernard Nathanson, then an agnostic Jew, to recognise the full humanity of his unborn patients! Swedish photographer Lennart Nilsson's classic *A Child Is Born* dramatically documented the humanity of the developing fetus. Of course, pro-abortionists hate and denounce the "emotional" photographs of tiny humans dismembered by abortion. The pro-abortion *Legal Handbook: A Speakers Notebook* by one Jimmye Kimmey advises: "It is also important to make the point with the audience that you do not have pictures to show them because what we are interested in is freedom and that isn't anything you can take a picture of" (19)!

Some twenty years ago I tried, as chairman of the Allen County (Indiana) Right To Life organisation, to advertise our annual Walk for Life with the aid of the photo, from Dr. and Mrs. Willke's *Handbook on Abortion*, showing a garbage bag full of tiny corpses discarded by a Canadian abortion facility. I assumed naively that the *conservative* one of our two daily newspapers would print such a paid advertisement. The picture was returned to me the next day, though, with the explanation that it was too gruesome for a family paper to print. "Very well," I suggested, "skip the picture, leave an empty space, and say: the photo of a rubbish bag full of discarded human babies from a Canadian abortion facility was too gruesome to print in a family newspaper." My suggestion was rejected, my money returned! The media are definitely not keen to "upset" the public with real evidence on the matter!

I must not conclude this section without referring to the fact that the unborn are known to be human not only physically, but also psychologically! A. W. (Sir William) Liley, the "father of foetology," wrote an article entitled "The Foetus as a Personality," in which he documented genuinely psychological behaviour in the unborn.

ABORTION AND THE PUBLIC SQUARE
Law, Morality, Politics

In my view, the anti-abortion movement in this country has hurt its own cause by often presenting itself, rhetorically and visually, as a Christian crusade. That, of course, sounds its own constitutional death-knell. The First Amendment—without any contemporary, unhistorical interpretation—certainly forbids the imposition by law of Christian tenets on the general public. The anti-abortion argument must be made in civil, secular terms, without invoking the specific beliefs of Christianity or any other religion. The clear distinction between the spiritual and the political powers passes muster not only biblically but also constitutionally!

First one needs to dispose of the *idee fixe* that morality is necessarily "religious," and that one cannot therefore "legislate morality." On the contrary: without morality, legislation becomes arbitrary and oppressive. Take robbery, for example. Do we have laws against it because it is wrong, or simply because it is inconvenient? Now, some crimes are crimes only by convention, not on moral grounds. For example, it is not inherently immoral to drive on the left side of the road. Yet the law cannot allow free choice of driving sides, and this for the sake of good order and public safety.

But murder, robbery, child abuse, etc., are outlawed not simply on prudential grounds but on moral grounds. Few would disagree that such crimes are inherently wrong. Even the most secularly minded judge imaginable would not put up with the following defence: "Your honour, I am an atheist and I reject the traditional Judaeo-Christian moral code. The statute against bank robbery, under which I am charged, is based on moral assumptions taken from the Jewish and Christian Fifth and Seventh Commandments, and therefore amounts to an 'establishment of religion.' I claim freedom from this religious law on the grounds of the First Amendment." And surely not even the most lunatic of simpering sentimentalists would argue that since no conceivable legislation will prevent future bank robberies, provisions should be made for "safe" bank robberies, under government supervision, so that nobody gets hurt. Yet the pro-abortion case rests on similar tissues of absurdities.

We simply have to distinguish between morality and religion, between crime and sin. Not every sin can be a crime, and it is conceivable that some "crimes" are not sins. Yet the mere fact that one or more religions hold abortion or robbery to be a sin does not mean that society cannot declare these acts to be crimes. They can be regarded as crimes on independent, rational moral grounds, without unconstitutional religious entanglements. So how does one provide purely reasonable moral grounds for the prohibition of abortion?

Of course it would be helpful to be able to appeal to natural theology (Rom. 1:19–20) and natural law (Rom. 2:14–15). That would be a purely philosophical argument, not one based on theology or biblical revelation. And that is exactly what the American Declaration of Independence did when it appealed to "the laws of Nature and of Nature's God." Since this Declaration is the real preamble to the U.S. Constitution, it is absurd that recent constitutional interpretation panics at the sight of the word "God," and would presumably hold Fourth of July celebrations to be unconstitutional, by virtue of the Declaration's "religious entanglement." Yet the new Canadian Constitution clearly grounds human rights not in fickle majorities but in God, by stating that "Canada is founded on principles which recognise the supremacy of God and the rule of law." The even newer Ukrainian Constitution is even more explicit: Ukraine recognizes that we are "responsible before God, conscience, and past, present, and future generations."

However, an appeal to natural law need not involve even a philosophical notion of God. One can simply appeal to people's innate sense of right and wrong. This can be enough to persuade a majority. Indeed, one might make a rational case against "abortion rights" even on the basis of a natural law substitute like that of John Rawls of Harvard. Rawls begins with a thought experiment which he calls the "initial situation." It is a meeting of rational persons for the purpose of agreeing to basic principles of justice which shall henceforth govern the relations among them. The most important proviso is that these persons act "under the veil of ignorance," which means that they do not know exactly what their place in society will turn out to be. Given this veil of ignorance, Rawls argues, whatever rational persons would agree upon, would be fair—for obviously if I do not know whether my lot will turn out to be that of a man or a woman, young or old, rich or poor, black or white, etc., I will not agree to any arrangements which would in principle disadvantage any of these groups in relation to the others. It is easy to show then that under this veil of ignorance I do not know whether I will turn out to be born or unborn, and will therefore not agree to any discrimination on those grounds. Indeed this very consideration is invited by Rawls' own insistence that "moral personality is here defined as a potentiality that is ordinarily realized in due course" (505). Again, "A being that has this capacity, whether or not it is yet developed, is to receive the full protection of the principles of justice. Since infants and children are thought to have basic rights (normally exercised on their behalf by parents and guardians), this interpretation of the requisite conditions seems necessary to match our considered judgments" (509).

Although abortion is not mentioned in Rawls' earlier work, *A Theory of Justice*, his more recent *Political Liberalism* amends his earlier proposals somewhat and adds an explicit endorsement of abortion. Having named "due respect for human life, the ordered reproduction of political society, . . . and finally the equality of women as equal citizens," he concludes that "any reasonable balance of these three values will give a woman a duly qualified right to decide whether or not to end her pregnancy during the first trimester." But this represents a total abrogation, not just a slight modification, of his whole original proposal. For that had insisted: "Thus to respect persons is to recognize that they possess an inviolability founded on justice that even the welfare of society as a whole cannot override" (586; for information about and competent criticism of Rawls' more recent book and his footnote on abortion, I am indebted to the splendid volume by George, especially 45–61).

Protection of those least able to protect themselves forms the very cornerstone of civilised law and jurisprudence. It stands out as the opposite of the law of the jungle. I regret that I cannot here offer the documentation, but I recall reading about the *Mignonette* case in a critique of the British

Abortion Act of 1967. If I am not mistaken, it occurred near the end of the Victorian age, and had to do with the case of survivors of a shipwreck who decided to kill their unconscious cabin boy for food. They pleaded necessity, yet the court held that this formed no justification. They might have cast lots among those who were freely able to consent, rather than picking on a helpless, unconscious person, whose rights therefore the court was especially duty-bound to uphold and vindicate.*

The real issue was well put in the notorious 1970 editorial of the California State Medical Association's Journal. It argued that scientific and cultural progress had produced a "new ethic," which placed "relative rather than absolute value on such things [sic!] as human lives." But a problem remained:

> ... since the old ethic has not been fully displaced it has been necessary to separate the idea of abortion from the idea of killing, which continues to be socially abhorrent. The result has been a curious avoidance of the scientific fact, which everyone really knows, that human life begins at conception and is continuous whether intra- or extra-uterine until death. The very considerable semantic gymnastics which are required to rationalize abortion as anything but taking a human life would be ludicrous if they were not often put forth under socially impeccable auspices. It is suggested that this schizophrenic sort of subterfuge is necessary because, while a new ethic is being accepted, the old one has not yet been rejected. (*California Medicine*, 67)

This is exactly the point. These "semantic gymnastics" are tolerated only because at the moment we simply have no public morality. What we have is a cruel and selective sentimentality, which favours those on whom the media bestow glamour and celebrity. Was it serious public morality when a former candidate for the U.S. vice presidency declaimed: "I am personally opposed to abortion, but I cannot force my own convictions on others." Let us substitute another class of humans here, like this: "I am personally opposed to the burning of Jews, but, if Hitler and company want to do it, who am I to force my convictions on them?" This is Monty Python moral discourse. The time has come to laugh it off the public stage.

---

* *Editor's note*: The case is *Regina v. Dudley and Stephens*, from 1884. Its story is told, in a way not especially sympathetic to the verdict eventually rendered, in A. W. Brian Simpson, *Cannibalism and the Common Law: The Story of the Tragic Last Voyage of the Mignonette and the Strange Legal Proceedings to Which It Gave Rise* (Chicago: The University of Chicago Press, 1984).

The Supreme Court decision of 1973 is just as wrong as the Dred Scott ruling of 1857, which held that slaves were property and not "persons" under the law! It took a Civil War to reverse that! The constitutional status of the unborn today is completely analogous. The moral and legal absurdity of our present situation is that while the corporations which slaughter the unborn for profit have full constitutional protection as (corporate) "persons" in law, their genuinely human victims do not. We cannot rest until this obscenity is reversed.

BIBLIOGRAPHY

BARCLAY, William

    1971   *Ethics in a Permissive Society.* London and Glasgow: Collins Fontana Books.

CALIFORNIA MEDICINE

    1970   Editorial, "A New Ethic for Medicine and Society," *California Medicine* 113 (September).

DeMAR, Gary

    1988   *The Debate Over Christian Reconstruction.* Ft. Worth: Dominion Press.

GEORGE, Robert P.

    2001   *The Clash of Orthodoxies.* Wilmington, DE: ISI Books.

HERTZ, Karl H., ed.

    1976   *The Two Kingdoms And One World.* Minneapolis: Augsburg.

HUTCHINSON, Dennis J.

    1998   *The Man Who Once Was Whizzer White: A Portrait of Justice Byron R. White.* New York: The Free Press.

K-W = KOLB, Robert and Timothy J. WENGERT, eds.

    2000   *The Book of Concord.* Minneapolis: Fortress Press.

LILEY, Sir William

    1972   "The Foetus as a Personality," *Australia and New Zealand Journal of Psychiatry,* vol. 6, pp. 99–105.

NATHANSON, Bernard

    1979   *Aborting America.* New York: Doubleday.

    1983   *The Abortion Papers.* New York: Frederick Fell Publishers.

    1996   *The Hand of God.* Washington: Regnery.

NILSSON, Lennart

 1966 *A Child Is Born.* New York: Delacorte.

NORMAN, Edward

 1979 *Christianity and the World Order.* Oxford University Press.

PIEPER, Francis

 1953 *Christian Dogmatics,* vol. III. St. Louis: Concordia.

RAWLS, John

 1971 *A Theory of Justice.* Cambridge, MA: The Belnap Press of Harvard University Press.

REICH, Warren T., ed.

 1978 *Encyclopedia of Bioethics.* New York: The Free Press.

STEPHENSON, John

 1981 "The Two Governments and the Two Kingdoms in Luther's Thought," *Scottish Journal of Theology,* vol. 34, pp. 321–337.

STRACK, Hermann L, and Paul BILLERBECK

 1924 *Kommentar zum Neuen Testament,* vol. 2. Munich: Oskar Beck.

SUPREME COURT OF THE UNITED STATES

 1973 *Roe et al. v. Wade.* In Paul Finkelman, ed.-in-chief, *Milestone Documents in American History: Exploring the Primary Sources that Shaped America.* Vol. 4: 1956–2003. Dallas: Schlager Group, 2008, pp. 1907–1928. [*Editor's note:* Marquart had cited the Government Printing Office publication of the *Roe v. Wade* decision. The above-listed publication is somewhat more durable, however, and hence more readily available.]

WILLKE, Dr. J. C. and Mrs.

 1997 *Why Can't We Love Them Both?* Cincinnati: Hayes Publishing Co.

WORLD COUNCIL OF CHURCHES

 1948 *The Church and the Disorder of Society: An Ecumenical Study Prepared under the Auspices of the World Council of Churches.* London: SCM Press.

KURT MARQUART BIBLIOGRAPHY

by Robert Paul

Editor's note: This bibliography makes no claim to be either comprehensive or exhaustive. It is not comprehensive because there has been no attempt to account for all of Kurt Marquart's published works such as, say, letters to the editor of a daily newspaper in Fort Wayne. It is not exhaustive because some of Marquart's essays appeared in print more than once, and in those cases this bibliography does not list every instance of publication. Instead, it reports only the most recent or durable forms in which these essays appeared. Even with these limitations, however, the present bibliography should serve those interested in learning still more from Professor Marquart.

Books, Monographs, Works

Anatomy of an Explosion: A Theological Analysis of the Missouri Synod Conflict. Fort Wayne, IN: Concordia Theological Seminary, 1978.

Church-Fellowship: Its Nature, Basis and Limits. Fort Wayne, IN: Concordia Theological Seminary Press, 1982.

Church & Fellowship: Evangelical Perspectives. Fort Wayne, IN: Concordia Theological Seminary Press, 1987.

Essays: Confessional and Doctrinal, vol. ii of *Truth, Salvatory and Churchly: Works of Kurt E. Marquart.* Luther Academy, 2017.

Essays: Historical and Historic, vol. iii of *Truth, Salvatory and Churchly: Works of Kurt E. Marquart.* Luther Academy, 2018.

Marquart's Works. Ten volumes. New Haven, MO: Lutheran News, 2014.

Ministry and Ordination: Confessional Perspectives. Fort Wayne, IN: Concordia Theological Seminary Press, 1983.

"*Prolegomena in Pieper and Aulen: A Comparison.*" BD Thesis, Concordia Seminary, St. Louis, MO, 1959.

The Church and Her Fellowship, Ministry, and Governance. Vol. ix of *Confessional Lutheran Dogmatics*, ed. Robert D. Preus. (Fort Wayne, IN: International Foundation for Lutheran Confessional Research, 1990).

The Saving Truth: Doctrine for Laypeople, vol. i of *Truth, Salvatory and Churchly: Works of Kurt E. Marquart.* Luther Academy, 2016.

Articles

"A Declaration and Plea." In *Marquart's Works*, vol. VIII, edited by Herman Otten, 1–7. New Haven, MO: Lutheran News, 2014.

"A Question of Fraud." In *Marquart's Works*, vol. V, edited by Herman Otten, 128–130. New Haven, MO: Lutheran News, 2014.

"A Response to Adequacy of Language and Accomodation." In *Essays: Confessional and Doctrinal*, vol. II of *Truth, Salvatory and Churchly: Works of Kurt E. Marquart*, 95–108. Luther Academy, 2017.

"A Tale of Two Books" *Concordia Theological Quarterly* 50, nos. 3 & 4 (July–October 1986): 183–186.

"Abortion and Luther's Two Kingdoms Theology." In *Essays: Historical and Historic*, vol. III of *Truth, Salvatory and Churchly: Works of Kurt E. Marquart*, 169–187. Luther Academy, 2018.

"An Earnest Fraternal Appeal from Overseas to Our Fellow Believers in The Lutheran Church—Missouri Synod on the Eve of the Denver Convention." In *Essays: Historical and Historic*, vol. III of *Truth, Salvatory and Churchly: Works of Kurt E. Marquart*, 17–30. Luther Academy, 2018.

"Apostasy in Valparaiso's *Cresset*." In *Marquart's Works*, vol. IX, edited by Herman Otten, 107–110. New Haven, MO: Lutheran News, 2014.

"Augsburg Confession VII: Our Evangelical and Ecumenical Magna Charta." Convention Essay, Lutheran Church—Canada, Regina, Sask., 21 Nov. 1979.

"Augsburg Confession VII Revisited." *Concordia Theological Quarterly*, vol. 45, nos. 1–2 (January–April 1981): 17–25.

"Augsburg Revisited." In *A Justification Odyssey: Papers Presented at the Congress on the Lutheran Confessions, Bloomingdale, Illinois, April 19–21, 2001*, ed. John A. Maxfield, 158–177. St. Louis, MO: Luther Academy, 2001.

"Aversion to Sanctification?" In *Marquart's Works*, vol. IX, edited by Herman Otten, 230–232. New Haven, MO: Lutheran News, 2014.

"Beyond Orthodoxy." In *Marquart's Works*, vol. VIII, edited by Herman Otten, 14–47. New Haven, MO: Lutheran News, 2014.

"Calling and Removing Ministers." In *Essays: Confessional and Doctrinal,* vol. II of *Truth, Salvatory and Churchly: Works of Kurt E. Marquart,* 185–188. Luther Academy, 2017.

"Central Lutheran Thrust for Today." *Concordia Journal* 8, no. 3 (May 1982): 86–91.

"C. F. W. Walther in Fact and Fiction." In *Essays: Historical and Historic,* vol. III of *Truth, Salvatory and Churchly: Works of Kurt E. Marquart,* 75–87. Luther Academy, 2018.

"Christian Giving." In *Marquart's Works,* vol. IX, edited by Herman Otten, 33–38. New Haven, MO: Lutheran News, 2014.

"Church and State: A Question of Principle." In *Marquart's Works,* vol. II, edited by Herman Otten, 106–109. New Haven, MO: Lutheran News, 2014.

"Church Fellowship." In *Essays: Historical and Historic,* vol. III of *Truth, Salvatory and Churchly: Works of Kurt E. Marquart,* 89–98. Luther Academy, 2018.

"'Church Growth' and Growth in Christ." In *We Believe, Teach, and Confess,* edited by Reijo Arkkila and Richard O. Olak, 69–82. International Lutheran Confessional Conference 21–24 April 1992, Matongo, Kenya. Helsinki: SLEY-Kirjat Oy.

"'Church Growth' as Mission Paradigm: A Confessional Lutheran Assessment." In *Church and Ministry Today: Three Confessional Lutheran Essays: Preus—Marquart—Weinrich,* edited by John A. Maxfield, 51–172. St. Louis, MO: Luther Academy, 2001.

"Communism, Western Civilization, and Christianity." In *Marquart's Works,* vol. II, edited by Herman Otten, 1–9. New Haven, MO: Lutheran News, 2014.

"Confession and Ceremonies." In *A Contemporary Look at the Formula of Concord,* edited by Robert D. Preus and Wilbert H. Rosin, 260–270. St. Louis: Concordia, 1978.

"Durchleutung der St. Louiser 'Affirmationen und Diskussionen.'" *Lutherischer Rundblick,* vol. 21, nos. 1 & 2, 1973, 77–85.

"Dr. Robert D. Preus: The Lutheran Confessions and the Idea of Confessional Lutheranism." In *The Theology and Life of Robert D. Preus: Papers Presented at the Congress on the Lutheran Confessions, Itasca, Illinois, April 8–10, 1999*, edited by Congress on the Lutheran Confessions, Jennifer H. Maxfield, and Bethany Preus, 122–135. St. Louis, MO: Luther Academy, 2009.

"ELCA Ecumenical Decisions." In *Essays: Historical and Historic*, vol. III of *Truth, Salvatory and Churchly: Works of Kurt E. Marquart*, 119–142. Luther Academy, 2018.

"Eucharist and Eschatology." In *Shepherd the Church: Essays in Honor of the Rev. Dr. Roger D. Pittelko*, edited by Roger D. Pittelko and Frederic W. Baue, 145–159. Fort Wayne, IN: Concordia Theological Seminary Press, 2002.

"Evolution in Shambles: From Paley to Darwin—and back." *The Northwestern Lutheran* (15 August 1983): 232–234.

"*Ex Oriente Lux*—Light from the East" including translation of "Declaration of the Constituting Synod of the Belorussian Evangelical Lutheran Church 2 December 2000" *Concordia Theological Quarterly* 65, no. 2 (April 2001): 174–177.

"Facts, Faith, and Proof: Eleven Theses on Apologetics." In *Essays: Confessional and Doctrinal*, vol. II of *Truth, Salvatory and Churchly: Works of Kurt E. Marquart*, 203–204. Luther Academy, 2017.

"Fellowship and Merger: Some Lutheran Commonplaces." *Concordia Theological Quarterly* 46, no. 4 (October 1982): 299–300.

"Fellowship or Communion vs. Unionism or Syncretism." In *Essays: Historical and Historic*, vol. III of *Truth, Salvatory and Churchly: Works of Kurt E. Marquart*, 103–108. Luther Academy, 2018.

"Forward to the Declaration of Independence!" In *Essays: Confessional and Doctrinal*, vol. II of *Truth, Salvatory and Churchly: Works of Kurt E. Marquart*, 205–208. Luther Academy, 2017.

"Foundations of Sola Scriptura Hermeneutics/Prolegomena." *Essays: Confessional and Doctrinal*, vol. II of *Truth, Salvatory and Churchly: Works of Kurt E. Marquart*, 69–72. Luther Academy, 2017.

"Francis Pieper on Church Fellowship," The Pieper Lectures, vol 2: *Church Fellowship*, edited by Chris Christophersen Boshoven, 57–82. St. Louis: Concordia Historical Institute and Luther Academy, 1998.

"From Paley to Darwin." In *Marquart's Works*, edited by Herman Otten, 18–24. New Haven, MO: Lutheran News, 2014.

"Germany and Australia: Ordination of Women?" including translation of "Theses for the 'Discussion Concerning the Ordination of Women into the Office of the Church in the SELK (Independent Evangelical Lutheran Church [Germany])." *Concordia Theological Quarterly* 63, no. 1 (January 1999): 50–52.

"Gold, Silver, and Bronze, and Closed Communion." In *Marquart's Works*, vol. VII, edited by Herman Otten, 104–106. New Haven, MO: Lutheran News, 2014.

"Helsinki, Doctrinal Unity, and Justification." In *Marquart's Works*, vol. VI, edited by Herman Otten, 16–25. New Haven, MO: Lutheran News, 2014.

"Hermann Sasse and the Mystery of Sacred Scripture," *Hermann Sasse: A Man for Our Times?* Essays from the Twentieth Annual Lutheran Life Lectures, St. Catharines, Ontario, Canada (30 October–1 November 1995). An International Theological Symposium marking the centennial of the birth of Dr. Hermann Sasse, edited by John R. Stephenson and Thomas M. Winger, 167–193. St. Louis: Concordia Academic Press, 1998.,167–193.

"Hermann Sasse and His Influence on the Lutheran Church of Australia: An Oral History." In *Essays: Historical and Historic*, vol. III of Truth, Salvatory and Churchly: Works of Kurt E. Marquart. Luther Academy, 2018: 3–13.

"How to Give Up the Confessions Without Seeming To." In *Marquart's Works*, vol. VII, edited by Herman Otten, 64–69. New Haven, MO: Lutheran News, 2014.

"In the Name of God . . . What 'False Doctrine'?" In *Marquart's Works*, vol. VIII, edited by Herman Otten, 80–107. New Haven, MO: Lutheran News, 2014.

"Integrity Barometer: Falling." In *Marquart's Works*, vol. IX, edited by Herman Otten, 89–92. New Haven, MO: Lutheran News, 2014.

"'Inter-Christian Relationships': A Minority Report." *Concordia Theological Quarterly*, vol. 57, nos. 1–2 (January–April): 41–94.

"Justification: Crown Jewel of Faith." In *Essays: Confessional and Doctrinal*, vol. 11 of Truth, Salvatory and Churchly: Works of Kurt E. Marquart, 123–134. Luther Academy, 2017.

"Justification: Let's Be Specific." In *Marquart's Works*, vol. vi, edited by Herman Otten, 64–67. New Haven, MO: Lutheran News, 2014.

"Law/Gospel and 'Church Growth' or Quo Vadis Lutheran Missiology?" In *Marquart's Works*, vol. ix, edited by Herman Otten, 159–169. New Haven, MO: Lutheran News, 2014.

"Let's Ask Scripture and Tradition About Scripture and Tradition." In *Marquart's Works*, vol. vi, edited by Herman Otten, 1–15. New Haven, MO: Lutheran News, 2014.

"Levels of Fellowship." In *Marquart's Works*, vol. ix, edited by Herman Otten, 116–118. New Haven, MO: Lutheran News, 2014.

"Liturgical Commonplaces." In *Marquart's Works*, vol. vii, edited by Herman Otten, 37–50. New Haven, MO: Lutheran News, 2014.

"Liturgy and Dogmatics." *Concordia Theological Quarterly*, vol. 67, no. 2 (April): 175–190.

"Liturgy and Evangelism." In *Lutheran Worship: History and Practice*, ed. Fred Precht, 58–73. St. Louis: Concordia, 1993.

"Luther and *Theosis*." *Concordia Theological Quarterly*, vol. 64, no. 3 (July 2000): 182–205.

"Luther's Theology of the Cross." In *Marquart's Works*, vol. vi, edited by Herman Otten, 52–57. New Haven, MO: Lutheran News, 2014.

"Lutheran Polity in the American Context." In *Church Polity and Politics: Papers Presented at the Congress on the Lutheran Confessions, Itasca, Illinois, April 3–5, 1997*, edited by John R. Fehrmann, and Daniel Preus, 177–206. Crestwood, MO: Luther Academy, 1997.

"Noted in Brief: Structured for Mischief." *Affirm*, May 1989, 4–6.

"Noted in Brief: The Ex-Lutheran Merger." *Affirm*, April 1983, 4–6.

"Noted in Brief: The Real Wichita." *Affirm*, April 1989, 4–6.

"O Worship the Lord in the Beauty of Holiness: Why We Go to Church." In *Marquart's Works*, vol. VII, edited by Herman Otten, 1–9. New Haven, MO: Lutheran News, 2014.

"Objective Justification." In *Marquart's Works*, vol. VI, edited by Herman Otten, 70–104. New Haven, MO: Lutheran News, 2014.

"Opinion of the Department of Systematic Theology" (re. Dr. Paul G. Bretscher's "The Sword of the Spirit.") *Concordia Theological Quarterly*, vol. 43, no. 4 (October 1979): 327–337.

"Our Lord's Baptism." *The Lutheran*, vol. 18, no. 5 (16 April 1984): 2–3.

"Our 'Worship Wars' at the Turn of the Millennium." In *Worship 2000: Papers Presented at the Congress on the Lutheran Confessions, Itasca, Illinois, April 27–29, 2000*, ed. Congress on the Lutheran Confessions, John A. Maxfield, and Jennifer H. Maxfield, 152–165. St. Louis, MO: Luther Academy, 2010.

"Putting Missouri Back on Track." In *Marquart's Works*, vol. IX, edited by Herman Otten, 208–217. New Haven, MO: Lutheran News, 2014.

"Quo Vadis Lutheran Witness?" In *Marquart's Works*, vol. IX, edited by Herman Otten, 18–26. New Haven, MO: Lutheran News, 2014.

"Reactions to the Official Results of Inter-Lutheran (LCUSA) Theological Discussions since 1972." In *Marquart's Works*, vol. IX, edited by Herman Otten, 93–97. New Haven, MO: Lutheran News, 2014.

"Regular Prayer and the Ministry." In *Marquart's Works*, vol. VII, edited by Herman Otten, 96–98. New Haven, MO: Lutheran News, 2014.

"Response to Cardinal Cassidy's Address." In *Essays: Historical and Historic*, vol. III of Truth, Salvatory and Churchly: Works of Kurt E. Marquart, Luther Academy, 2018: 143–150.

"Response to Presentation II." In *The Collected Papers of The 150th Anniversary Theological Convocation of The Lutheran Church—Missouri Synod*, edited by Jerald C. Joerz and Paul T. McCain, 100–112. St. Louis, MO: Office of the President, The Lutheran Church Missouri Synod, 1998.

"Robert D. Preus, from *The Handbook of Evangelical Theologians*." In *Marquart's Works*, vol. IX, ed. Herman Otten, 127–142. New Haven, MO: Lutheran News, 2014.

"Santa Claus Theology." In *Marquart's Works*, vol. IX, edited by Herman Otten, 112–115. New Haven, MO: Lutheran News, 2014.

"Science: Sacred Cow or Sacred Calling?" In *Reading God's World: The Scientific Vocation*, edited by Angus J. L. Menuge, 271–294. St. Louis, MO: Concordia Pub. House, 2004.

"Seven Deadly Sins." In *Marquart's Works*, vol. I, edited by Herman Otten, 53–69. New Haven, MO: Lutheran News, 2014.

"Some Aspects of a Healthy Church Life." In *Marquart's Works*, vol. III, edited by Herman Otten, 34–47. New Haven, MO: Lutheran News, 2014.

"Some Important Doctrinal Points." In *Essays: Historical and Historic*, vol. III of Truth, Salvatory and Churchly: Works of Kurt E. Marquart. Luther Academy, 2018: 15–16.

"Thanks, Lutheran Witness and LLL." In *Essays: Historical and Historic*, vol. III of Truth, Salvatory and Churchly: Works of Kurt E. Marquart. Luther Academy, 2018: 99–101.

"The Case Against Evolution." In *Marquart's Works*, vol. IV, edited by Herman Otten, 1–8. New Haven, MO: Lutheran News, 2014.

"The Christian Church and Communism." In *Marquart's Works*, vol. II, edited by Herman Otten, 11–32. New Haven, MO: Lutheran News, 2014.

"The Church in the Twenty-first Century: Will There Be a Lutheran One?" In *Marquart's Works*, vol. IX, edited by Herman Otten, 170–186. New Haven, MO: Lutheran News, 2014.

"The Church, Its Mission, and Its Ministry of Mercy: Theological Reflections." In *Essays: Confessional and Doctrinal*, vol. II of Truth, Salvatory and Churchly: Works of Kurt E. Marquart. Luther Academy, 2017, 145–184.

"The Crisis in Christendom." In *Marquart's Works*, vol. V, edited by Herman Otten, 34–77, New Haven, MO: Lutheran News, 2014.

"The Contemporary Significance of the Formula of Concord." In *Essays: Confessional and Doctrinal*, vol. II of Truth, Salvatory and Churchly: Works of Kurt E. Marquart. Luther Academy, 2017, 31–68.

"The Doctrine of Justification." In *Marquart's Works*, vol. VI, edited by Herman Otten, 27–61. New Haven, MO: Lutheran News, 2014.

"The Double-Edged Sword of God's Word." In *Marquart's Works*, vol. v, edited by Herman Otten, 105–109. New Haven, MO: Lutheran News, 2014.

"The Dogma of Evolution," *The Australian Lutheran* (6 May, 1964): 144.

"The Evolution Humbug." In *Essays: Confessional and Doctrinal*, vol. ii of Truth, Salvatory and Churchly: Works of Kurt E. Marquart, 189–202. Luther Academy, 2017.

"The Fate of Christians Under Communism." In *Marquart's Works*, vol. ii, edited by Herman Otten, 54–71. New Haven, MO: Lutheran News, 2014.

"The Gifts of the Spirit Today." In *Marquart's Works*, vol. iii, edited by Herman Otten, 90–108. New Haven, MO: Lutheran News, 2014.

"The Gospel Ministry: Distinctions Within and Without." Faculty Paper. Ft Wayne, IN: Concordia Theological Seminary Press, 1995.

"The Gospel Ministry—in the Lutheran Confessions." In *We Believe: Essays on the Catechism As Drawn from For the Life of the World*, edited by Scott C. Klemsz, 111–113. Fort Wayne, IN: Concordia Theological Seminary Press, 2000.

"The Historical-Critical Method and Lutheran Presuppositions." In *Marquart's Works*, vol. viii, edited by Herman Otten, 110–136. New Haven, MO: Lutheran News, 2014.

"The Holy Spirit in the Augsburg Confession." In *Essays: Confessional and Doctrinal*, vol. ii of Truth, Salvatory and Churchly: Works of Kurt E. Marquart, 3–15. Luther Academy, 2017.

"The Incompatibility between Historical-Critical Theology and the Lutheran Confessions." *In Essays: Confessional and Doctrinal*, vol. ii of Truth, Salvatory and Churchly: Works of Kurt E. Marquart, 73–94. Luther Academy, 2017.

"The Issue of Church Fellowship and Unionism in the Missouri Synod and Its Associated Churches." *Logia* xii, no. 1 (Epiphany, 2003): 17–26.

"The Lord's Supper." In *Marquart's Works*, vol. vii, edited by Herman Otten, 70–77. New Haven, MO: Lutheran News, 2014.

"The Marks of the Church." In *Marquart's Works*, vol. iii, edited by Herman Otten, 3–26. New Haven, MO: Lutheran News, 2014.

"The Meaningful Use of the Means of Grace as the Source of Spiritual Life." In *Marquart's Works*, vol. VII, edited by Herman Otten, 18–35. New Haven, MO: Lutheran News, 2014.

"The Ministry, Confessionally Speaking: Just What Is Divinely Instituted?" In *The Office of the Holy Ministry*. Papers Presented at the Congress on the Lutheran Confessions, edited by John R Fehrmann and Daniel Preus, 6-33. Crestwood, MO and Minneapolis, MN: Luther Academy and Association of Confessional Lutherans, 1996.

"The Mysteries of God." *The Lutheran*, vol. 18, no. 4 (26 March 1984): 2–4.

"The New Missiology." *Concordia Theological Quarterly*, vol. 59, nos. 1–2 (January–April 1995): 99–100.

"The 'New Maths' of Christ." In *Marquart's Works*, vol. I, edited by Herman Otten, 29–40. New Haven, MO: Lutheran News, 2014.

"The Opinion of the Department of Systematic Theology on 'Meta-Church.'" *Concordia Theological Quarterly*, vol. 59, no. 3 (July 1995): 219–224.

"The Question of Procedure in Theological Controversies." In *Marquart's Works*, vol. IV, edited by Herman Otten, 94–103. New Haven, MO: Lutheran News, 2014.

"The 'Realist Principle' of Theology," *Logia*, vol. V, no. 3 (Holy Trinity 1996): 15–17.

"The Reformation Roots of 'Objective Justification.'" In *Essays: Confessional and Doctrinal*, vol. II of Truth, Salvatory and Churchly: Works of Kurt E. Marquart, 109-122. Luther Academy, 2017.

"The Sacrament, An Easter Affair." In *Marquart's Works*, vol. VII, edited by Herman Otten, 58–62. New Haven, MO: Lutheran News, 2014.

"The Sacramentality of Truth." In *And Every Tongue Confess: Essays in Honor of Norman Nagel on the Occasion of His Sixty-fifth Birthday*, edited by Gerald S. Krispin and Jon D. Vieker, 86-99. Dearborn MI: The Nagel Festschrift Committee, 1990.

"The Sacraments in the Pastor's Life and Ministry." In *Essays: Confessional and Doctrinal*, vol. II of Truth, Salvatory and Churchly: Works of Kurt E. Marquart, 135-144. Luther Academy, 2017.

"The Shape and Foundation of Faith." In *Marquart's Works*, vol. IX, edited by Herman Otten, 192–205. New Haven, MO: Lutheran News, 2014.

"The Spirit and His Gifts," Convention Essay, Lutheran Church of Australia, Tanunda, South Australia, 1975.

"The Swing of the Pendulum: An Attempt to Understand the St. Louis 'Affirmations and Discussions'." In *Essays: Historical and Historic*, vol. III of Truth, Salvatory and Churchly: Works of Kurt E. Marquart, 31-74. Luther Academy, 2018.

"The Trouble with the Task Force Proposals." In *Essays: Historical and Historic*, vol. III of Truth, Salvatory and Churchly: Works of Kurt E. Marquart, 109-118. Luther Academy, 2018.

"The Two Realms ("Kingdoms") in the Lutheran Confessions." In *God and Caesar Revisited*, edited by John Stephenson, 37-46. Luther Academy Conference Papers, Spring 1995.

"Truth and/or Consequence." In *Marquart's Works*, vol. VIII, edited by Herman Otten, 9–13. New Haven, MO: Lutheran News, 2014.

"Turbulence and Division." In *Marquart's Works*, vol. VII, edited by Herman Otten, 81–87. New Haven, MO: Lutheran News, 2014.

"Two Documents on Church and State." In *Marquart's Works*, vol. II, edited by Herman Otten, 97–104. New Haven, MO: Lutheran News, 2014.

"Unreal Language About the Real Presence." In *Marquart's Works*, vol. VII, edited by Herman Otten, 78–80. New Haven, MO: Lutheran News, 2014.

"Walther and Grabau Revisited"—Reply to Lowell Green, *Logia*, vol. VI, no. 2 (Eastertide): 31–36.

"War." In *Essays: Historical and Historic*, vol. III of *Truth, Salvatory and Churchly: Works of Kurt E. Marquart*, 151-167. Luther Academy, 2018.

"What Does Baptism Mean for Daily Living?" In *Marquart's Works*, vol. VII, edited by Herman Otten, 89–95. New Haven, MO: Lutheran News, 2014.

"What is Theology Or: In Defense of Dogma." In *Marquart's Works*, vol. V, edited by Herman Otten, 80–98. New Haven, MO: Lutheran News, 2014.

"What is the Church?" *The Lutheran*, vol. 18, no. 9 (9 July 1984): 7–9.

"When is Prayer a Matter of Church Fellowship?" In *Contemporary Issues in Fellowship: Confessional Principles and Application: Papers Presented at the Congress on the Lutheran Confessions, Bloomingdale, Illinois, April 24–26, 2003*, ed. Congress on the Lutheran Confessions, and John A. Maxfield, 29–35. St. Louis, MO: Luther Academy, 2004.

"Why Not Effective Parental Choice of Schools?" *Concordia Theological Quarterly*, 41 (April 1977): 72–74.

Book Reviews

"A Tale of Two Books," Review. In *Marquart's Works*, vol. VIII, edited by Herman Otten, 149–152. New Haven, MO: Lutheran News, 2014.

Review of *Catholic, Lutheran, Protestant* by Gregory L. Jackson. *Concordia Theological Quarterly* 60, nos. 1 & 2 (January–April 1996): 147–150.

Review of *Church and Ministry* by C. F. W. Walther. *Concordia Theological Quarterly* 52, no. 4 (October 1988): 311–313.

Review of *Die Rechtfertigung des Suenders* by Gottfried Martens. *Concordia Theological Quarterly* 60, nos. 1 & 2 (January–April 1996): 134–141.

Review of *Die Theologie Martin Luthers nach seinen Predigten* by Ulrich Asendorf. *Concordia Theological Quarterly* 55, nos. 2 & 3 (April–July 1991): 214–216.

Review of H. Senkbeil, *Dying to Live*, in *Logia*, vol. IV, no. 2 (Eastertide/April 1995): 57–59.

"Escape From Reason," Review. In *Marquart's Works*, vol. IV, edited by Herman Otten, 56–59. New Haven, MO: Lutheran News, 2014.

"Evangelical Grace vs. Ecumenical Pressure," Review of *Grace Under Pressure*. In *Marquart's Works*, vol. III, edited by Herman Otten, 28–33. New Haven, MO: Lutheran News, 2014.

"Evolution: Some Serious Theoretical Flaws," Review of A.E. Wilder Smith's "Man's Origin, Man's Destiny." In *Marquart's Works*, vol. IV, edited by Herman Otten, 9–16. New Haven, MO: Lutheran News, 2014.

"From Luther to Kierkegaard," Review. In *Marquart's Works*, vol. IV, edited by Herman Otten, 50–55. New Haven, MO: Lutheran News, 2014.

"Killing with Kindness, A Review of Eldon Weisheit, *Should I Have an Abortion.*" In *Marquart's Works*, vol. IV, edited by Herman Otten, 72–76. New Haven, MO: Lutheran News, 2014.

"Realism: Lessons in Christian Duty—By An Agnostic," Review of Frank Knopfelmacher, *Intellectuals and Politics*. In *Marquart's Works*, vol. II, edited by Herman Otten, 83–88. New Haven, MO: Lutheran News, 2014.

"A Review of Harry Blamires—The Christian Mind." In *Marquart's Works*, vol. I, edited by Herman Otten, 81–85. New Haven, MO: Lutheran News, 2014.

"Review of J.W. Montgomery's "The Factual Basis of Christianity." In *Marquart's Works*, vol. V, edited by Herman Otten, 100–103, New Haven, MO: Lutheran News, 2014.

"Your Personal Guide to Head-Shrinking." Review of Schoeck and Wiggins, *Psychiatry and Responsibility*. In *Marquart's Works*, vol. I, edited by Herman Otten, 75–80. New Haven, MO: Lutheran News, 2014.

Translation

Schmidt, F.A. *Justification, Objective and Subjective: A Translation of the Doctrinal Essay Read at the First Convention of the Synodical Conference in 1872*, translated by Kurt E Marquart. Fort Wayne, IN: Concordia Theological Seminary Press, 1982.

"Associate Membership in the LWF," by Gottfried Hoffmann, *Concordia Theological Quarterly*, vol. 57, nos. 1–2 (January–April 1993): 125–133.

INDICES

SACRED SCRIPTURE INDEX

LUTHERAN CONFESSIONS INDEX

NAME AND SUBJECT INDEX

.

www.ingramcontent.com/pod-product-compliance
Lightning Source LLC
Chambersburg PA
CBHW030924090426
42737CB00007B/308